IMAGES
of America

BLAND COUNTY

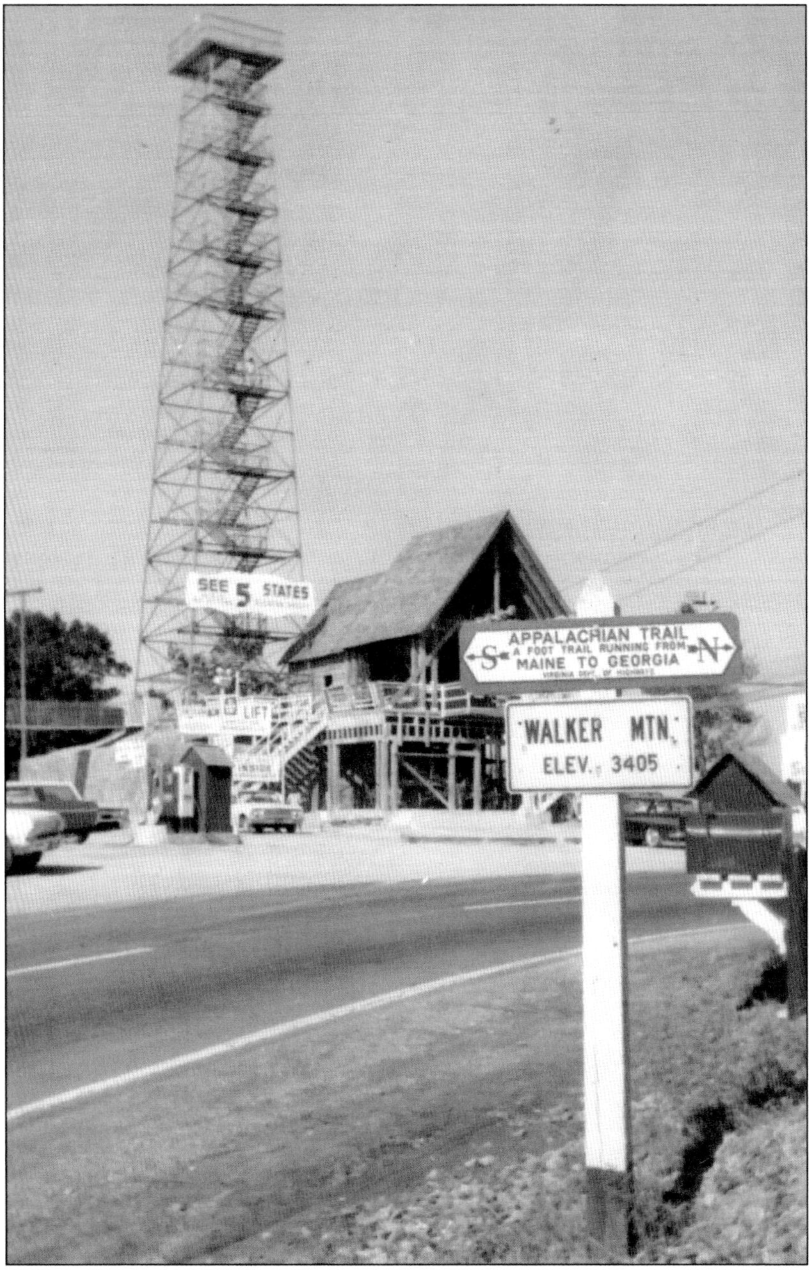

Sitting on Top of the World. The Big Walker Lookout atop Big Walker Mountain in Bland County, Virginia, near the Wythe County line, has been a regional landmark for more than a half a century. The lookout is the highest privately owned and operated scenic attraction in Virginia. (Courtesy of Ron Kime.)

On the Cover: Shall They Gather. Several members of the congregation of the Honaker Chapel, of the Rocky Gap Methodist Church in Rocky Gap, are shown in this 1932 photograph. Families represented in the photograph include the following: Goodman, Graves, French, Conley, Hare, Bailey, McBride, Sands, Lambert, Gibson, Harman, Hunter, Tuggle, Cecil, and Rucker. (Courtesy of Nannie Rose Tiller.)

IMAGES
of America

BLAND COUNTY

William R. "Bill" Archer

ARCADIA
PUBLISHING

ISBN 978-0-7385-8733-2

Published by Arcadia Publishing
Charleston, South Carolina

Printed in the United States of America

Library of Congress Control Number: 2010936402

For all general information, please contact Arcadia Publishing:
Telephone 843-853-2070
Fax 843-853-0044
E-mail sales@arcadiapublishing.com
For customer service and orders:
Toll-Free 1-888-313-2665

Visit us on the Internet at www.arcadiapublishing.com

I dedicate this book to my friends, Jeanie Owens, president of the Bland County Historical Society, and her husband, Rick Owens; my longtime friend and colleague, Ray Glover; the late Nannie Rose Tiller, who contributed to this project on the eve of her passing; and my wife, Evonda Archer, who, like the others mentioned here, worked tirelessly to make this book a reality.

Contents

ACKNOWLEDGMENTS

When my editor at Arcadia Publishing, Elizabeth Bray, asked me to consider working on a book about Bland County, Virginia, for Arcadia's Images of America series, I hesitated a little. However, I knew that Bland County has a great story to tell, and my friend Jeanie Owens, the president of the Bland County Historical Society, proved a veritable fountainhead of information. Historical society members brought in the images, and my colleague, Ray Glover, transformed precious family photographs into digital images so contributors did not have to wait long to get their photographs back. I also made new friends while working on this book, including Georgia Stacy Havens, a gifted historian from Bastian, Virginia; Marie Groseclose, the widow of Henry C. Groseclose, the father of the Future Farmers of America; Ron Kime, who keeps his parents' dream of the Big Walker Lookout alive; Nannie Rose Tiller and Billy Jean (Walters) Carty, whose awesome collections made this book come to life; Mary Little, who has preserved the history of Bland County's African American community; and other friends like Denise Smith, Mary Jane (Johnston) Pennington, Wanda Blankenship, Mel Grubb, Henry Blessing, Walter Lawson, Woody Bailey, Bob Colley, Bill Shrader, Eric DiNovo, Gordon Hamilton, Promise Sloane, JoAnne Tickle Scott, Wanda Burton Reynolds, Robert Waddle, Rick Owens, Ann Briton, Sue Repass, and so many more. Thanks also to Betty Hubble, Alan Ashworth, Howard and Reva Crabtree, Brenda King, Harry Thompson, Doris Sink, Jean Blevins, and the Bogle Library, as well as *Bluefield Daily Telegraph* publisher Darryl Hudson and managing editor Samantha Perry.

INTRODUCTION

The awe-inspiring, rugged scenic mountain beauty of Bland County, Virginia, has shielded it from unwanted intrusions through the years. The forest-covered mountains, tight-winding valleys, and rolling pastureland that appears to reach out toward eternity have served as a fertile nurturing ground for people with progressive ideas and a willingness to work hard to help their neighbors, their state, and their nation. Although unassuming and humble, Bland County is a unique place in Southwest Virginia mountain country.

Living in the idyllic, rural mountains and pastures of Southwest Virginia has its share of challenges. Some of the earliest settlers of Bland County faced horrible attacks from Native Americans who were not eager to share their lands with European Colonial settlers. Before America declared its independence from England, five members of the Sluss family, who settled in the rolling hills between Garden Mountain to the north and Big Walker Mountain to the south, died from wounds they received in a Shawnee Indian attack on August 2, 1774. After the United States gained its independence, in March 1793, John Goolman Davidson died at the base of East River Mountain on Laurel Fork, near Rocky Gap, Virginia, in a Native American attack.

The population of Bland County grew slowly in the years after the American Revolutionary War. Many surrounding counties of Virginia were purchased by land speculators like Moses Austin to the south and Robert Morris to the north, who selected sites based on potential profits from mineral or natural resources development. Some Revolutionary War veterans who received land grants for their military service made Bland County their home, but growth was slow. Finally, in the late 1850s, the population of the region had reached a sufficient level as to create a new county from portions of Wythe, Giles, and Tazewell Counties. The act creating Bland County passed the Virginia General Assembly on March 30, 1861. The new county was named for Richard E. Bland, a native of Prince George County, Virginia, and the "Virginian Antiquary," who served as an advocate for the Revolutionary War.

Less than three weeks after it became a political entity, Bland County became part of the Confederate States of America when Virginia seceded from the United States on April 17, 1861. Young men from Bland County entered military service in the Confederacy and served with the Bland Rangers in the Battle of Pigeon Roost in Mercer County, West Virginia, in May 1862, and also served with Company B, 47th Virginia Battalion; Company F, 8th Virginia Cavalry; Company F, 51st Virginia Infantry; Company G, 36th Virginia Infantry; and Company F, 45th Virginia Infantry; as well as other Confederate units. Soldiers from Bland County participated in key engagements regionally to defend against Union armies seeking to destroy the railroad in Wytheville, Virginia, and salt works in Saltville, Virginia, but after four years of warfare, the Union was preserved.

The peace was uneasy for many Virginians dealing with a transformation from an agrarian-based economy and entering a modern industrial age. Dynamic leaders like Bland County's Capt. Samuel Newberry led the fight in the Virginia General Assembly as the voice of the "Big Four" to keep the Old Dominion a Democratic state in the face of the Reconstruction movement. As a new, diverse future evolved, Virginia remained true to the strengths of its historic past. During the postwar years, several black families moved into the Dry Fork area of Bland County and peacefully farmed the fertile soil alongside their white neighbors.

The New River, Holston & Western Railway pushed into Bland County at the dawn of the 20th century, as timber companies like Mermian Lumber and Virginia Hardwoods began harvesting the mountain timber reserves. While part of the county grew due to the influx of lumberjacks and other workers associated with the industry, a brilliant young farm boy from a pioneer family, Henry C. Groseclose, studied the trend in the United States of young people leaving farms in the American heartland for jobs in urban areas and decided that rural areas would need new leaders to survive the challenges. Groseclose developed the Future Farmers of Virginia (later the Future Farmers of America) to help its farm boy members learn parliamentary procedure and Robert's Rules of Order as part of their animal husbandry and agricultural learning.

Other Bland County residents made a mark on national and world history. The inventor John Allen Newberry developed a cable-splicing device that is used extensively on ships at sea. In later years, Newberry became a big game hunter and donated his trophies to the county at his death.

East River Mountain to the north and Big Walker Mountain to the south presented barriers to growth in Bland County, but in the early 1970s, that all changed when the federal interstate highway system located Interstate 77 in the heart of Bland County. In addition to opening the county to new opportunities, the new highway construction uncovered part of Bland County's pre-Columbian past when road builders encountered a Native American village site that had to be excavated and relocated in advance of paving crews. History of that time is preserved and on display at the Wolf Creek Indian Village near Bastian, Virginia.

The Wolf Creek Indian Village is just one of the attractions that Bland County can celebrate in its sesquicentennial year and for years to come. The county offers unrivaled scenic beauty, as thousands of hikers on the Appalachian Trail can attest. Bland County provides a wealth of outdoor activities for anglers, hunters, campers, and people who just want to enjoy nature. The Bland County Prison Farm provides jobs for many people in the region, and several successful businesses call Bland County home. The Boy Scouts of America have enjoyed Camp Roland for decades, and Wolf Creek Golf Course is one of the county's hidden gems. Dismal Falls provides a natural setting of incredible beauty, and the county plays host to many fairs and festivals each spring, summer, and fall. Perhaps above all, the spirit of volunteer service is alive and well in Bland County, where neighbors are always prepared to help their neighbors, as volunteer firefighters and paramedics from Bland, Rocky Gap, Grapefield, Ceres, Hollybrook, and Bastian are always ready to help.

Thousands of travelers pass through Bland County daily on Interstate 77, and they see tree-covered mountains. Yet, the fascinating history beneath the Jefferson National Forest canopy is rarely seen by folks passing through at an uninterrupted 65-miles-per-hour clip. Bland County history is steeped in tradition and ripe with potential. This year, 2011, marks a great milestone in Bland County history—the 150th anniversary of the county's formation. This book seeks to tell part of Bland County's incredible history as the county celebrates its past and looks forward to its future.

One

The Heart of the Virginias

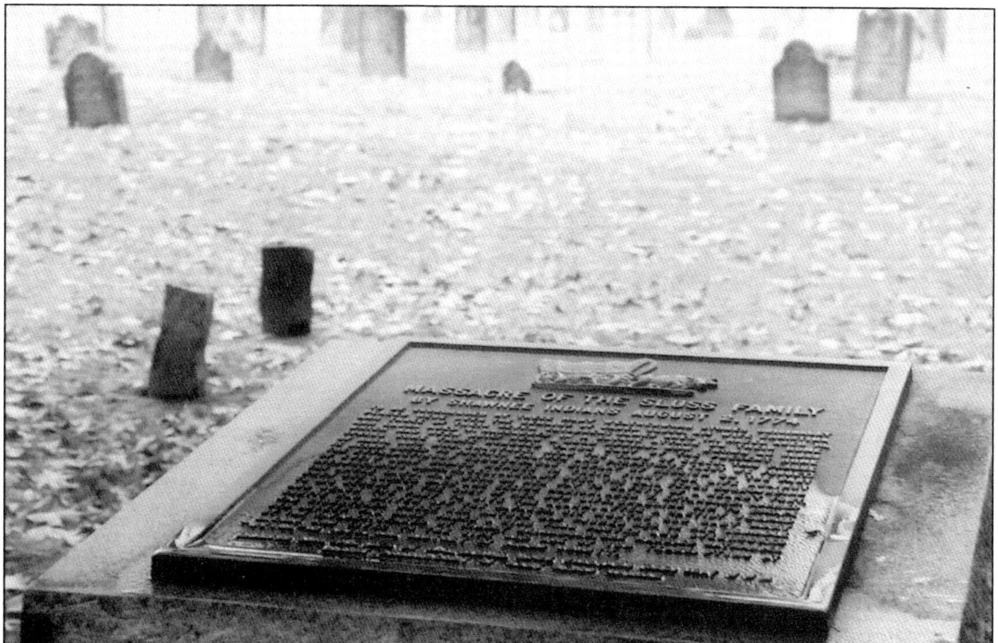

High Cost of Freedom. Jared and Christina Sluss settled on land in the southwestern part of Bland County in the 1770s. On August 2, 1774, while Jared and his 12-year-old son, James, were at work in a field near their home, Christina and her daughters, Laura, age 4, and Hazel, age 10, were attacked and killed at the residence. Jared and James Sluss returned home and were also killed by the Shawnee Indian raiding party. Three of the Sluss children survived the attack. The stones marking the graves of the Sluss family members killed in the massacre are in the front of the Sharon Lutheran Church Cemetery in Ceres, Virginia. (Author's.)

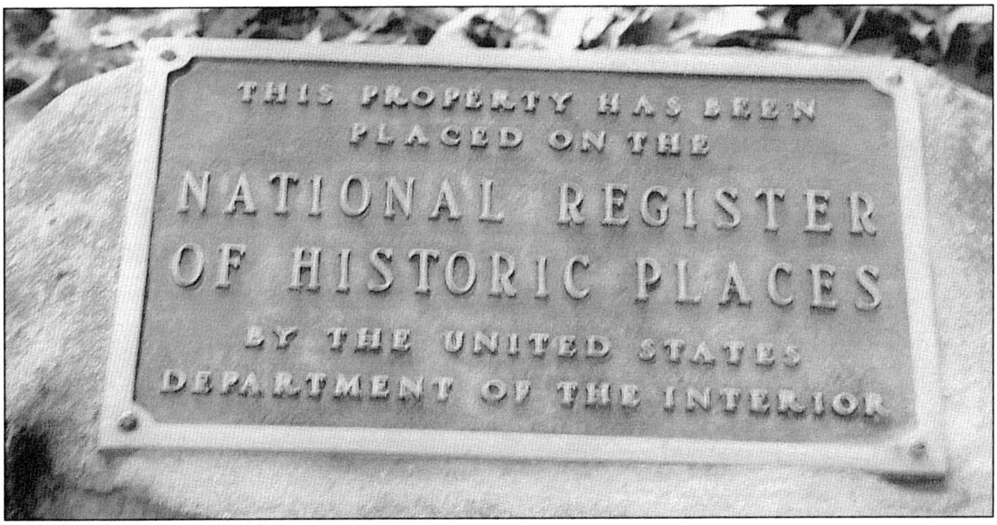

A Place in Time. The historic Sharon Cemetery, located on a hillside behind Sharon Lutheran Church, serves as the final resting place for Sluss family members killed in the 1774 massacre as well as some other notable area residents, like Henry C. Groseclose of Ceres, the father of the Future Farmers of America. (Author's.)

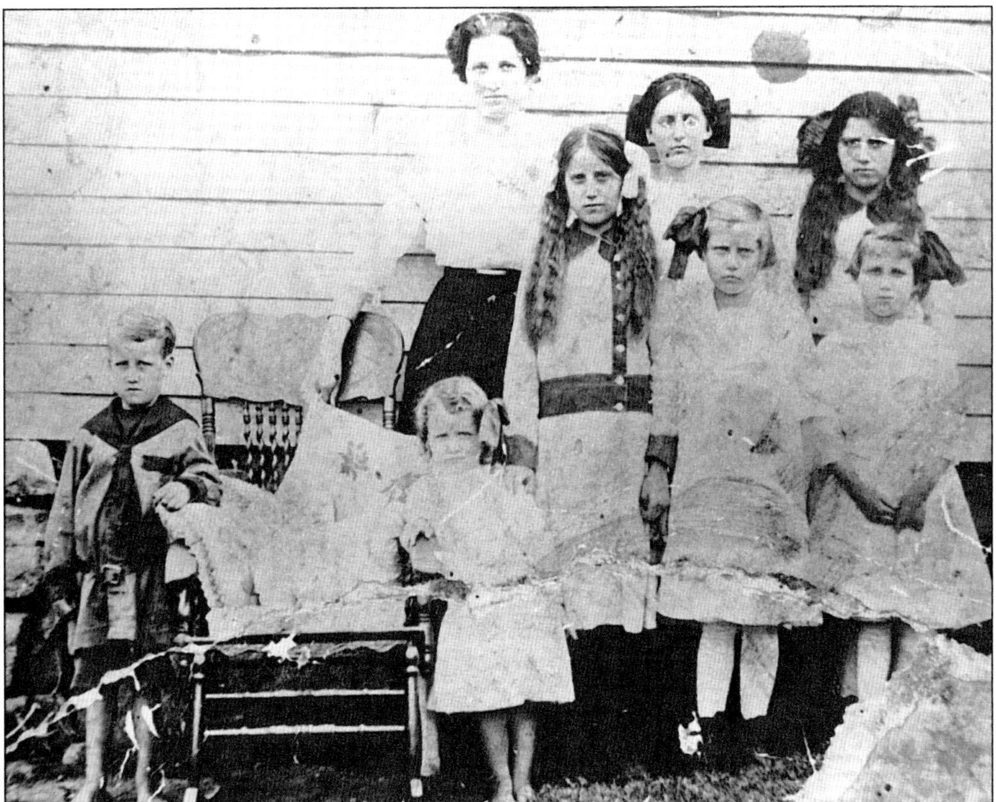

All Clear. Bland County, Virginia, proved to be a good place to raise families like the Walters family of Clearfork, shown here. Those pictured are, from left to right, Bill, Blanch (infant), Glorena, Clara, Gladys, Ada, Kathleen, and Virgie Walters. (Courtesy of Billy Jean [Walters] Carty.)

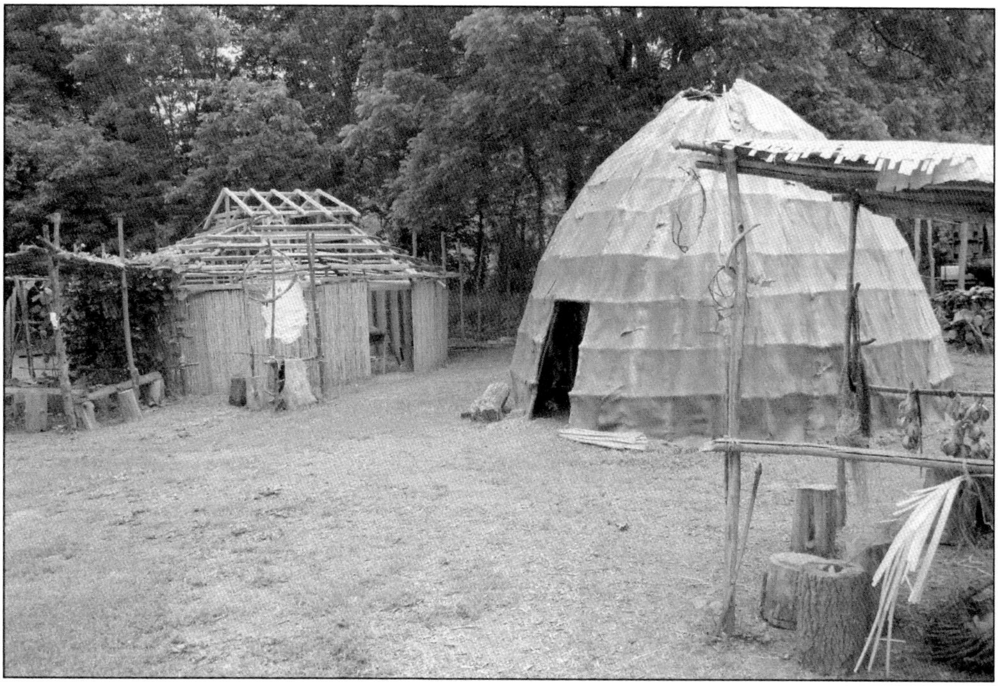

Home and Hearth. For thousands of years before the arrival of European settlers, Native Americans inhabited the region that would become Virginia. Volunteers with the Bland County Historical Society, with the support of the Bland County administration, have recreated the lodges and work sites of Native Americans as they lived in Bland County around 1490–1530. (Photograph by Eric DiNovo.)

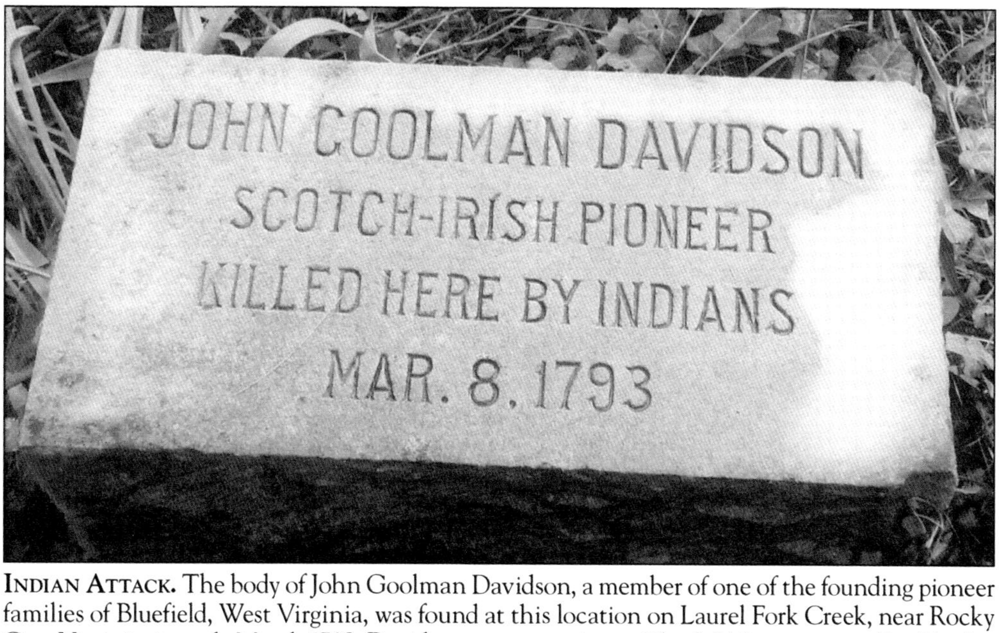

Indian Attack. The body of John Goolman Davidson, a member of one of the founding pioneer families of Bluefield, West Virginia, was found at this location on Laurel Fork Creek, near Rocky Gap, Virginia, in early March 1793. Davidson was returning to Bluefield from a trip to Rockbridge County, Virginia, and passed through Rocky Gap on March 8, 1793. His body was discovered several days later, and he was buried on the spot. (Author's.)

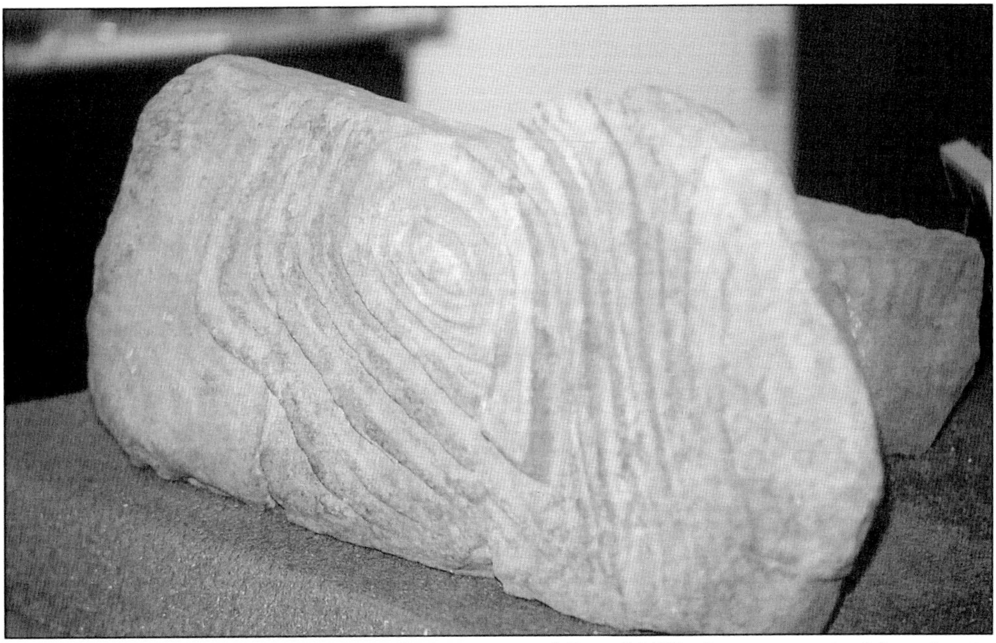

Early Bland County Map. Maxwell, Stewart, and Donald Wright were squirrel hunting in the southeast section of Bland County in the late 1950s or early 1960s when they came upon this large rock with an unusual carving on the surface. It is believed to be of Native American origin. (Author's.)

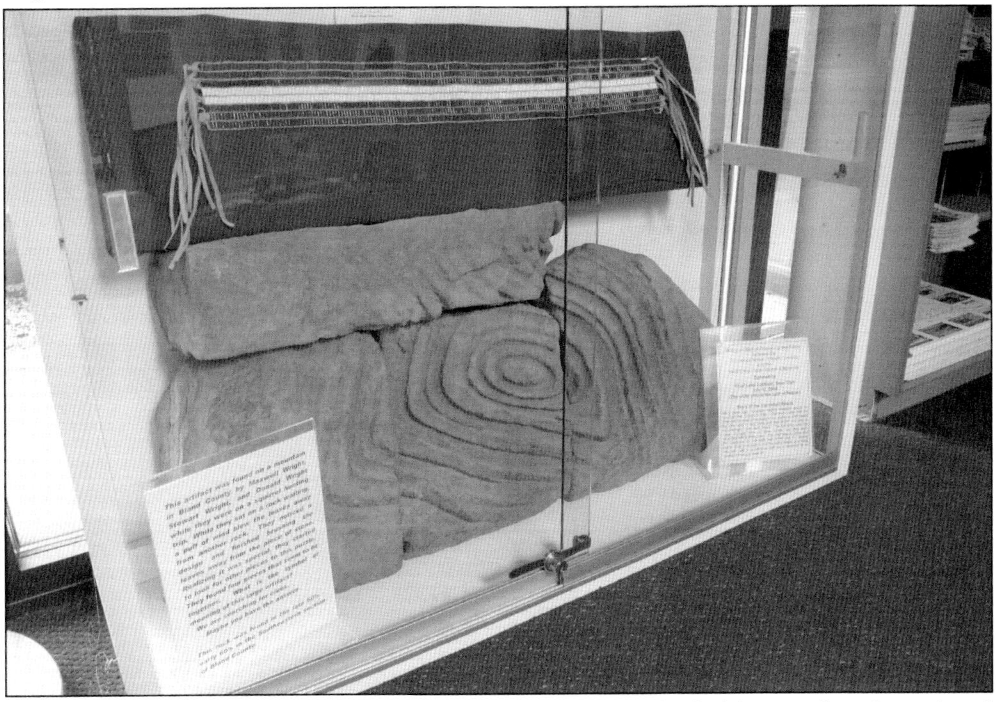

Between a Rock and a Glass Case. Thanks to the incredible find of the Wrights, the rock and its sections are now on display in the museum of the Wolf Creek Indian Village, near Bastian, Virginia. (Photograph by Eric DiNovo.)

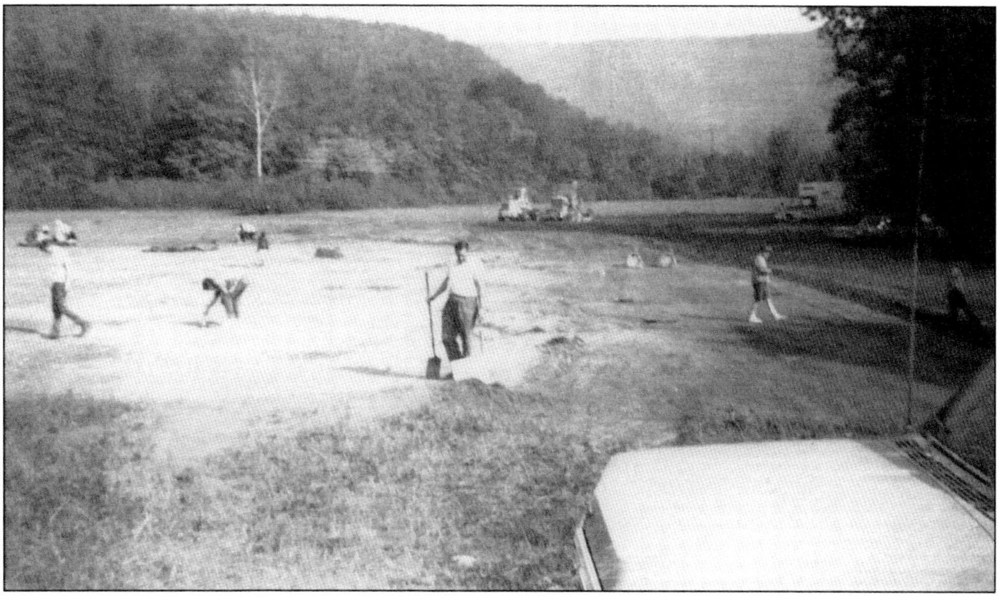

History Discovered. In the spring of 1970, as highway construction crews were busy building Interstate 77 through Bland County, Virginia, workers came upon the area shown here, which they believed to be a Native American burial ground. Volunteers from Bland County joined regional archaeologists to excavate and preserve the site. (Courtesy of Mary Jane [Johnston] Pennington.)

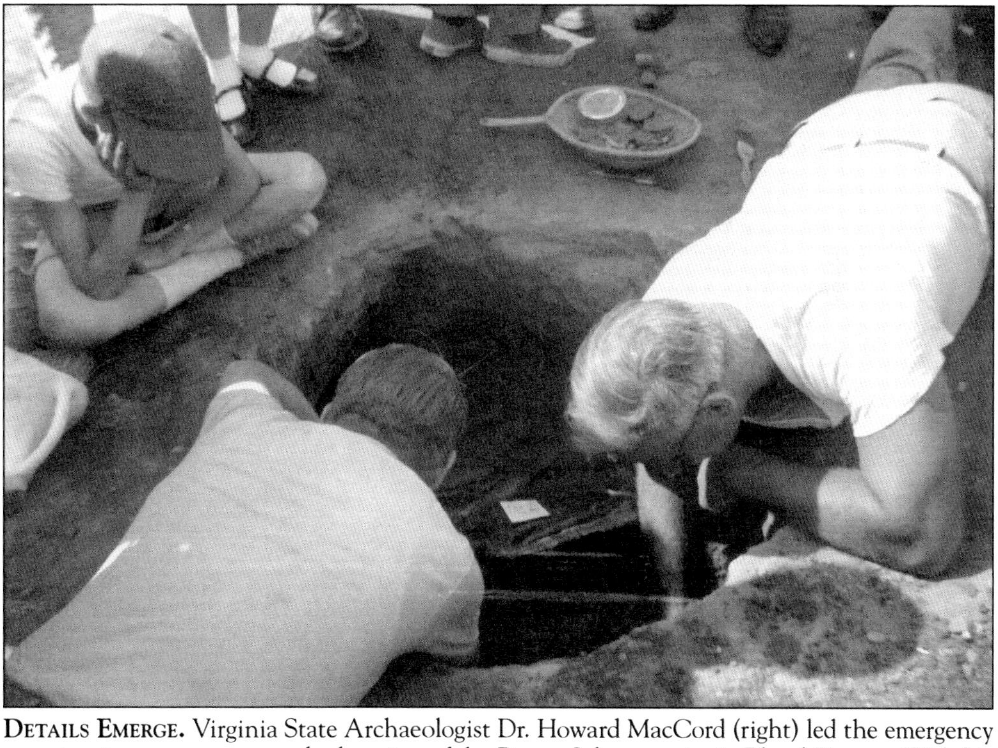

Details Emerge. Virginia State Archaeologist Dr. Howard MacCord (right) led the emergency examination, excavation, and relocation of the Brown Johnston site in Bland County. With his back to the camera, the property owner, Brown Johnston, is in the foreground of the photograph above. (Courtesy of Mary Jane [Johnston] Pennington.)

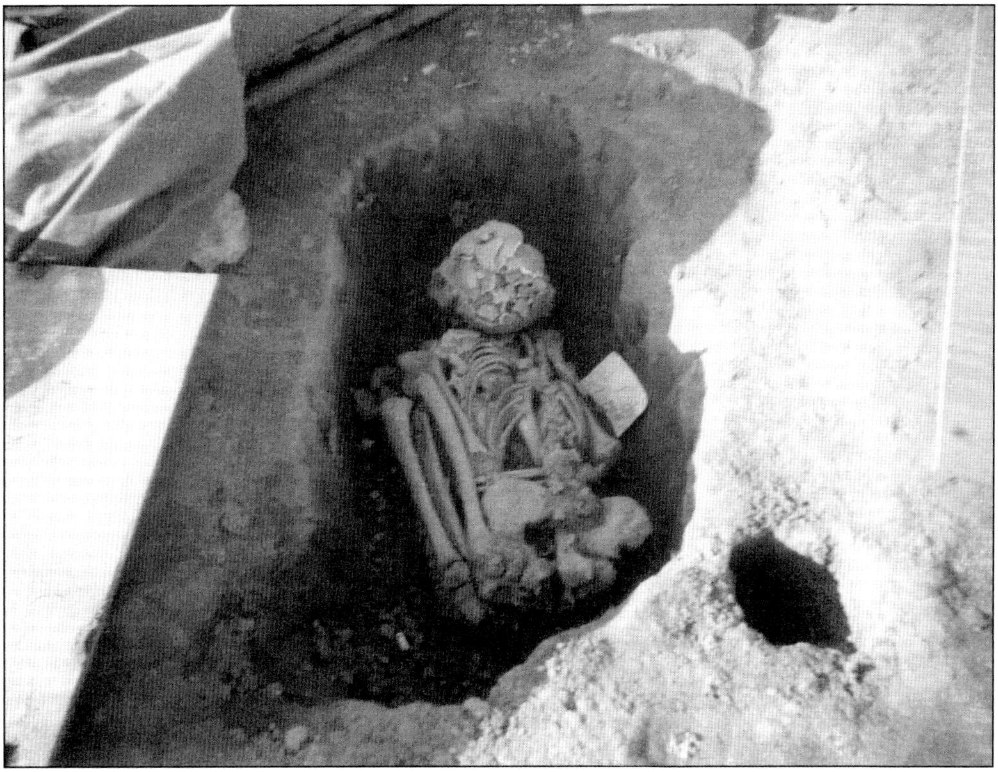

History Revealed. Dr. Howard MacCord and his team of regional experts, as well as volunteers, painstakingly removed the remains of Native Americans buried at the site prior to transporting the remains to another site, safe from the highway disturbance and the rerouting of Wolf Creek. (Courtesy of Mary Jane [Johnston] Pennington.)

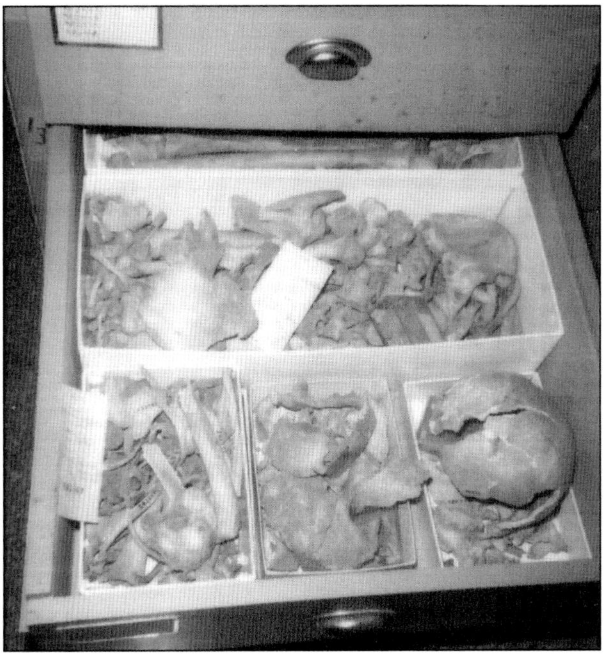

Stop in the Nation's Capital. Some remains uncovered at the Brown Johnston site were temporarily taken to the Smithsonian Museum in Washington, DC, for additional study. The Johnston family was invited to visit the museum to see how the remains were stored until to their return to Bland County for reinterment. (Courtesy of Mary Jane [Johnston] Pennington.)

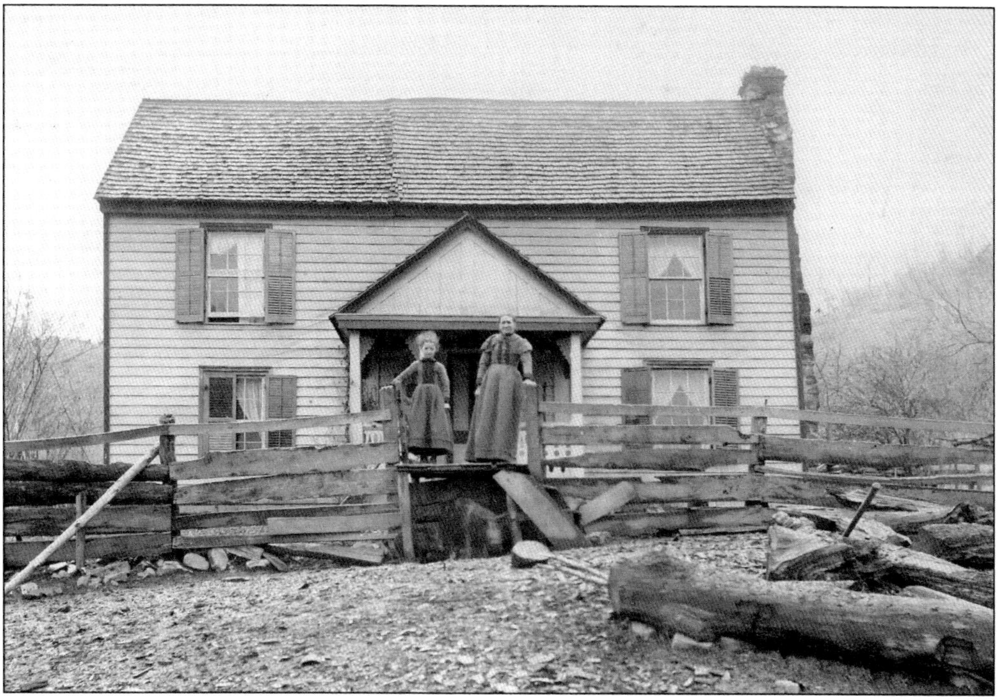

Pioneer Settlers. Marion Radford (left) and her mother, Mary Emma Lou Burton Radford, are shown here standing in front of the county home place. (Courtesy of Wanda Blankenship.)

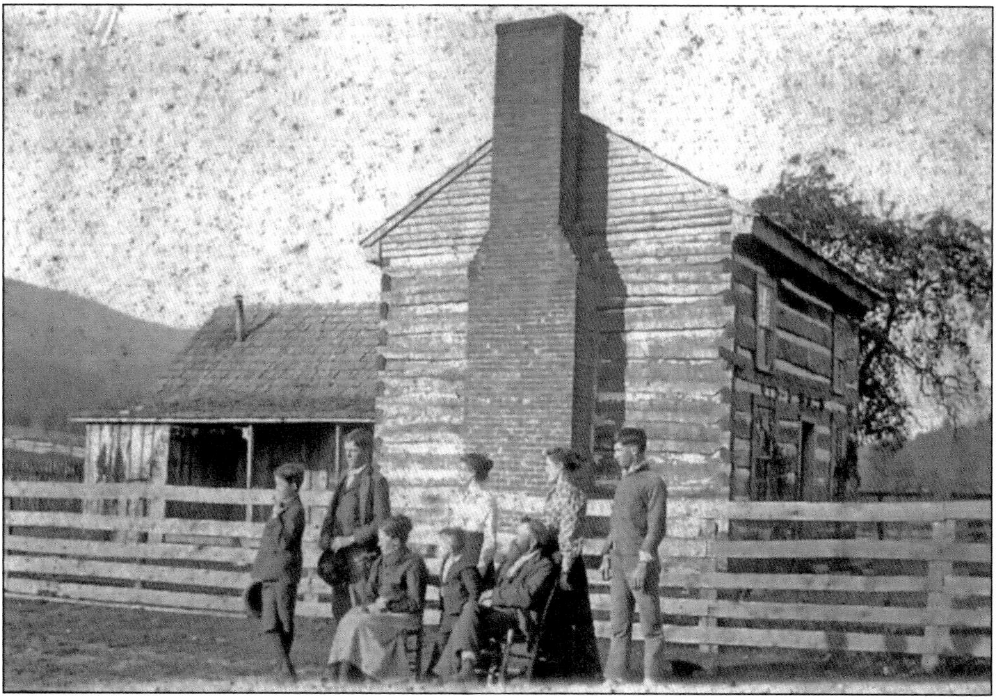

Life in the Wilderness. The Burton family is shown here standing in profile in front of their home in the Wilderness Section of Bland County, Virginia. The Wilderness Section is located between South Gap and Dismal. (Courtesy of Wanda Blankenship.)

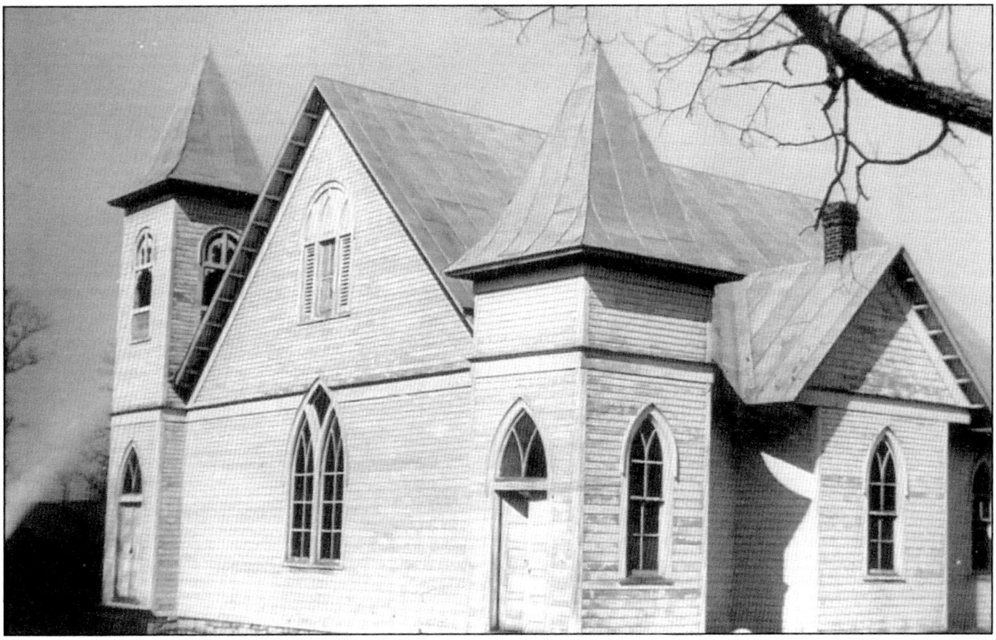

On the Mechanicsburg Charge. Mount Zion Church, shown here, was located on Walkers Creek and was erected on land donated to the church in 1869 by Hiram and Ruth Stinson. (Courtesy of Bland County Historical Society.)

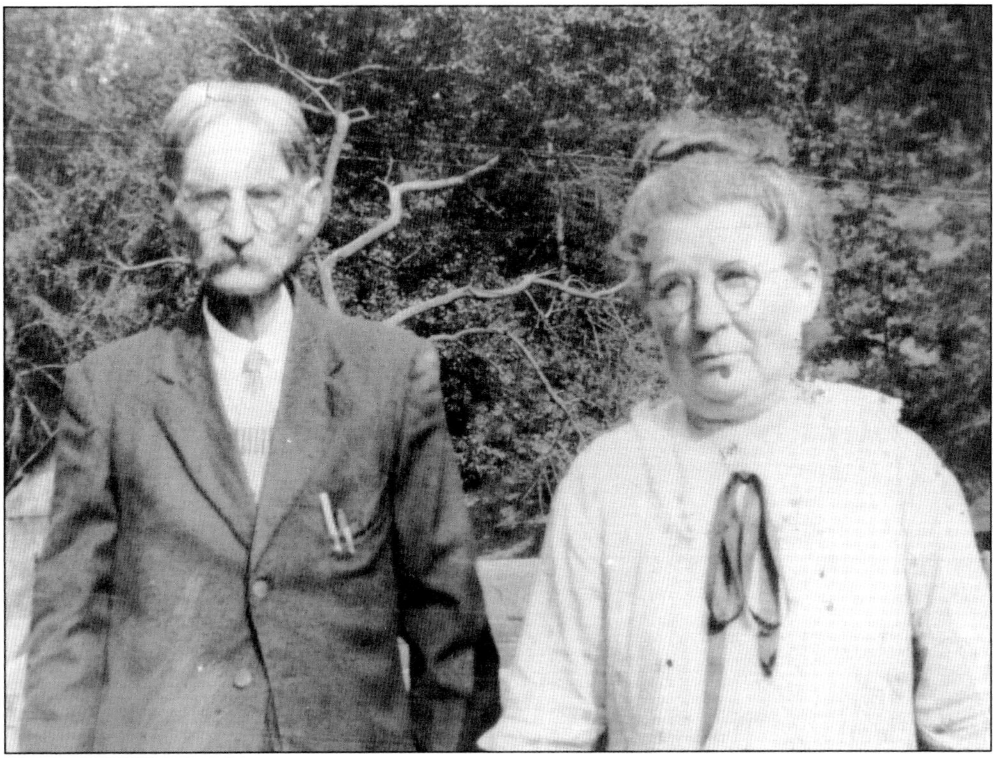

The Family. Marion Radford (left) and his wife, Mary Emma Lou Burton Radford, are shown here at their home in the Wilderness Section of the county. (Courtesy of Wanda Blankenship.)

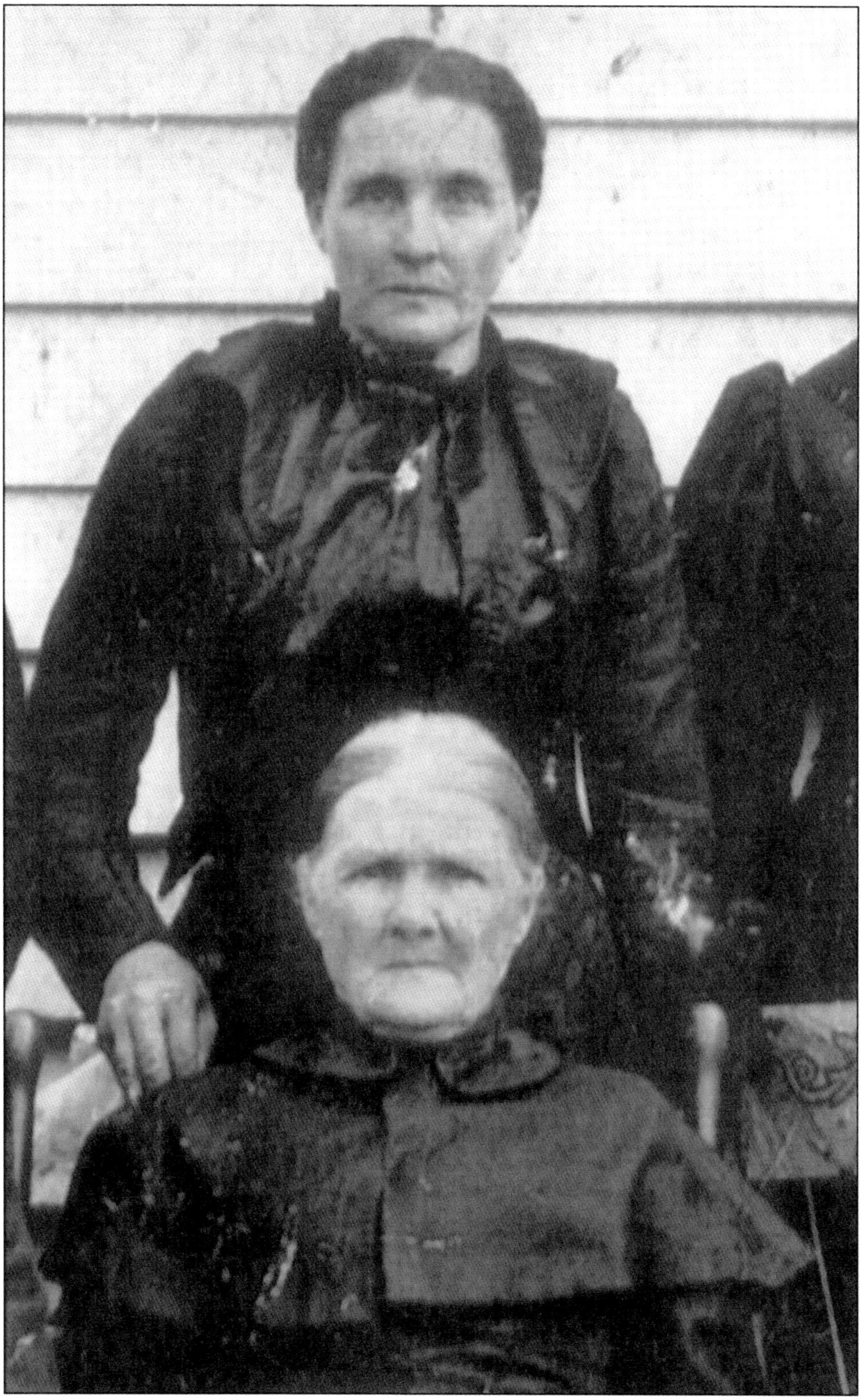

Mother and Daughter. Mary Absher Wingo is shown here seated with her daughter standing behind her. Her daughter's name is not known. The Reverend James Wingo was one of the early pastors of Hornbarger's Chapel, a Christian church that was the first church built in Bastian, Virginia, on land that was donated to the church in 1875 by the William P. Hornbarger family. (Courtesy of Wanda Blankenship.)

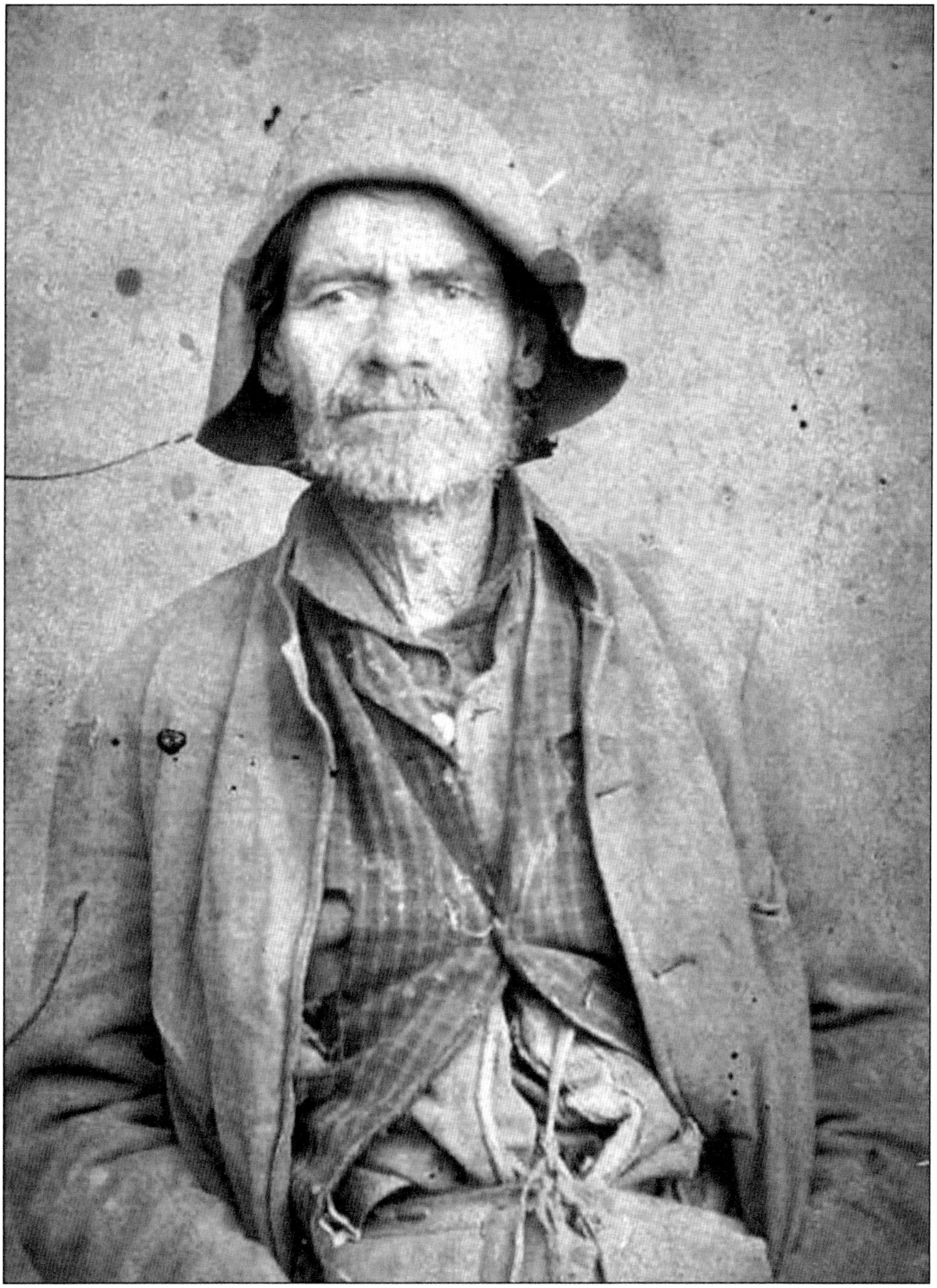

AN INTERESTING LIFE. Jimmy Surat, shown here, was believed to be Bland County's oldest resident when he passed away at age 120 in 1915. He lived on Brushy Mountain and registered to vote on September 15, 1902. He slept on a pallet in front of his fireplace and never slept in a bed. He was said to have been half Blackfoot Indian. He escaped to Bland County when the eastern Indian tribes were moved 2,000 miles to the west on the infamous Trail of Tears. (Courtesy of Robert Waddle.)

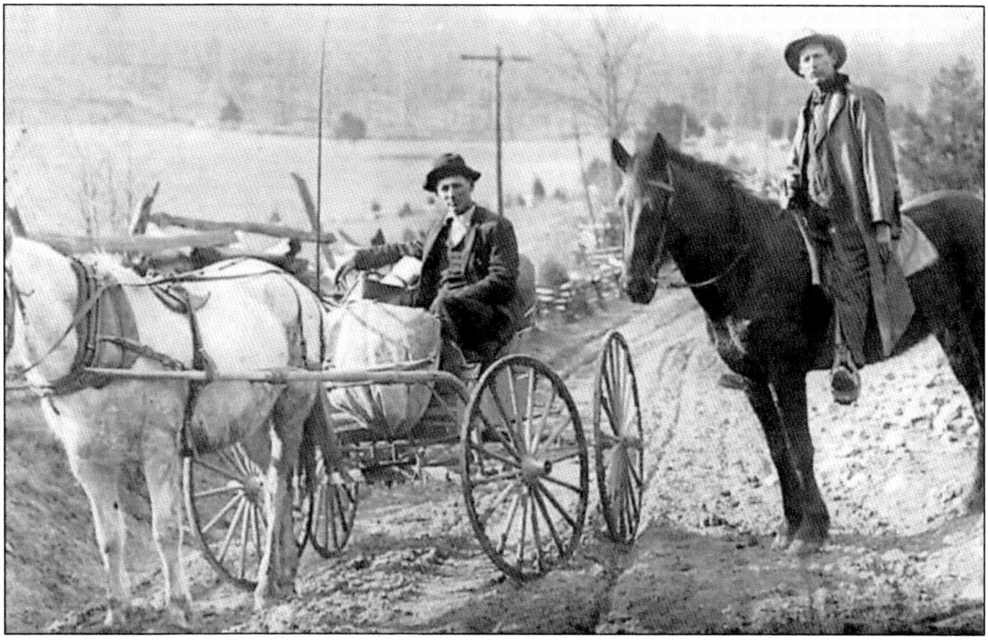

MEANS OF TRAVEL. Getting around in Bland County during the early days could be difficult because of the mountains and rocky ground, as the unidentified carriage driver and horse rider could attest. (Courtesy of the Bland County Historical Society.)

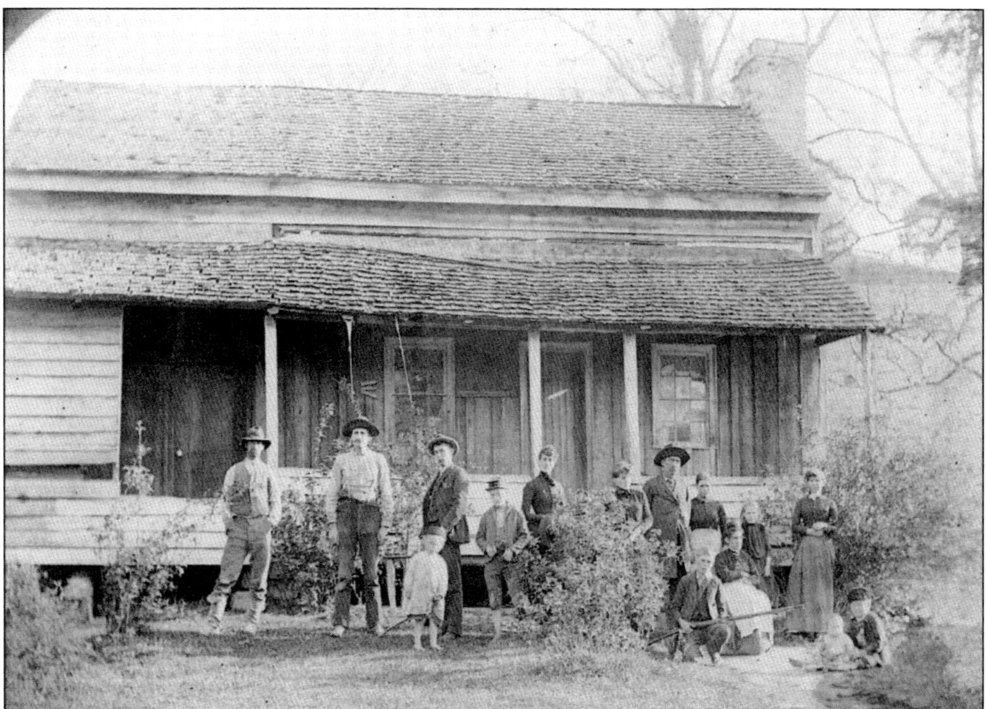

DOWN ON THE FARM. Bland County families worked the land and carved their future out of the mountain forests of Southwestern Virginia. (Courtesy of the Bland County Historical Society.)

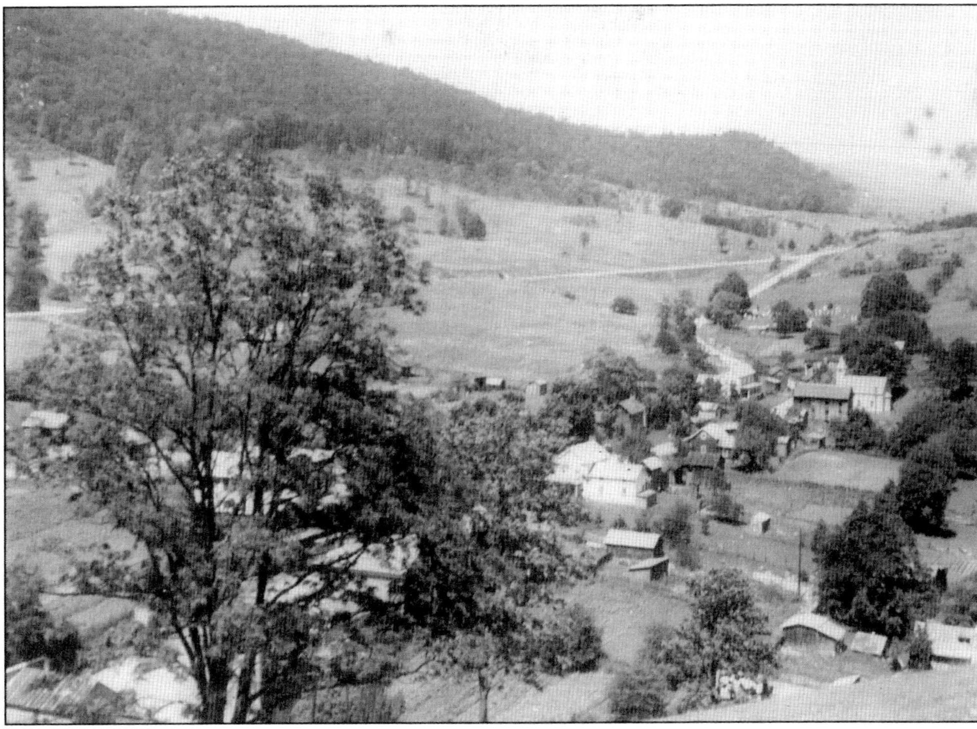

MECHANICSBURG. The Mechanicsburg community was laid out in 1830 and soon became one of the busiest communities in Bland County, Virginia. The community is remembered as the home of the Keister Hotel, which featured plenty of good food and lodging for travelers. (Courtesy of the Bland County Historical Society.)

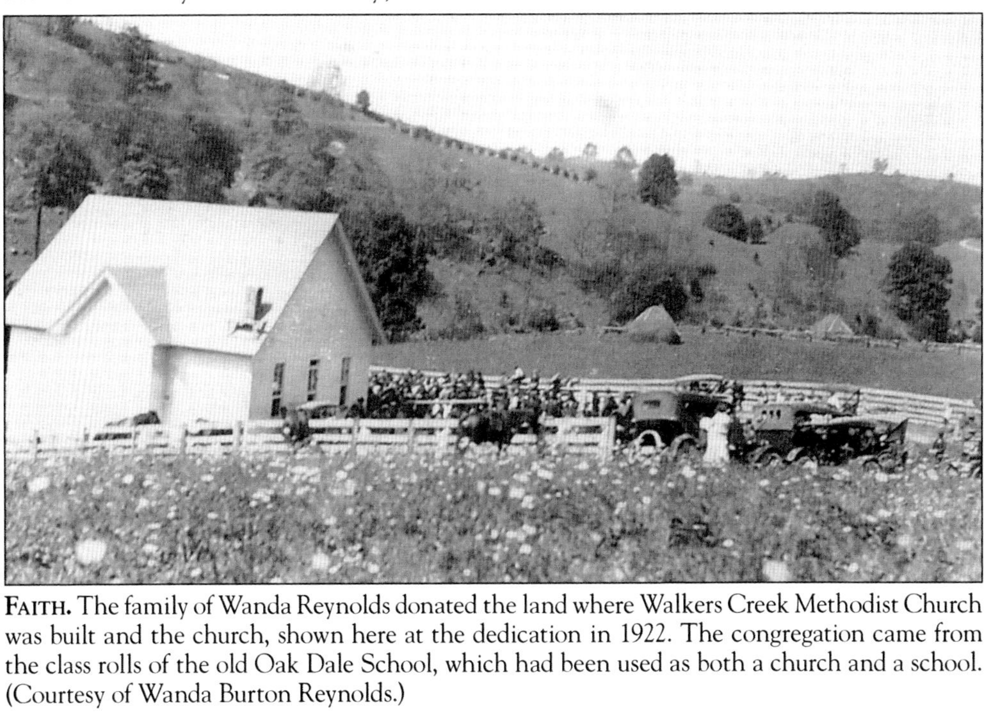

FAITH. The family of Wanda Reynolds donated the land where Walkers Creek Methodist Church was built and the church, shown here at the dedication in 1922. The congregation came from the class rolls of the old Oak Dale School, which had been used as both a church and a school. (Courtesy of Wanda Burton Reynolds.)

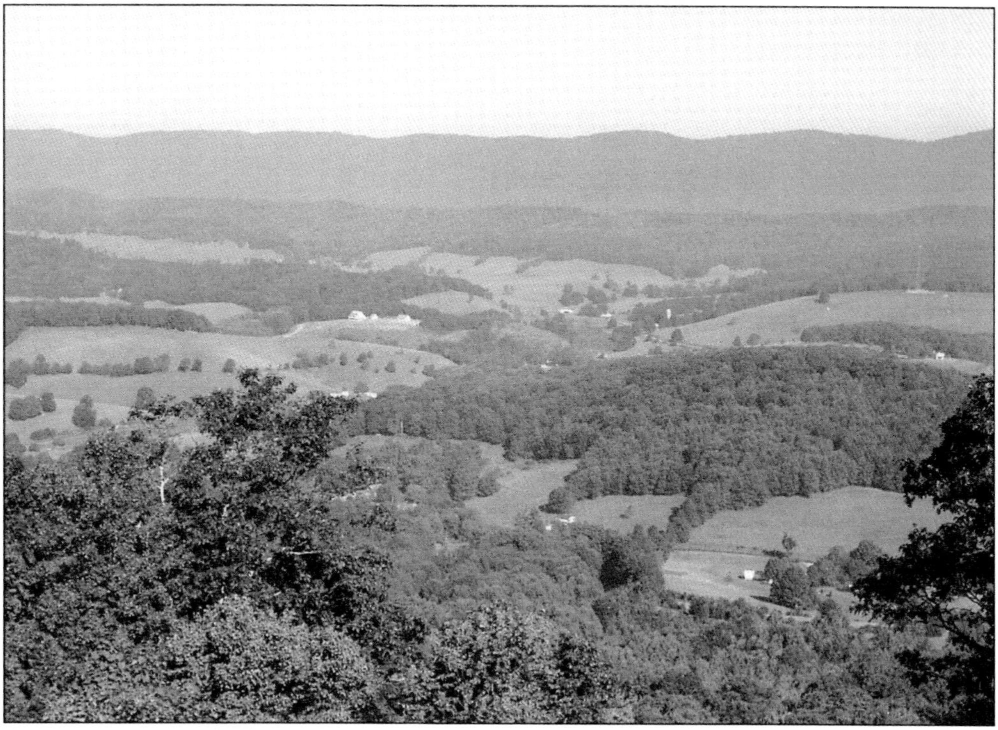

On a Clear Day. Bland County, seen here looking north from the top of Big Walker Mountain, is a spectacular view in any season of the year. (Author's.)

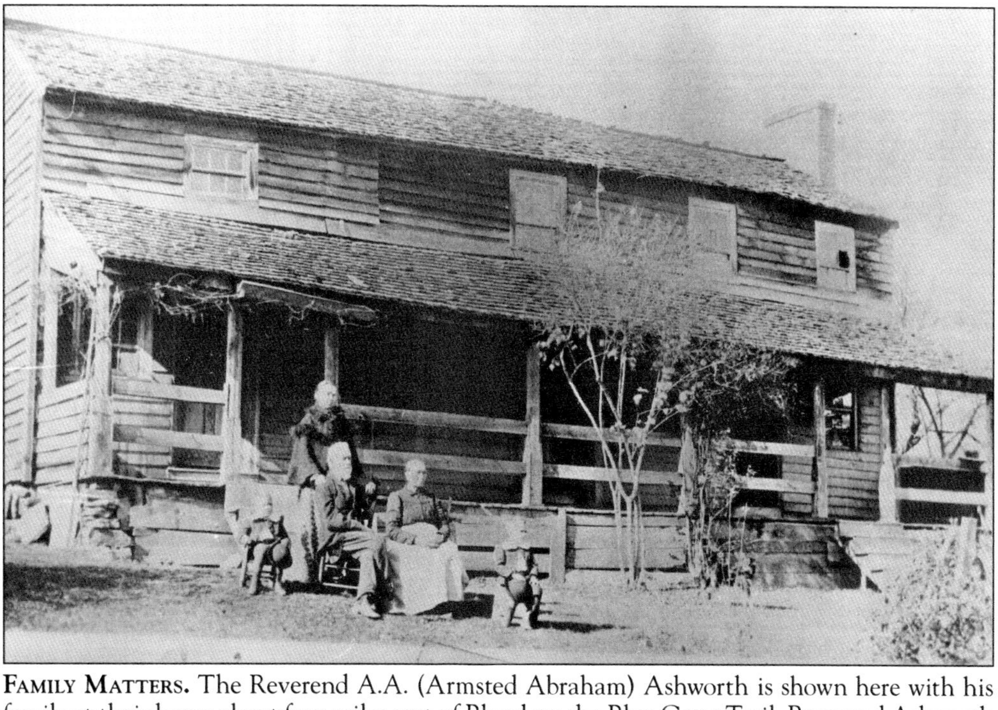

Family Matters. The Reverend A.A. (Armsted Abraham) Ashworth is shown here with his family at their home about four miles east of Bland on the Blue Grass Trail. Reverend Ashworth was pastor of the Baptist church at Bland Courthouse. (Courtesy of Alan Ashworth.)

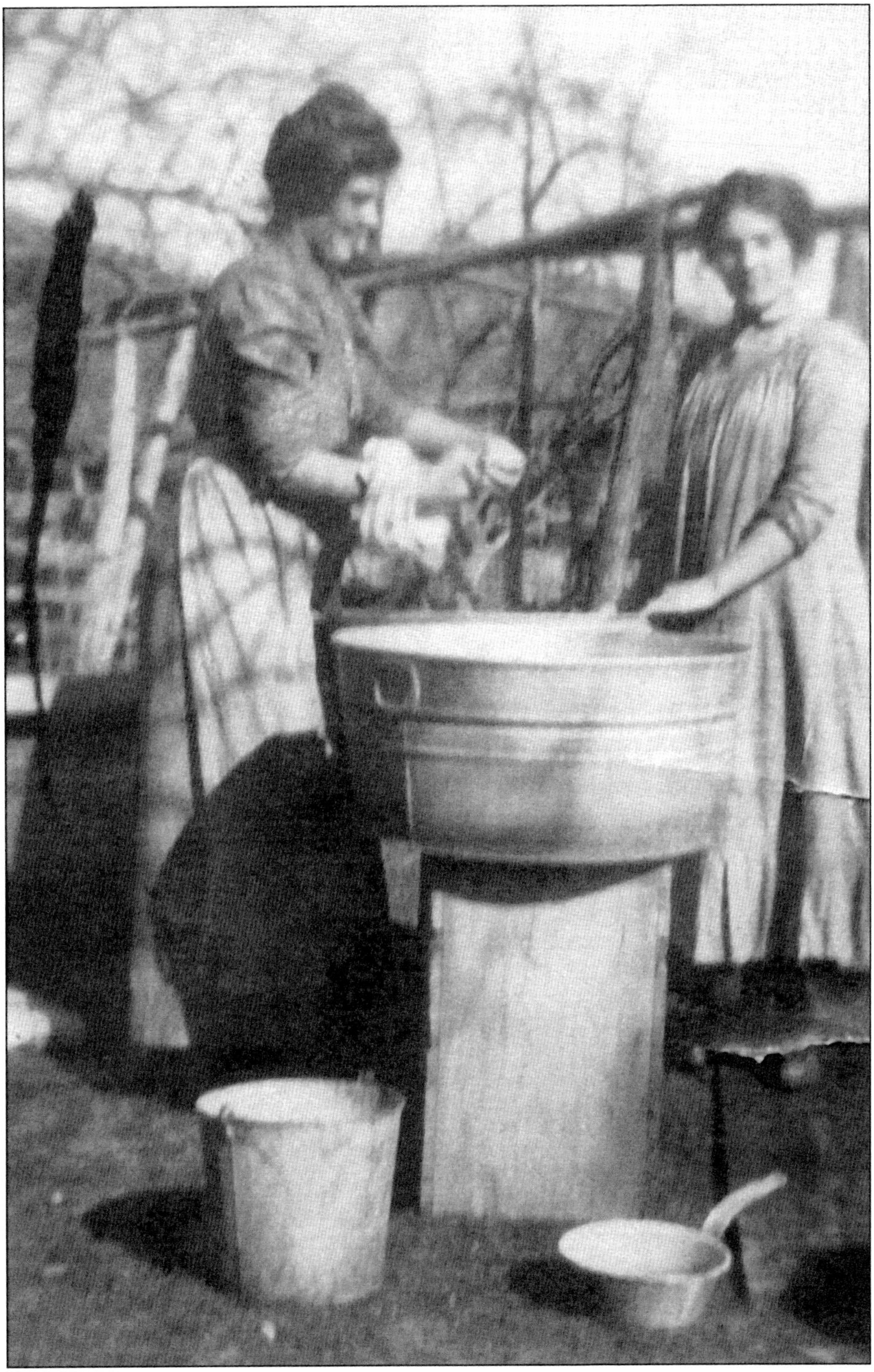

WASH DAY. Margaret Harvey Shufflebarger and her daughter, Naomi Helvey, are shown here washing clothes. Bland County was once humorously referred to as "The home of hard-working women and shade-loving men," but in truth, there was always plenty of work for everyone in the rugged mountains of Southwest Virginia. (Courtesy of Billy Jean [Walters] Carty.)

Two

America at War

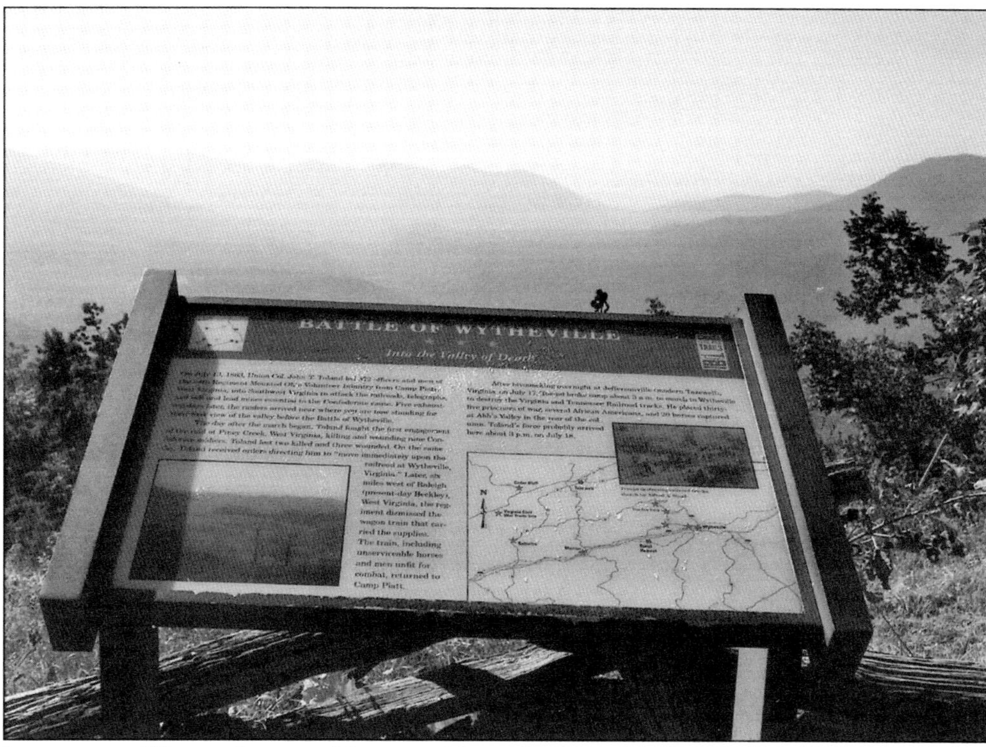

Invasion of Wythe County, Virginia. Union brevet general John T. Toland and the 1,000 cavalry troops in his command looked out on essentially the same vista as the one pictured here after moving through Burke's Garden, across Brushy Mountain, and over Big Walker Mountain on July 17, 1863. Toland's army was on the way to destroy the (then) Virginia & Tennessee Railway, which passed through Wytheville. (Author's.)

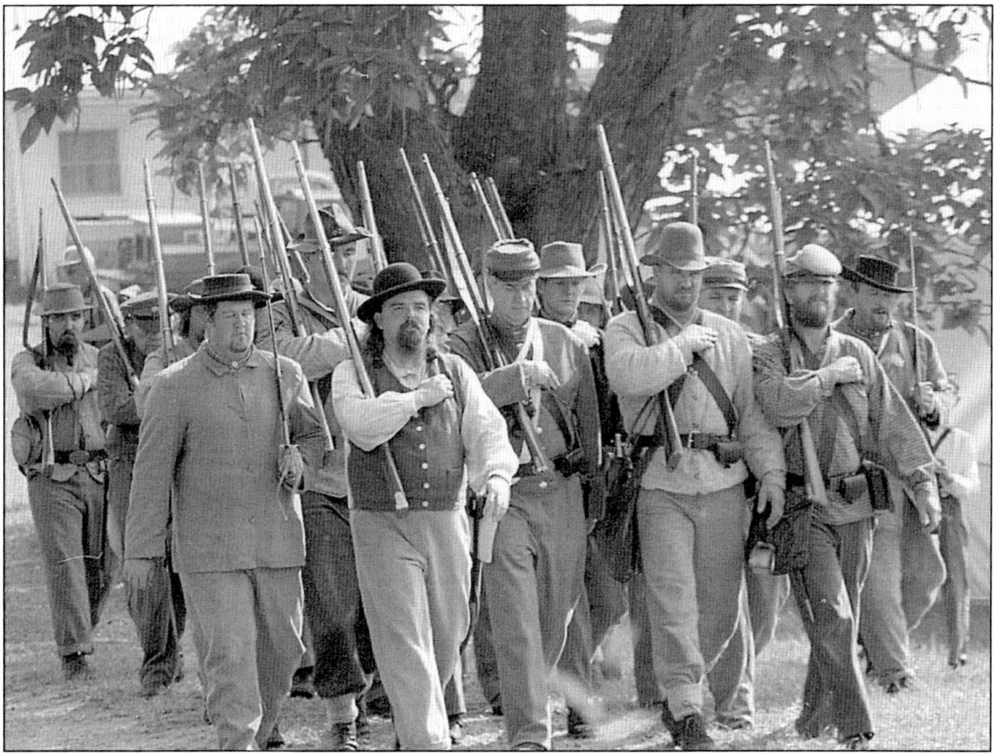

DEFENSE OF THE HOMELAND. Confederate troops camped in the vicinity of the Cove in Tazewell County, Virginia, under the command of Col. A.J. May. They pursued Toland and caught up with his forces at Stony Fork, about six miles northwest of Wytheville. Confederate reenactors are shown here demonstrating close-order drill techniques at Saltville, Virginia, in 1998. (Author's.)

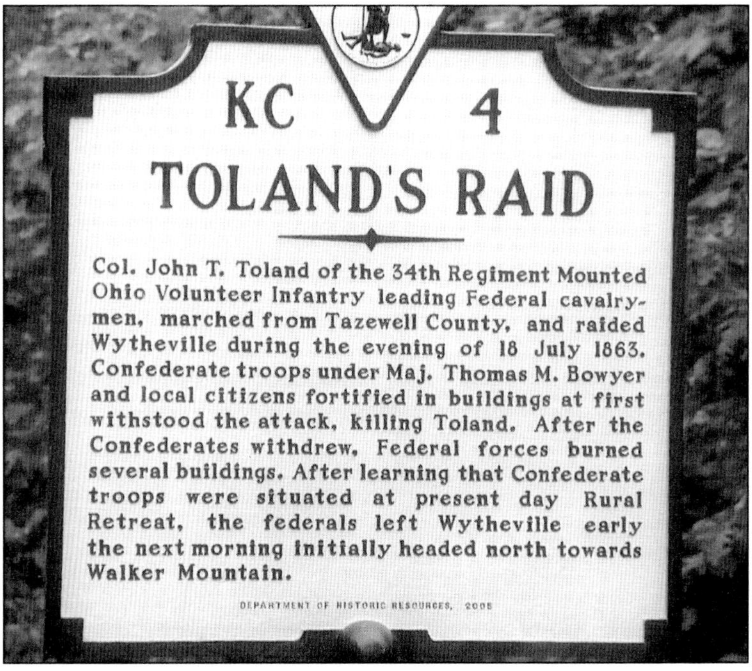

LIVING HISTORY. The historic marker on US Route 52 at the top of Big Walker Mountain tells the story of Toland's raid through Tazewell and Bland Counties into Wythe County, Virginia. (Author's.)

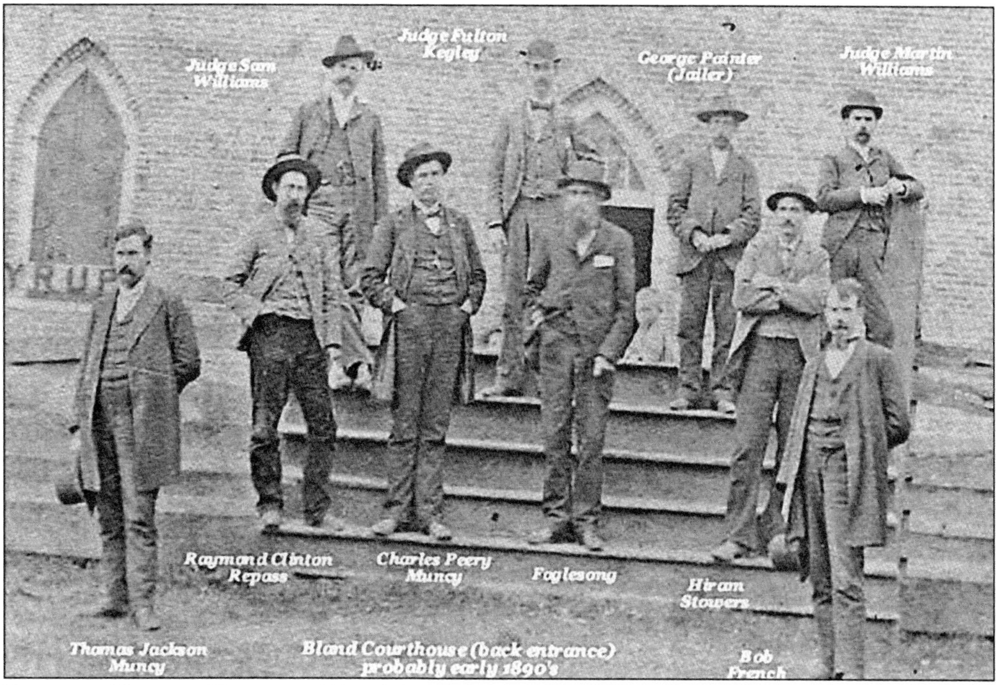

Birth of Bland, Virginia. Bland County was created by an act that passed the Virginia General Assembly on March 30, 1861, less than three weeks before Virginia seceded from the Union at the start of the American Civil War. Several of Bland County's early founders are shown here. Those pictured are, from left to right, (first row) Thomas Jackson Muncy and Bob French; (second row) Raymond Clinton Repass, Charles Peery Muncy, ? Foglesong, and Hiram Stowers; (third row) Judge Sam Williams, Judge Fulton Kegley, George Painter (jailer), and Judge Martin Williams. (Courtesy of the Bland County Historical Society.)

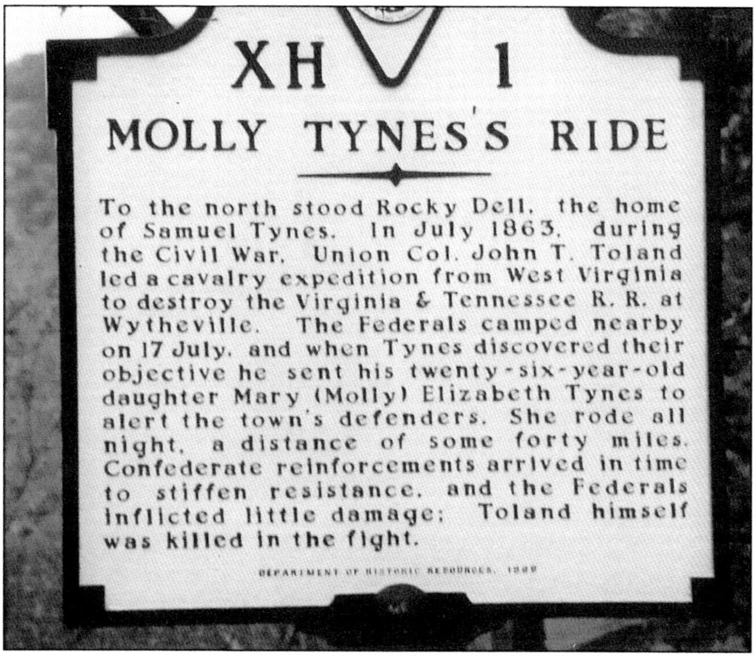

Heroine of the Battle of Wytheville. Molly Tynes, 26, was at home in Tazewell County, Virginia, in the summer of 1863 when she overheard Union soldiers discuss the attack on Wytheville, Virginia. Tynes rode to Wytheville to alert Confederate defenders of the coming attack by the troops commanded by Gen. John P. Toland. (Author's.)

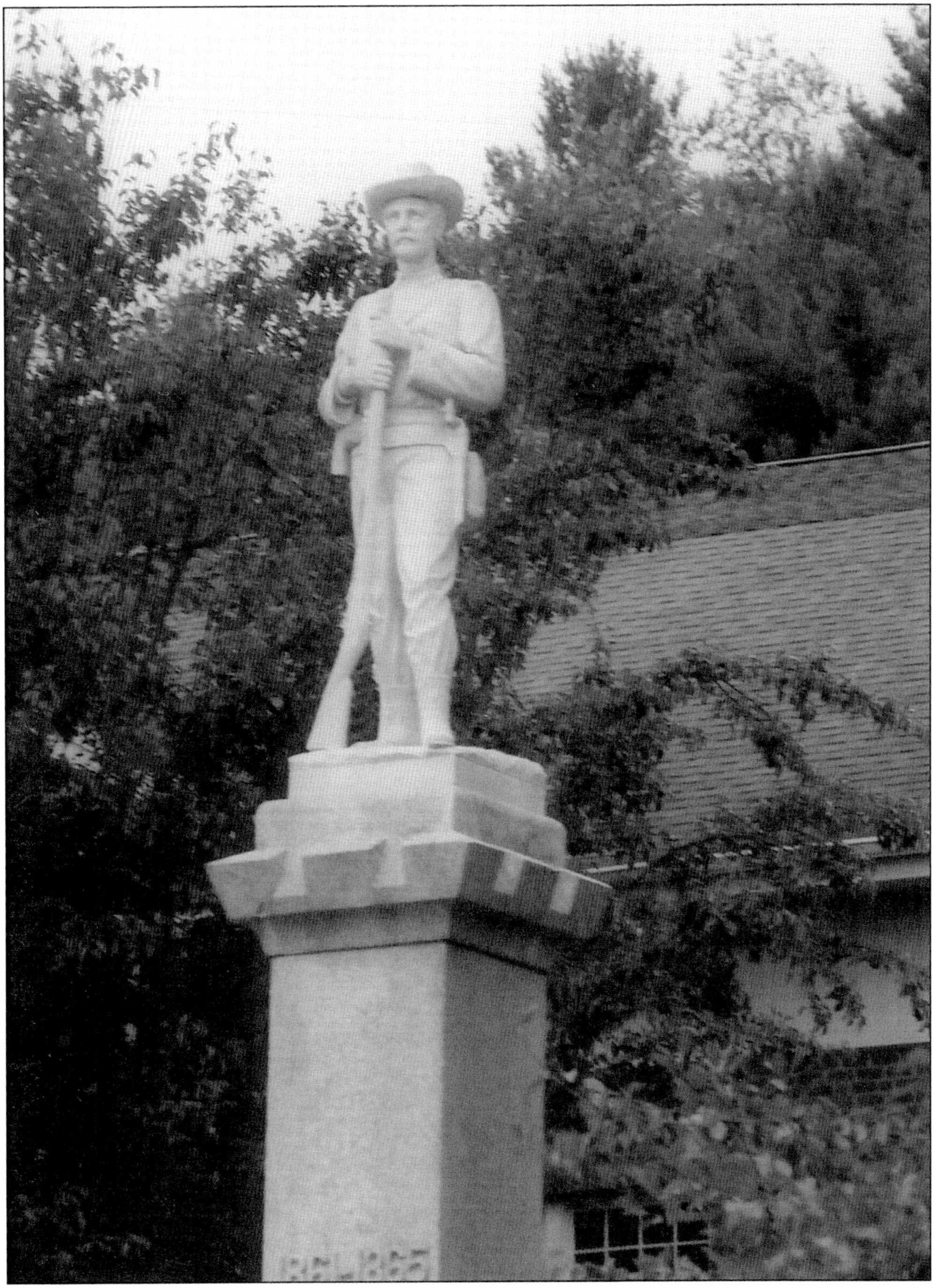

SENTINEL. The Bland Chapter of the United Daughters of the Confederacy dedicated this monument in front of the Bland County Courthouse in August 1911. It states the following: "To the gallant sons of Bland County who gave their lives in defense of their beloved Southland. Fate denied them victory but crowned them with glorious immortality." The monument includes notations honoring five companies of the Virginia infantry and cavalry including the 51st, 36th, and 45th infantry divisions; the 47th battalion; and the 8th cavalry. (Author's.)

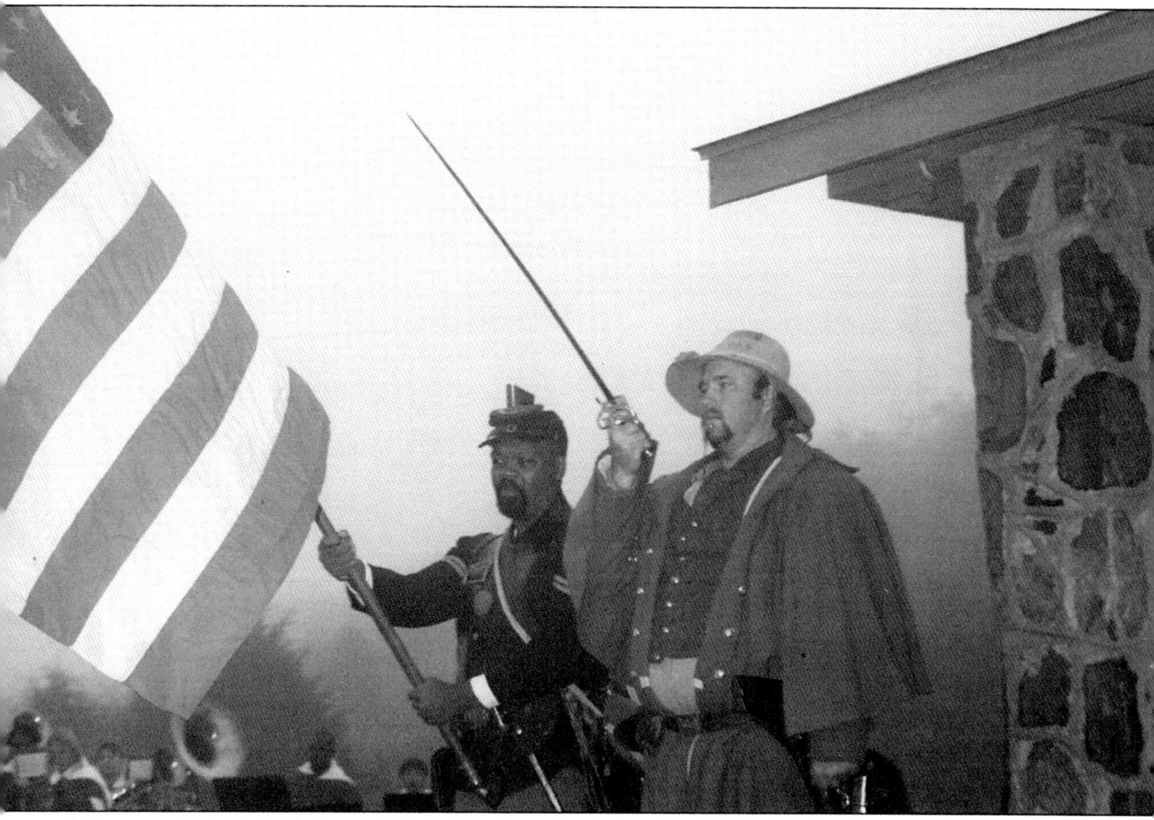

COMBINED SALUTE. Charles Rawlins (left), a reenactor with the 54th Massachusetts Regiment, and Capt. Jim Boardwine, a reenactor with the 22nd Virginia Cavalry, are shown here on October 3, 1999, in a combined salute to the soldiers who died in the October 2, 1864, battle of Saltville. The dawn service was conducted at the Battlefield Overlook in Saltville, Virginia. Reenactors like Rawlins and Boardwine serve as living historians and help people understand the American Civil War. (Author's.)

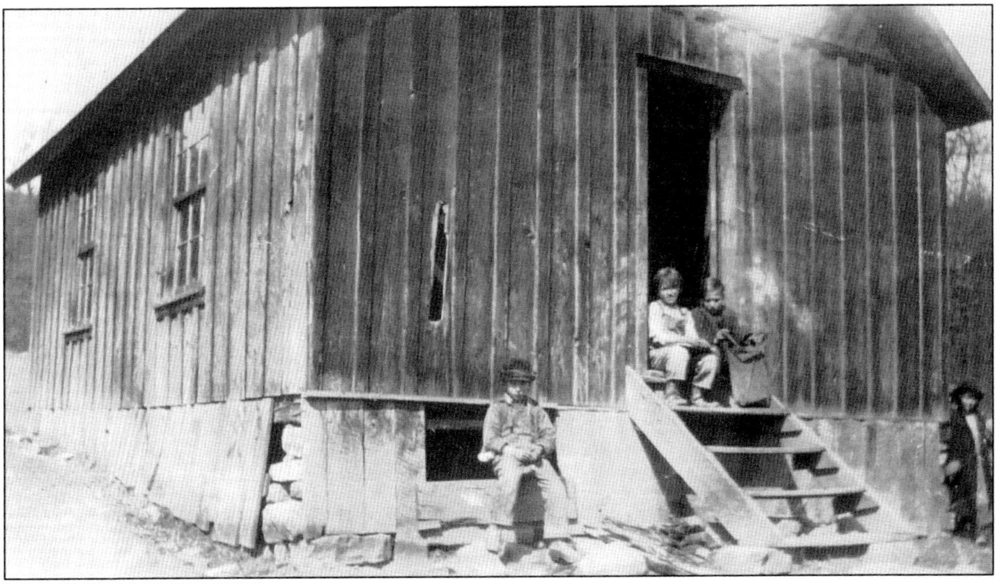

Aftermath. The war left Virginia with many new challenges as the nation worked to reunite. Public schools in rural areas faced extreme conditions like the Bogle School on Wolf Creek, shown here. (Courtesy of Billy Jean [Walters] Carty.)

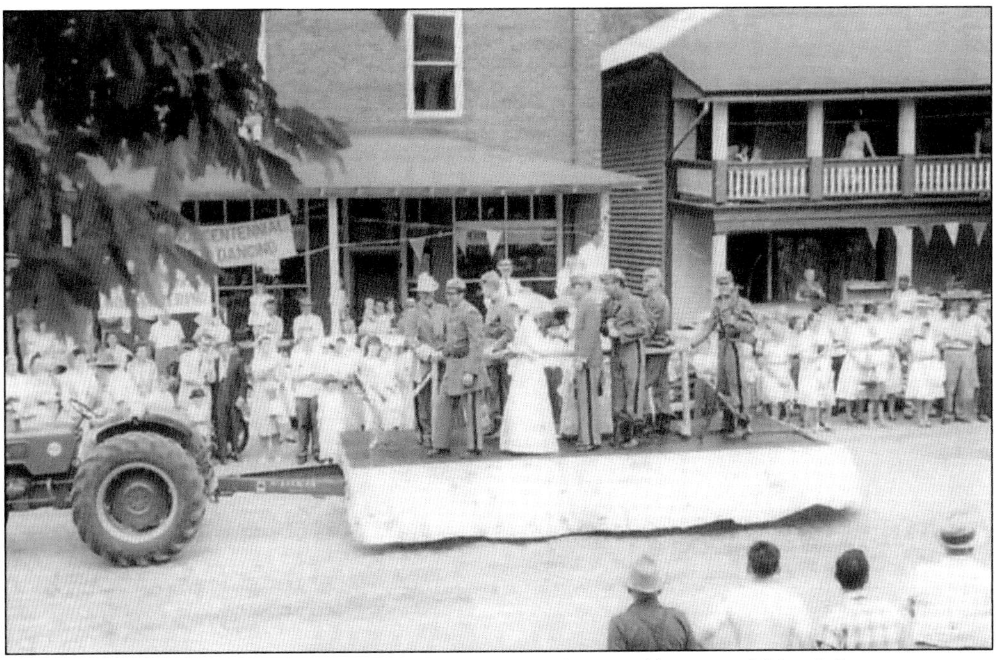

Heritage on Parade. Although the Virginia General Assembly created Bland County prior to secession, the county government was organized in May 1861, which was after Virginia had become part of the Confederacy. The county honored its Southern heritage during Bland's centennial parade in 1961 with the float shown above. (Photograph from the Bogle Library Collection; courtesy of the Bland County Historical Society.)

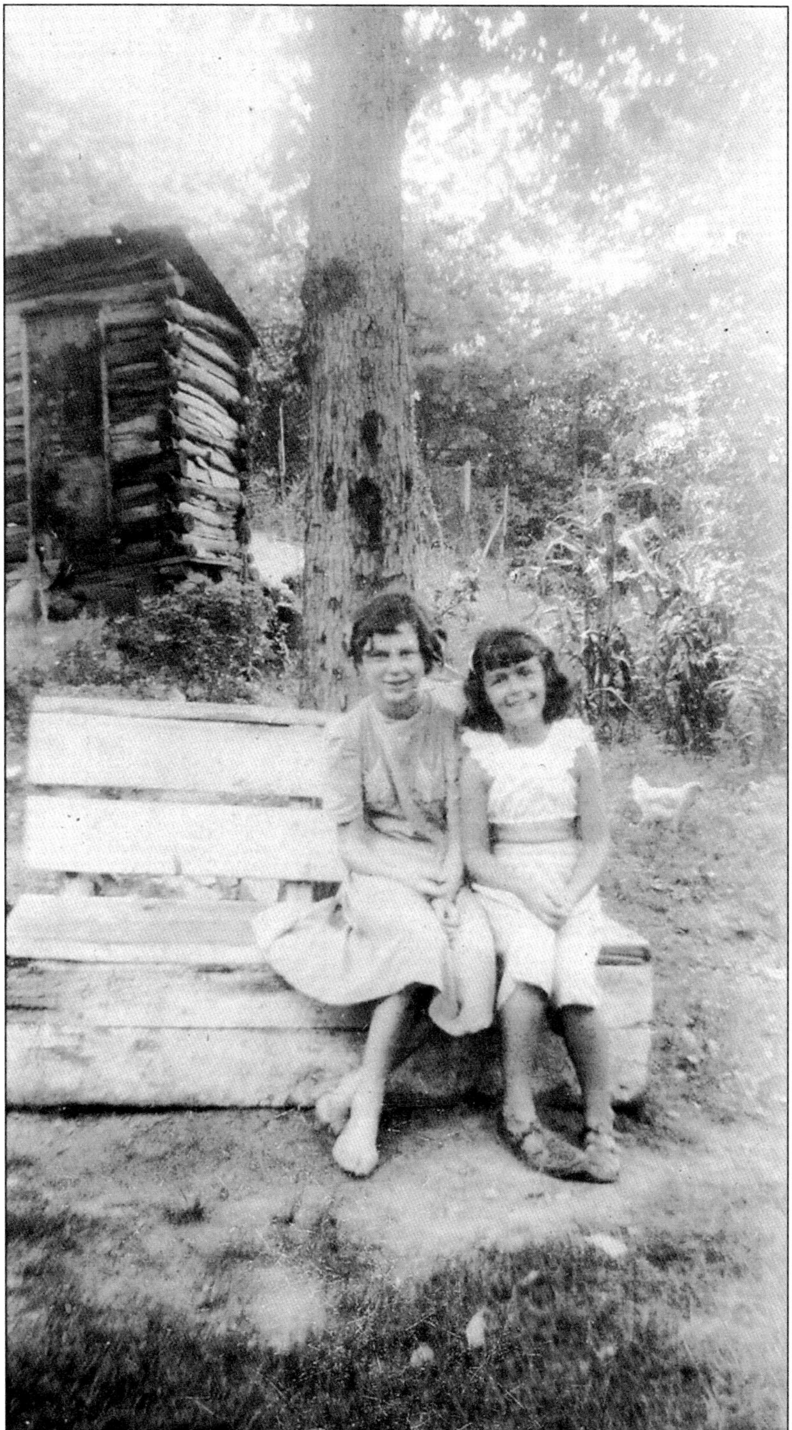

FRIENDS. While rural life has its challenges, friends like Jean Shrewsbury (left) and Felicia Hurley can still enjoy an afternoon sitting on a handcrafted bench in the sunshine and just talking at the Dangerfield cabin on Laurel Fork. (Courtesy of Rick Owens.)

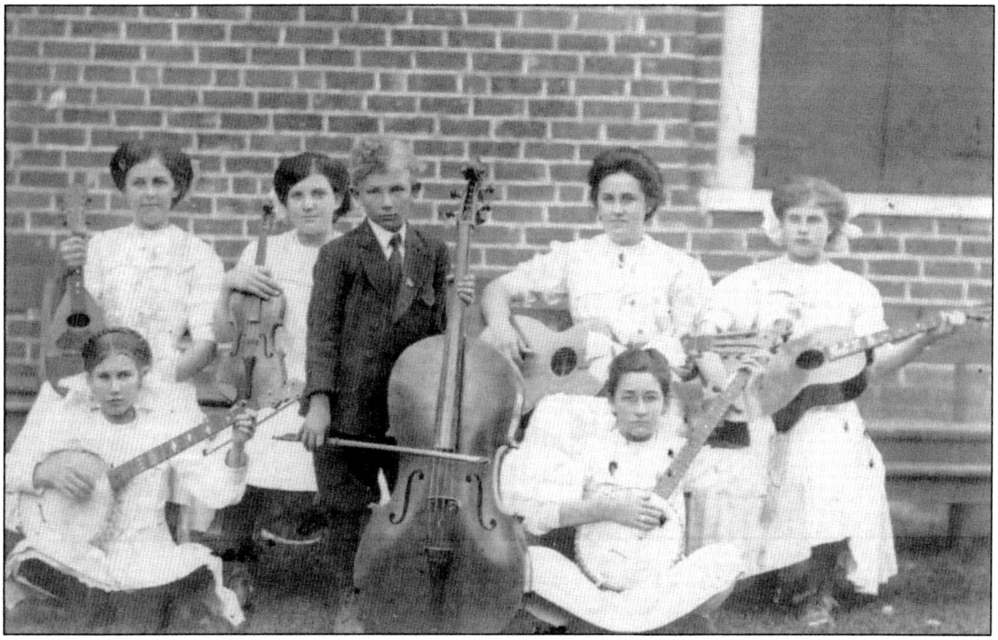

Music. The popular Tickle Family Band from Bland is shown here. Group members shown include, in no set order, Elizabeth Estelle Tickle, Effie Kate Tickle, Lilly Cecil Tickle, Robert Mason Tickle, Virginia E. Tickle, Ruby Olive Tickle, and Annie Melissa Tickle. (Courtesy of Wanda Burton Reynolds.)

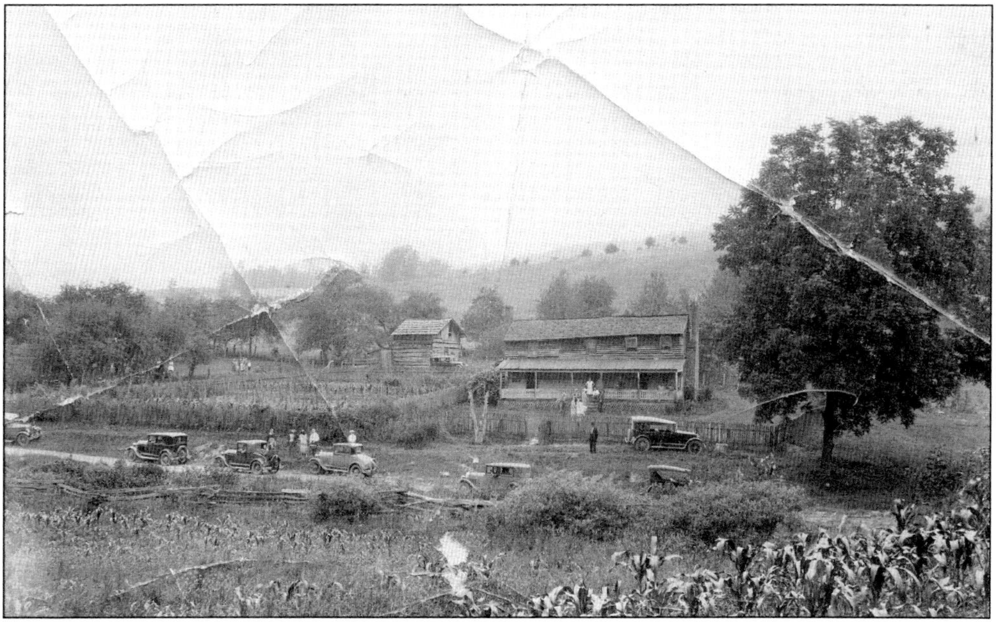

Big Valley. The Rev. A.A. Ashworth home on the Blue Grass Trail was located a few miles from the Bland community. (Courtesy of Alan Ashworth.)

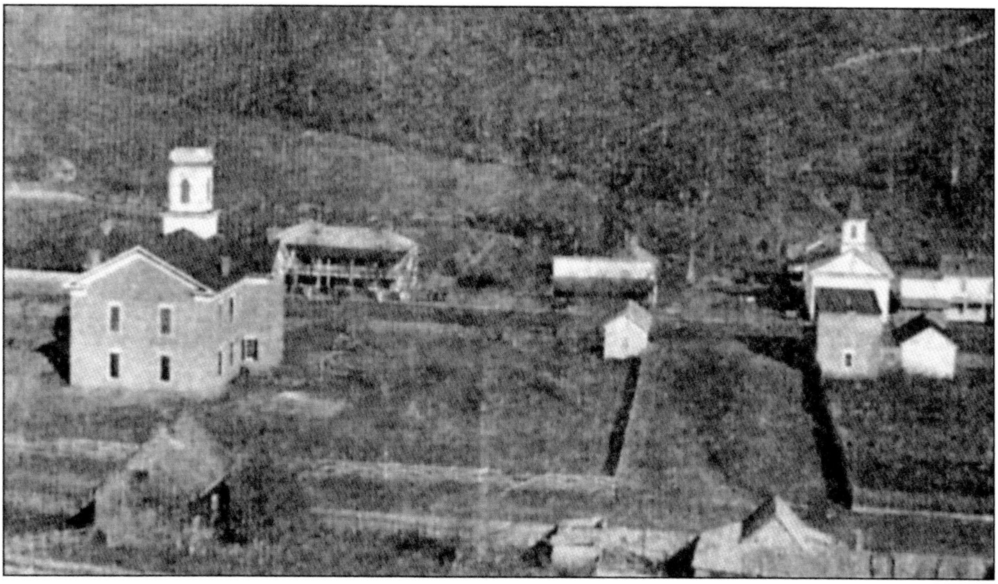

Early Times. This photograph of Bland from the early days was included in the county centennial brochure in 1961. (Courtesy of the Bland County Historical Society.)

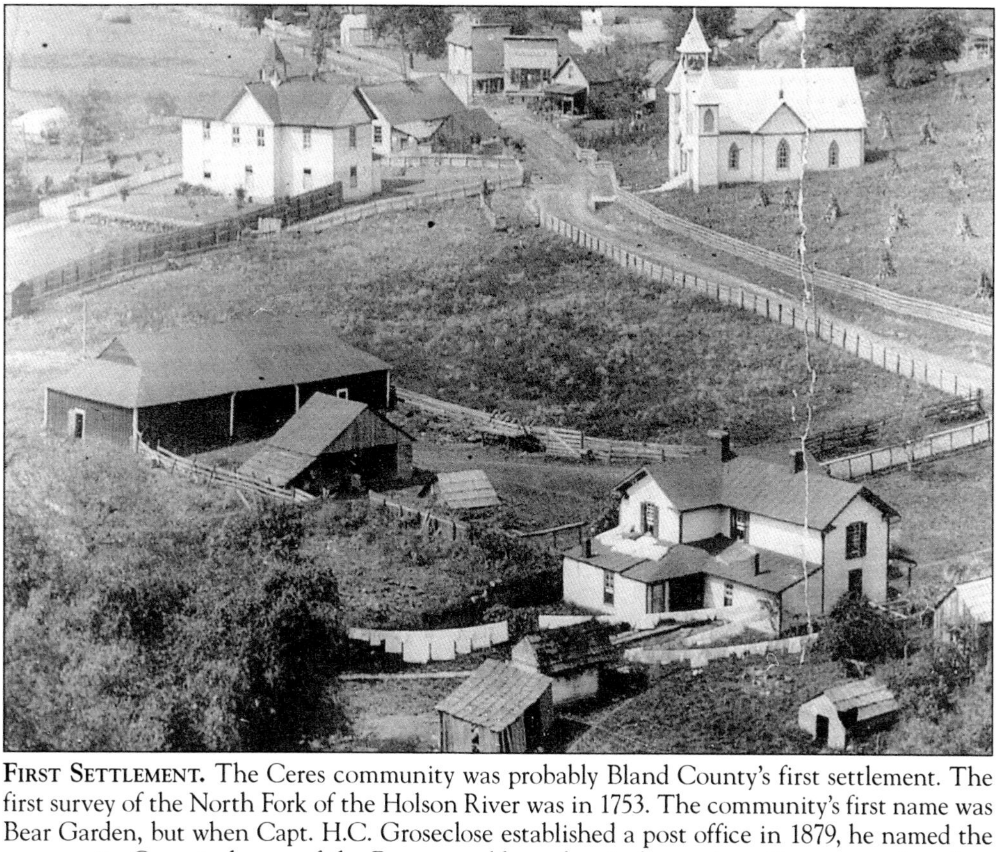

First Settlement. The Ceres community was probably Bland County's first settlement. The first survey of the North Fork of the Holson River was in 1753. The community's first name was Bear Garden, but when Capt. H.C. Groseclose established a post office in 1879, he named the community Ceres in honor of the Roman goddess of agriculture, since Ceres was primarily a farming community. (Courtesy of the Ceres Alumni Association.)

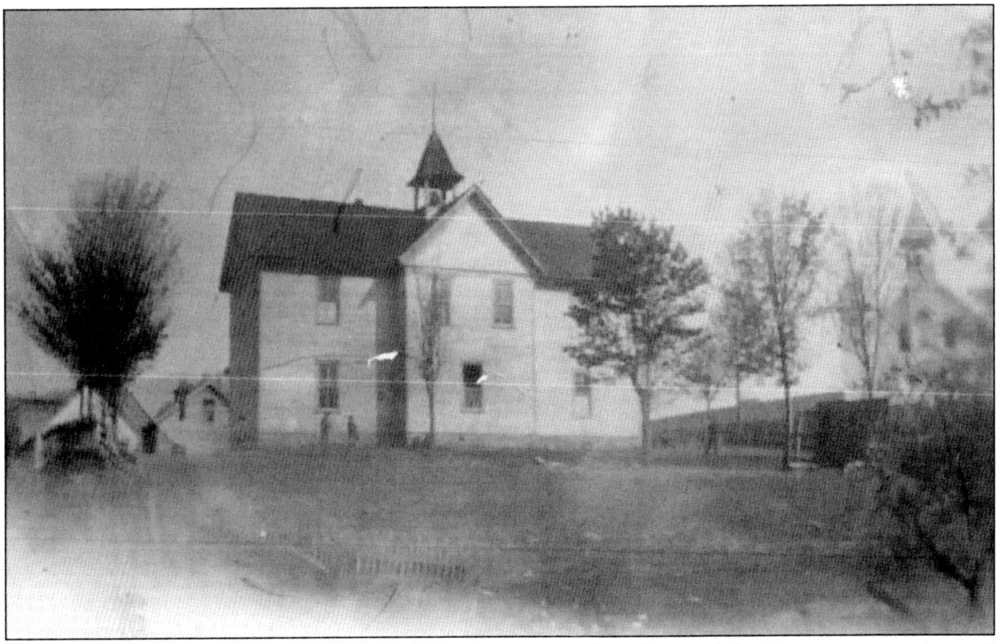

Old School. The Ceres High School, shown here, served students of the Ceres community and beyond. (Courtesy of the Ceres Alumni Association.)

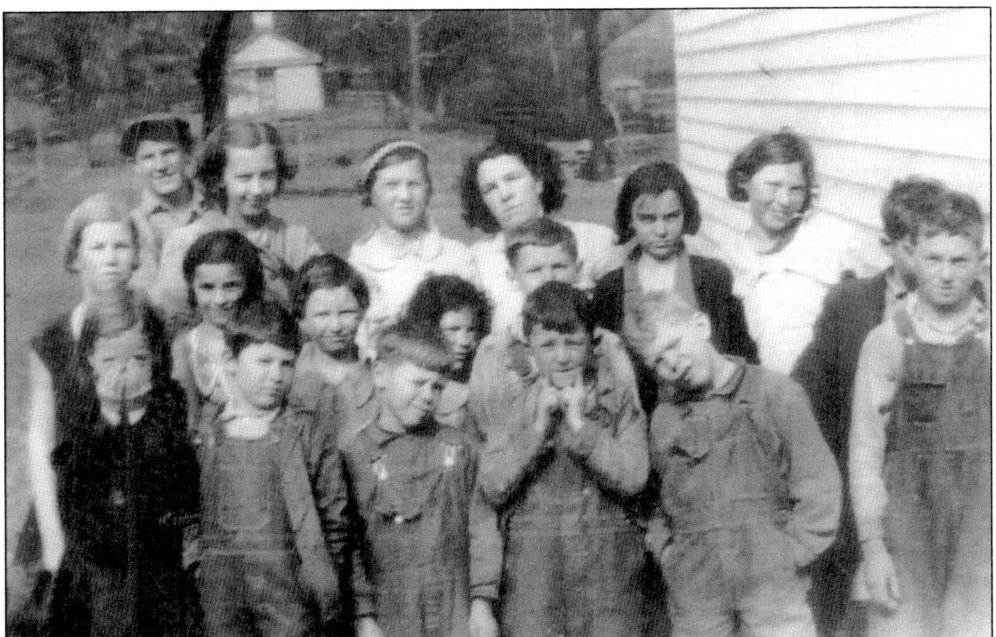

Student Body. Some students of a Bland County public school are shown here assembled for a school picture. Education has always been a high priority in Bland County. (Courtesy of the Bland County Historical Society.)

Centennial Attire. Nannie Rose Tiller is shown here decked out in her pioneer finest during the Bland County Centennial Celebration in 1961. (Courtesy of Nannie Rose Tiller.)

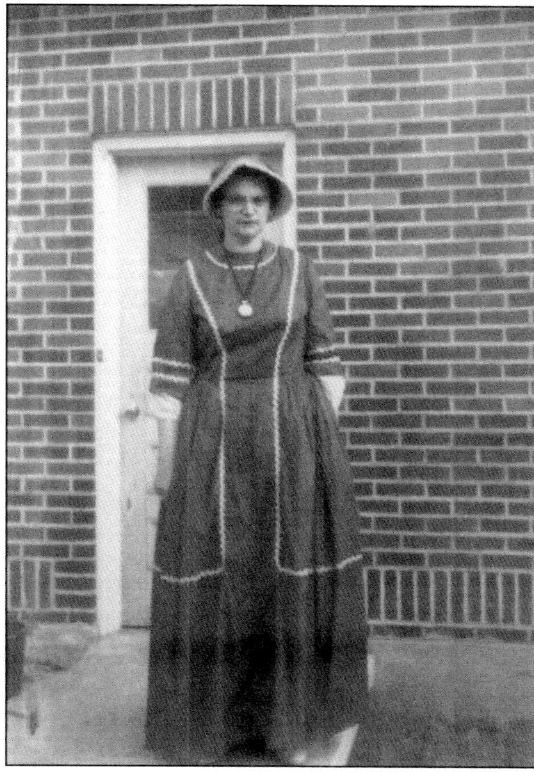

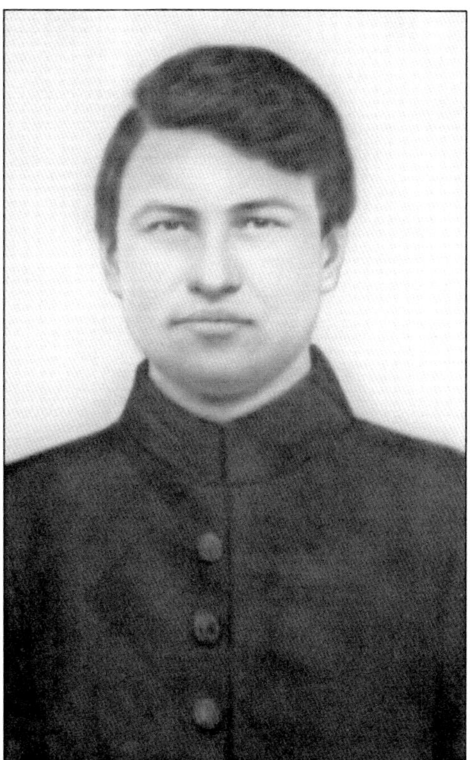

Returning Soldier. Berry Blankenship served in the Confederate army, which included service in Company F, 8th Cavalry Regiment, also known as the Bland Rangers. He was a prisoner of war at Camp Case, Ohio, at the end of the war. (Courtesy of Wanda Blankenship.)

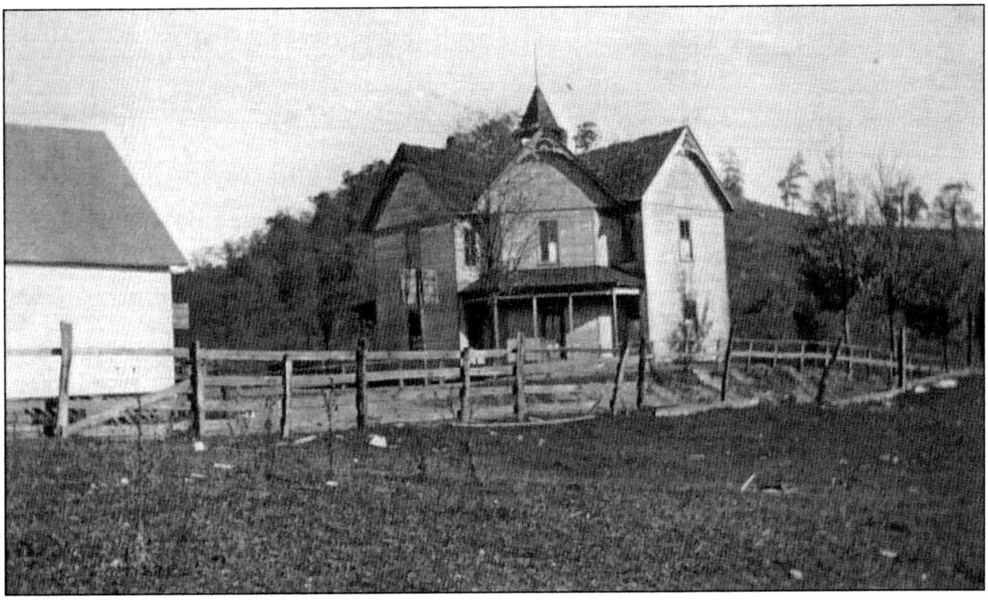

SAME SCHOOL. This is another view of Ceres High School. Note the ornate lattice work in the front of the building. (Courtesy of the Ceres Alumni Association.)

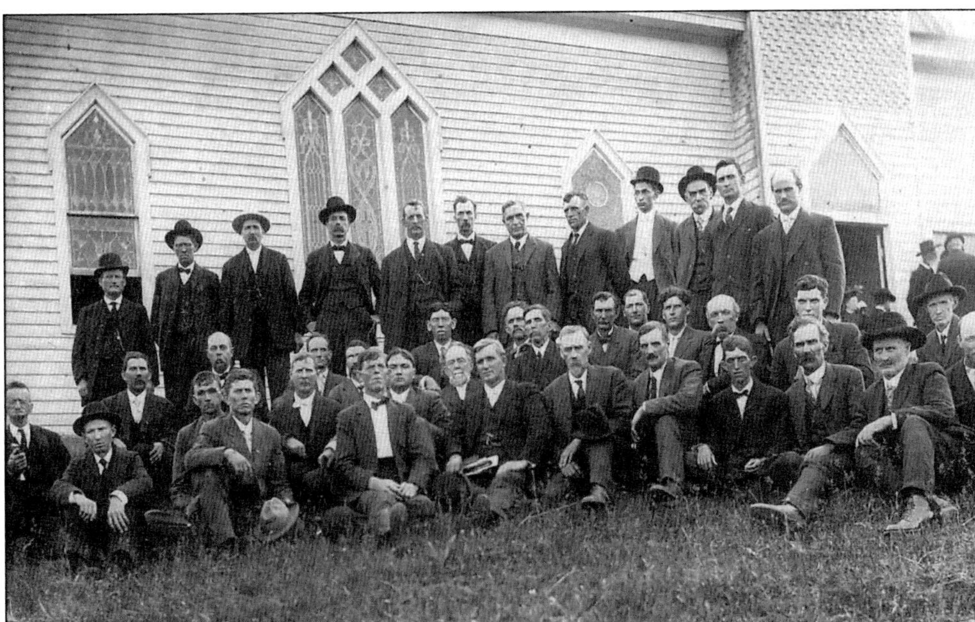

CONFERENCE CALL. Members of the Methodist District Conference are shown here discussing matters of religion during a meeting in Bland in May 1908. (Courtesy of the Bland County Historical Society.)

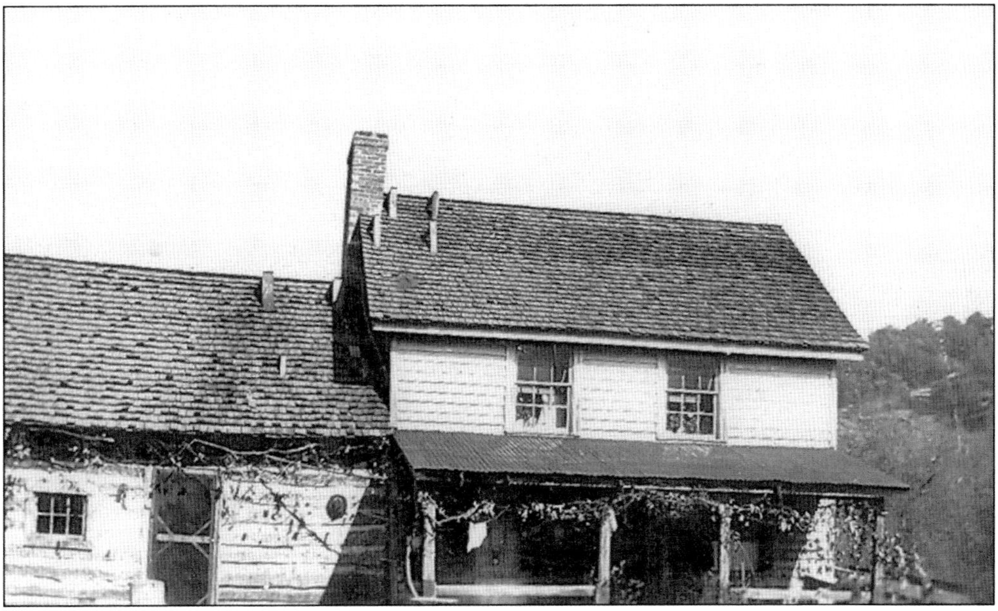

OLD HOME PLACE. The Giles Henderson and Callie Dixie Burton home was located on Walkers Creek and built in 1859. (Courtesy of Wanda Burton Reynolds.)

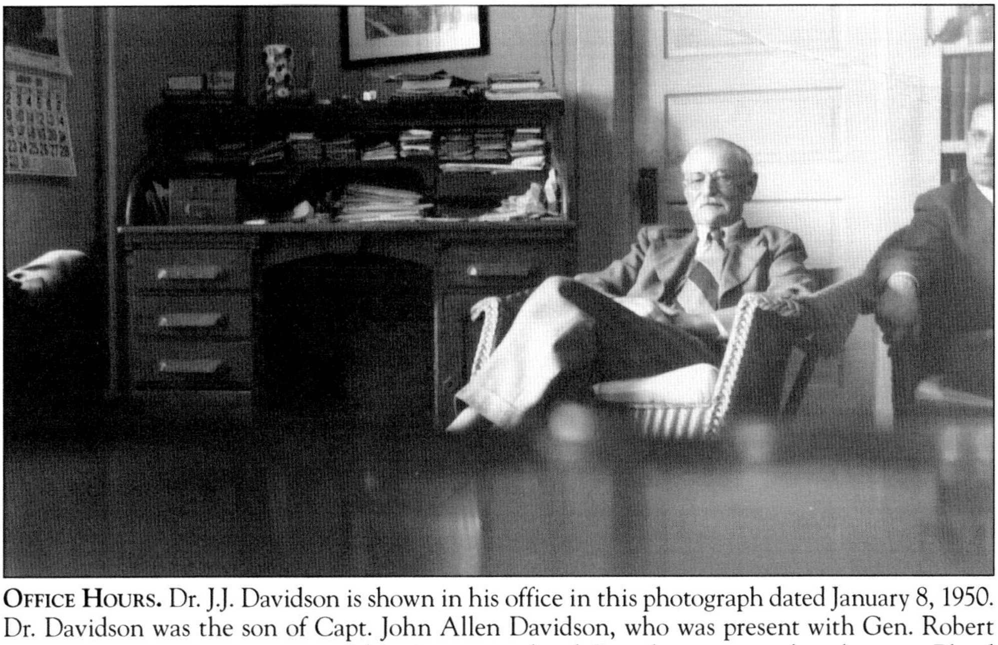

OFFICE HOURS. Dr. J.J. Davidson is shown in his office in this photograph dated January 8, 1950. Dr. Davidson was the son of Capt. John Allen Davidson, who was present with Gen. Robert E. Lee at Appomattox, Virginia, when Lee surrendered. Davidson practiced medicine in Bland County from 1908 until his death on December 31, 1952. (Photograph from the Bogle Library Collection; courtesy of the Bland County Historical Society.)

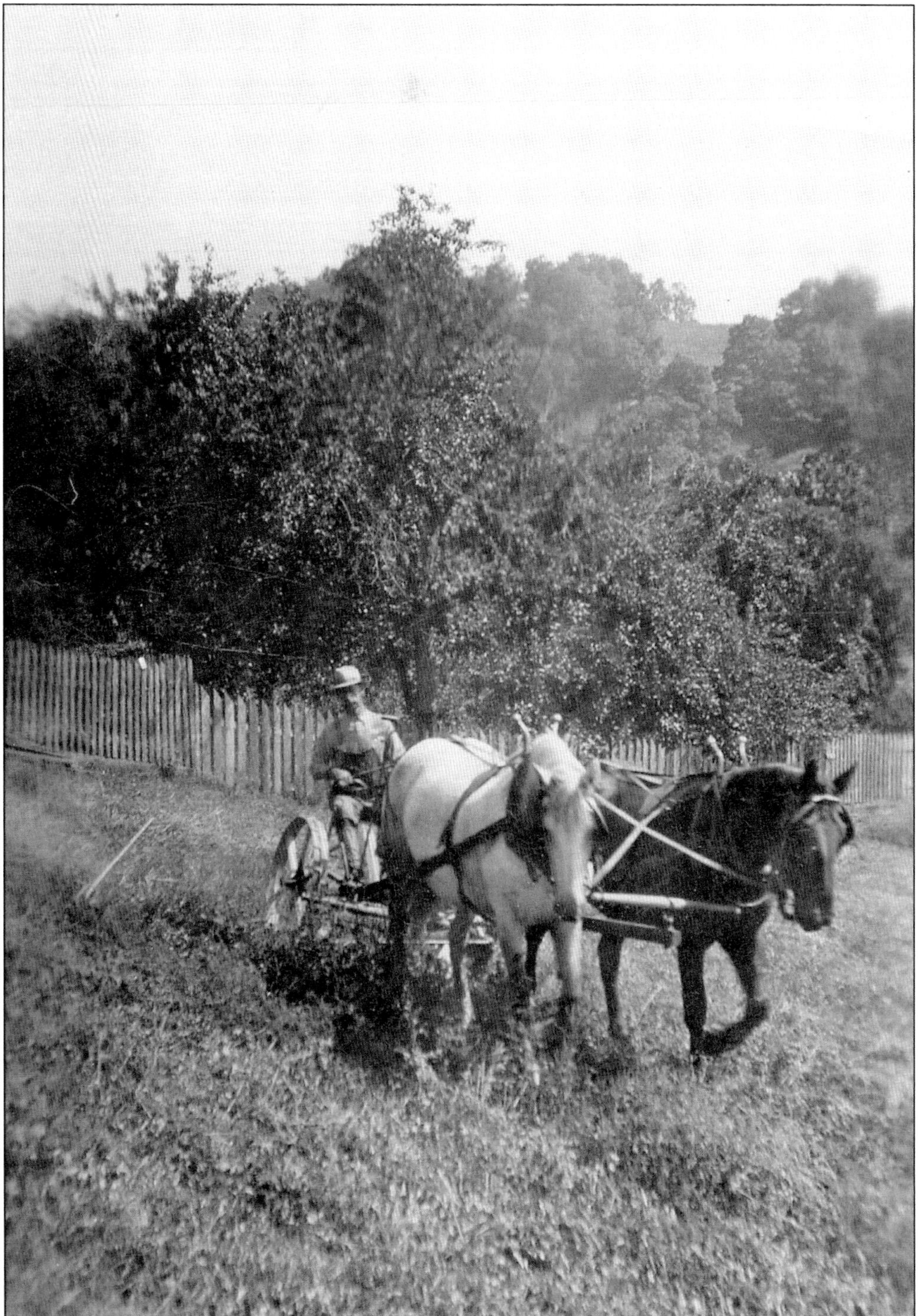

Haying Time. L.D. (Dell) Burton is shown here mowing hay with a team of horses at the family farm on Walkers Creek in 1935. Many Bland County farmers continued to use horses to work their fields well into the 20th century. (Courtesy of Wanda Burton Reynolds.)

Play Ball. Members of the Silver Creek Elementary School softball team are shown here ready to play a game. (Courtesy of Wanda Blankenship.)

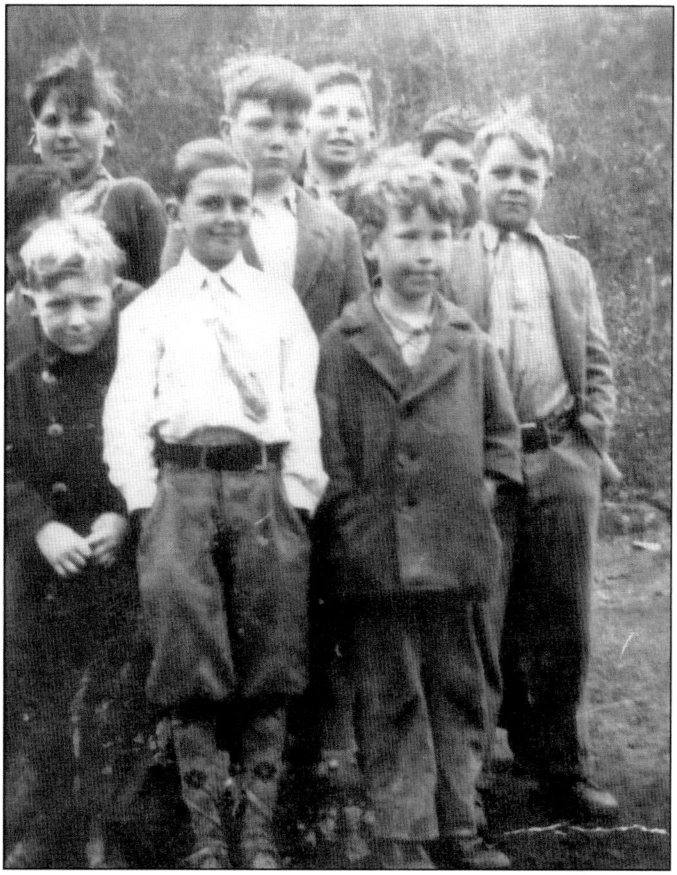

Rebuilding Effort. Bland County was home to Capt. Samuel H. Newberry. He was the leader of the "Big Four" of the Virginia State Senate who fought to preserve Virginia as a Democratic state during the post–Civil War Reconstruction period. Newberry called his home Eagle Oak. (Author's.)

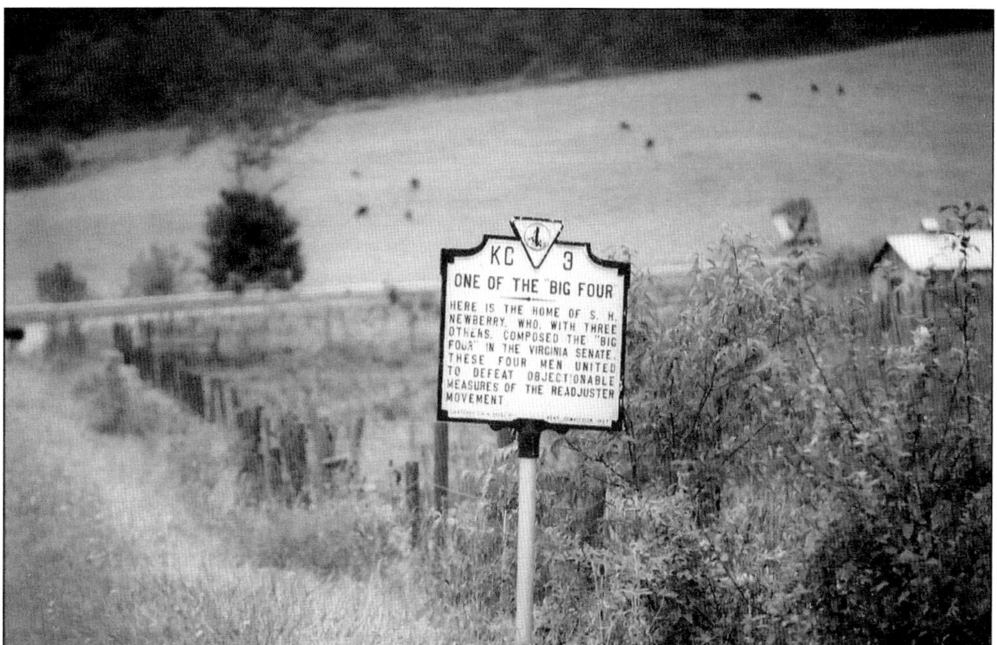

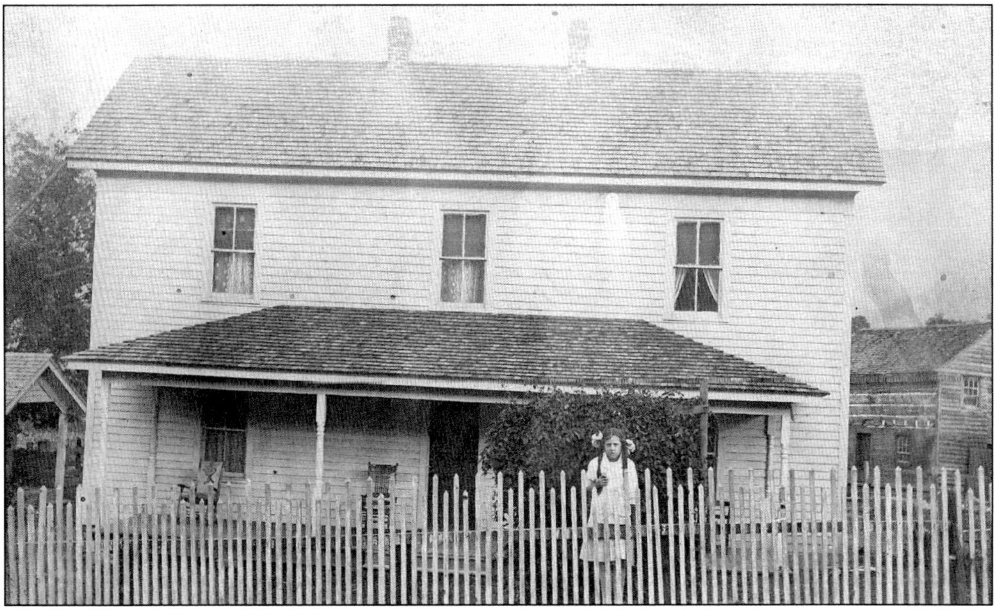

New Home. An unidentified girl is shown here standing in front of the new Shufflebarger house that was built to replace the family's former home, which was destroyed by fire. The residence is now the home of Billy Jean's Flowers on US Route 52 in Bastian, Virginia. (Courtesy of Billy Jean [Walters] Carty.)

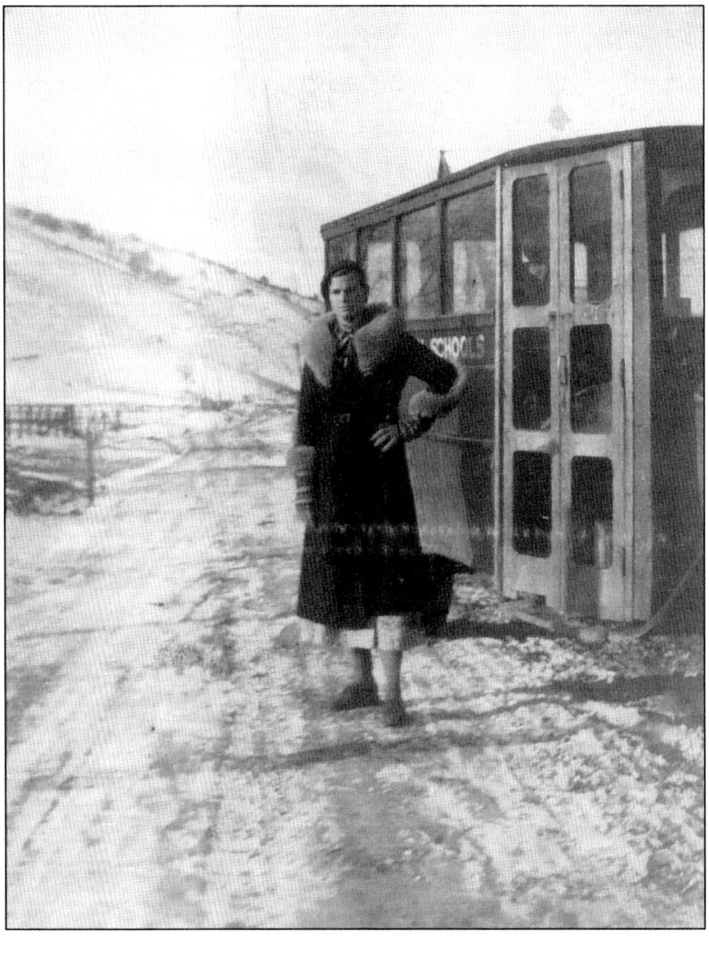

School Spirit. Cecil Robinette Bruce, the wife of Guy Bruce, is shown here standing in front of a school bus in Bastian, Virginia. Cecil Bruce was the principal at the school in Bastian, which was built by the Virginia Hardwood Lumber Company in 1927. (Courtesy of Georgia Stacy Havens.)

Three

Taming the Mountains

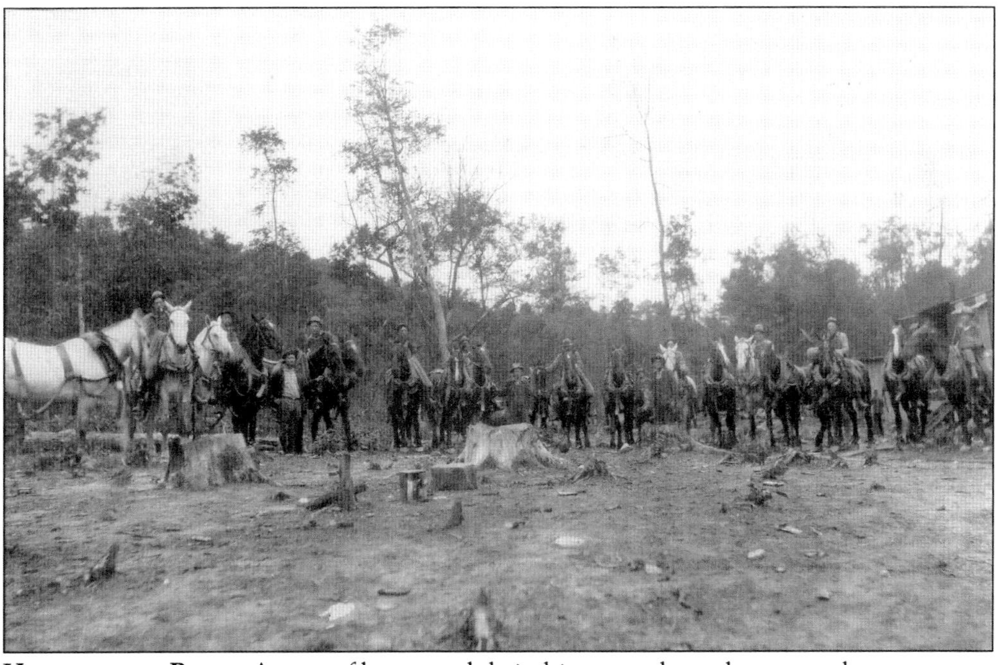

Horses at the Ready. A gang of horses and their drivers are shown here as workers prepare to clear ground for the Virginia Hardwood Lumber Company camp at Bastian, Virginia. (Courtesy of Georgia Stacy Havens.)

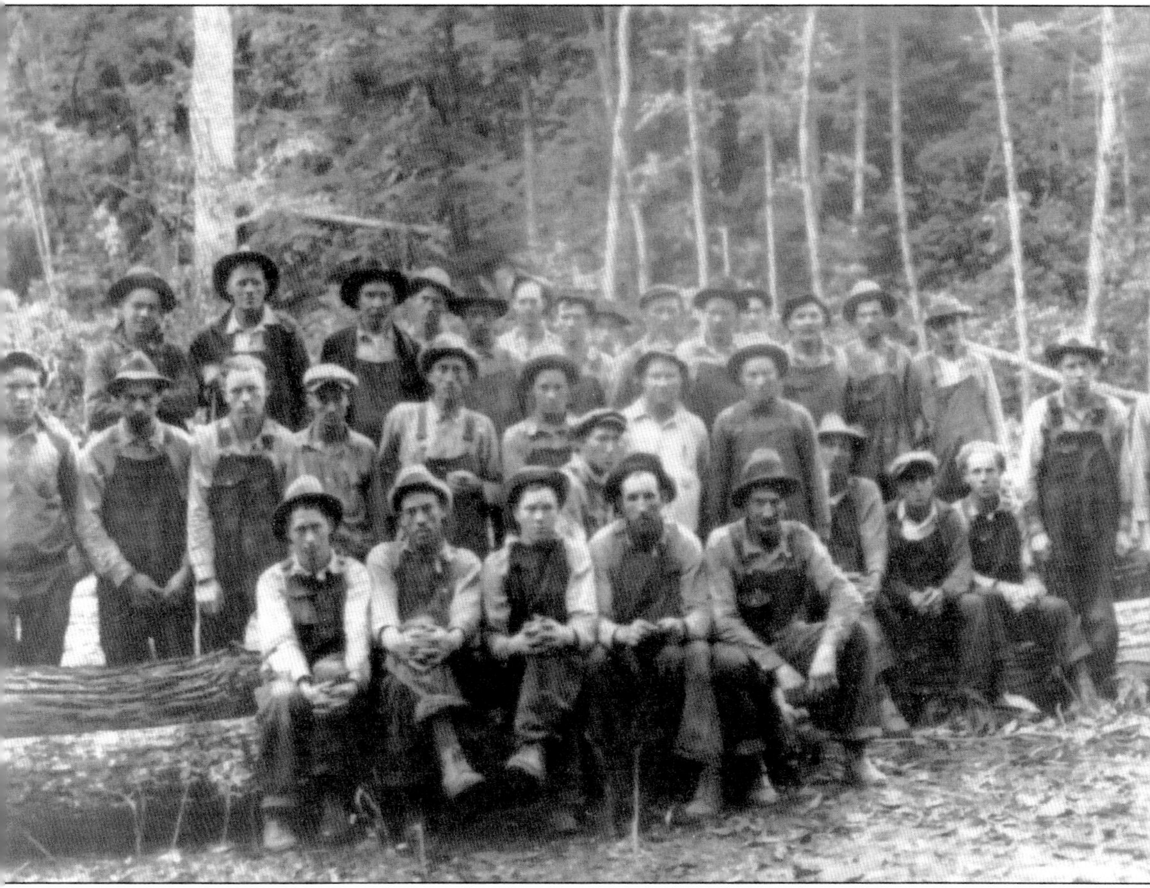

Lumber Crew. Several workers of the Virginia Hardwood Company mill, some green lumber, and a shop are shown in this August 28, 1928, photograph taken at the camp in Crab Orchard, near Suiter. The workers who were present for the photograph include Otis Estep, Bill Page, John Winegar, Ted Linkenfelter, Albert Pauley, William Vanover, Eck Neal, Chafe Paule, Pat Griffith, Kearney Puckett, Alfonso Puckett, Mose Sarver, Bill Paige, Elmer Clemens (or Hoyt McConnell), Clarence Presley, Ira Cox, John S. Cassell, Tyler Kidd, Felix Cummings, Ellie Sams, Martin Kitts, Ike Pauley, Max Vermilya, Ernest Clements, Lloyd Quillen, J.D. Bliss, Julius "Dummy" Prater, Sheffie Hancock, Straley Kitts, Jack Barton, Ace Tolliver, Arch Wimmer, Lafayette Sexton, Graham Brickey, Paul Kidd, Emmit Stone, Lee Hall, Charlie Linkenfelter, ? Bentley, and John Beard. (Courtesy of Georgia Stacy Havens.)

Log Roll. Loggers with the Virginia Hardwood Lumber Company used Hunting Camp Creek in Bland County to transport logs to the mill at Suiter. (Courtesy of Georgia Stacy Havens.)

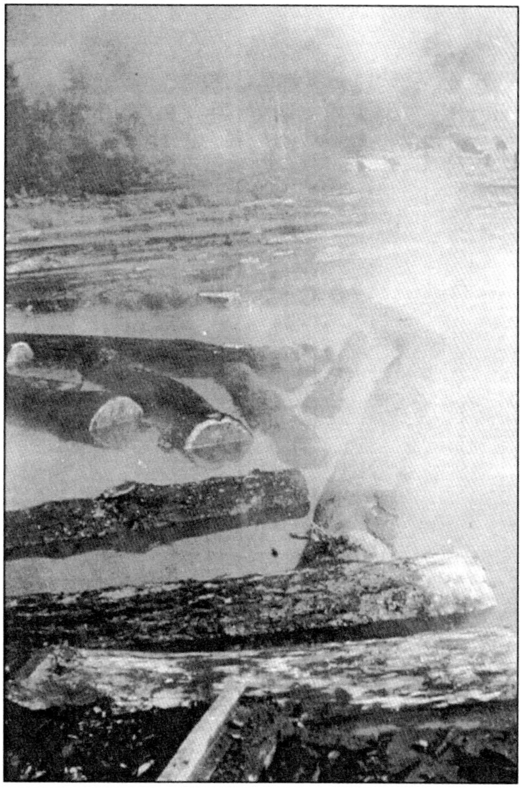

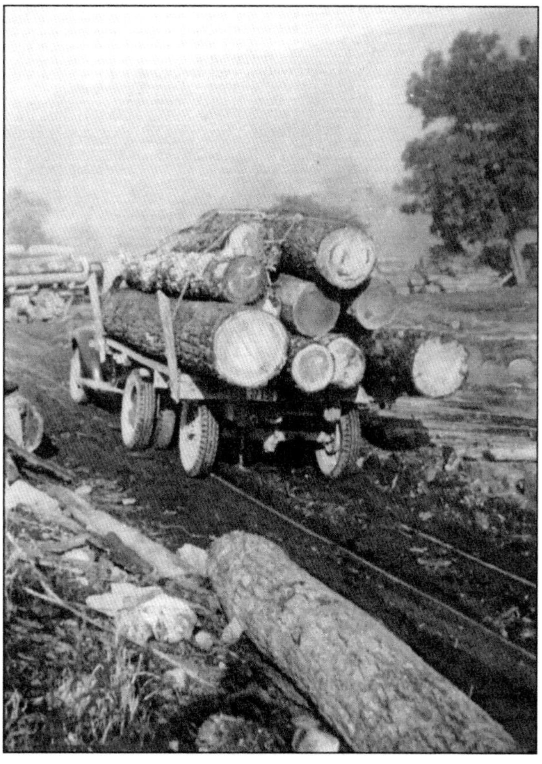

Lumber Overland. Loggers also used trucks to transport logs to the Virginia Hardwood Lumber Company mill. (Courtesy of Georgia Stacy Havens.)

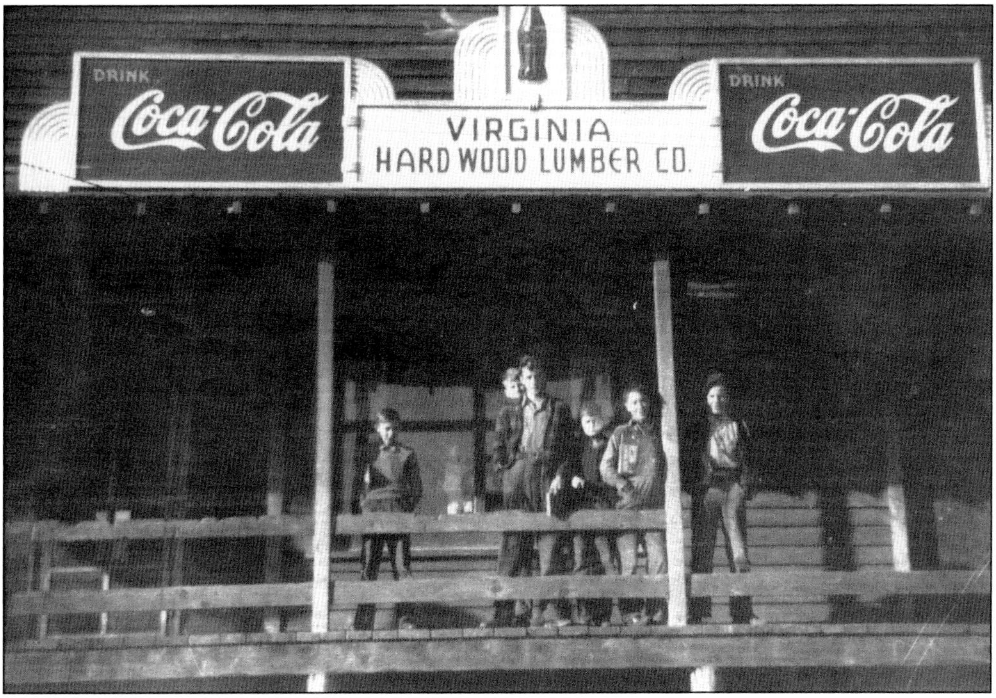

OWE MY SOUL. Several Virginia Hardwood Lumber Company employees are shown here in front of the old company store. Those pictured are, from left to right, Dean Cox, Edwin Mullins, Red Quillen, Frank Hall, and Elmer Pauley. (Courtesy of Georgia Stacy Havens.)

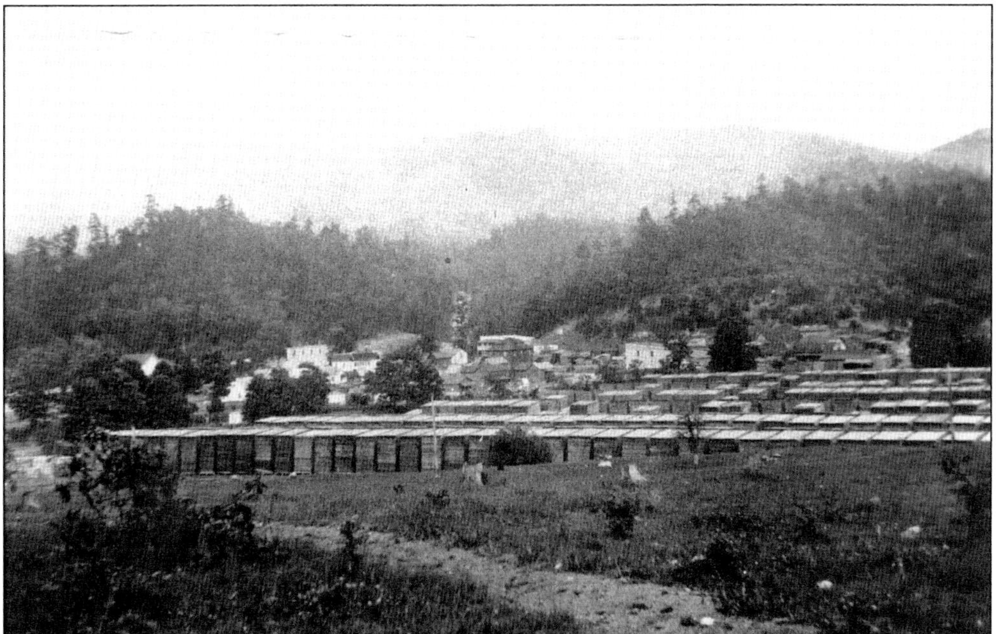

RACKED AND STACKED. Piles of cut lumber are shown here in Bruce Field, where lumber was stored before shipping. According to Georgia Havens, the first shipment of wood from Bland County went to England for use in the ship building industry. (Courtesy of Georgia Stacy Havens.)

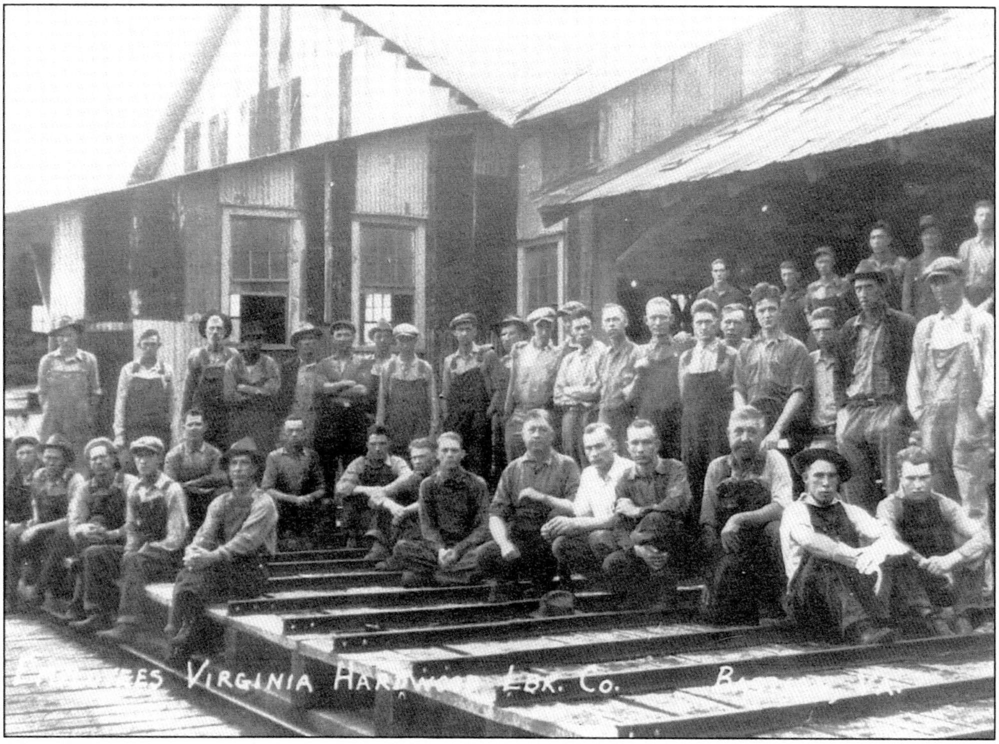

MILL WORKERS. Several Virginia Hardwood Lumber Company workers are shown here at the lumber mill in Suiter. (Courtesy of Georgia Stacy Havens.)

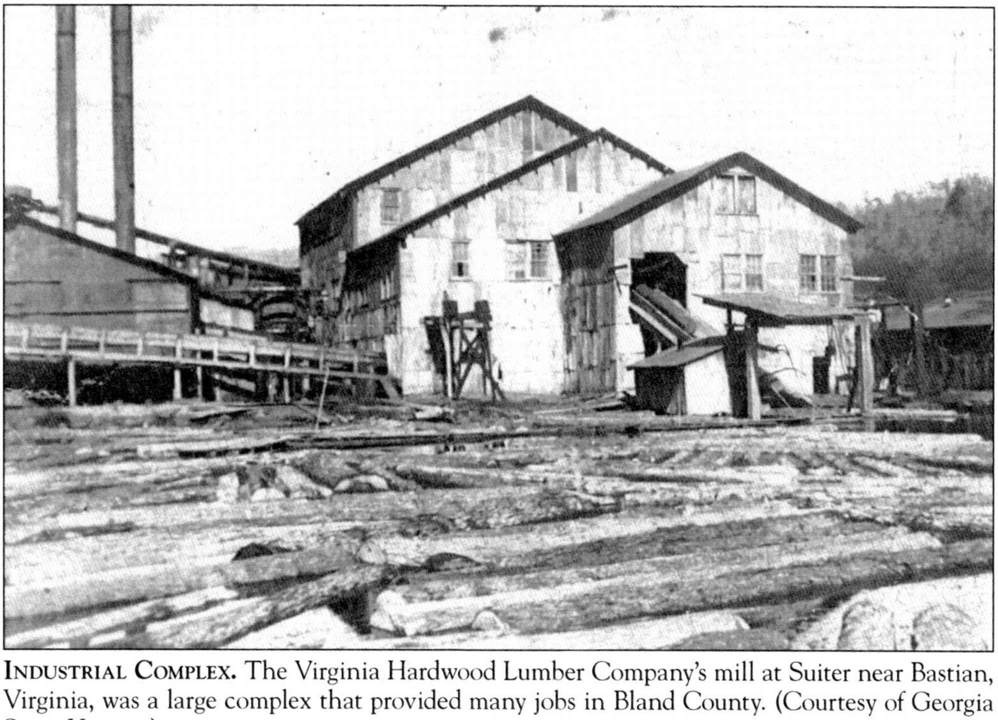

INDUSTRIAL COMPLEX. The Virginia Hardwood Lumber Company's mill at Suiter near Bastian, Virginia, was a large complex that provided many jobs in Bland County. (Courtesy of Georgia Stacy Havens.)

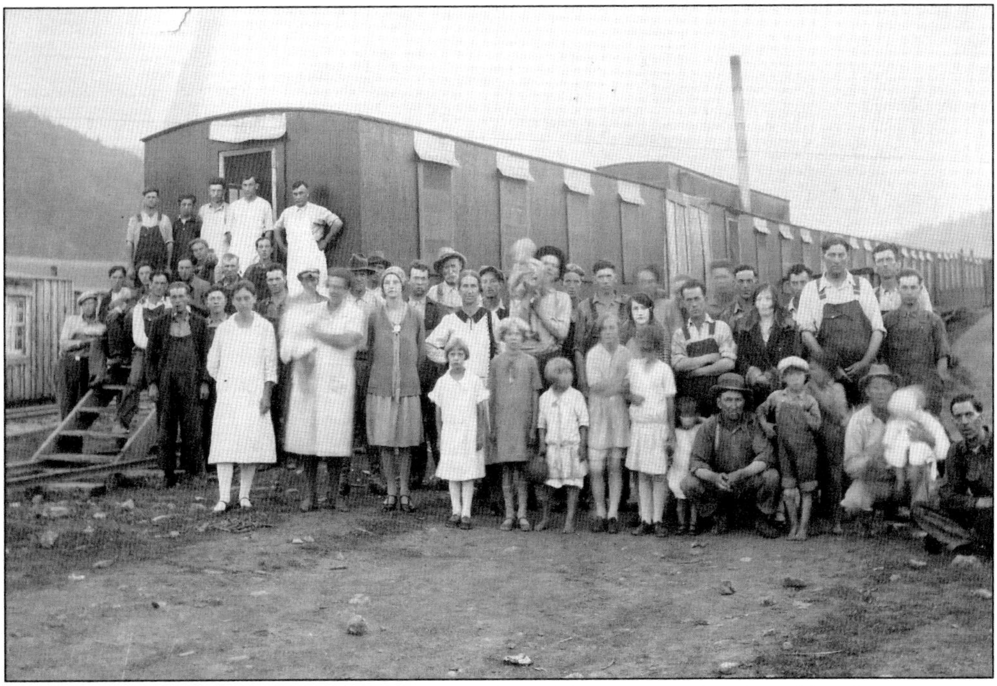

Rolling Wheels Estate. The families and workers of the Virginia Hardwood Lumber Company moved from one base of operation to another in the mountains of Bland County and lived in company-owned mobile housing that was parked on a railroad siding until time to move again. (Courtesy of Georgia Stacy Havens.)

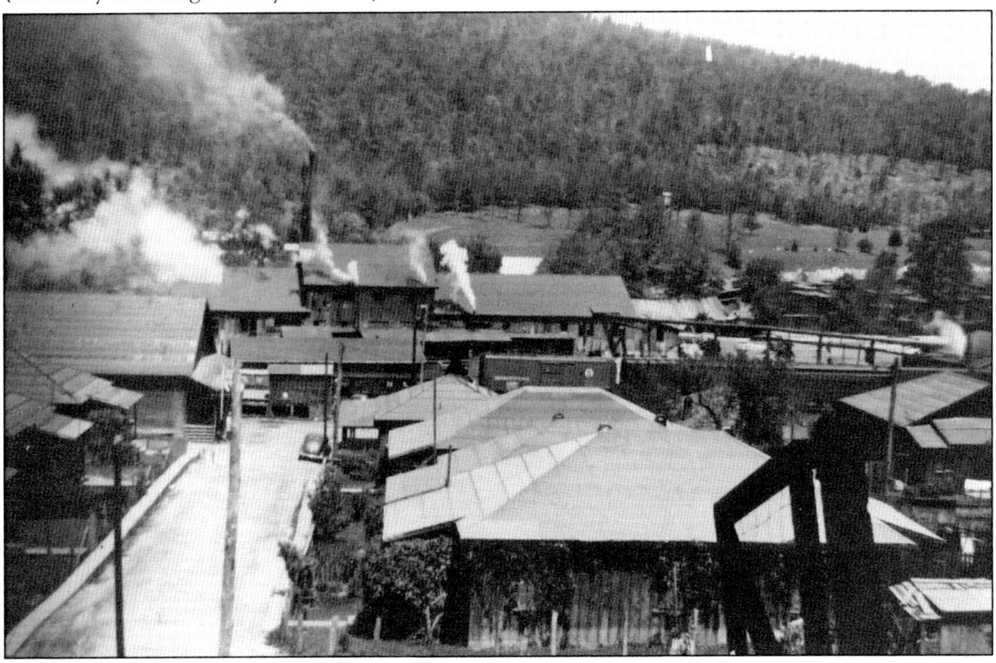

Company Town. The Virginia Hardwood Lumber Company built homes for workers at the mill in the Suiter-Bastian area. Several old company houses are shown here. (Courtesy of Georgia Stacy Havens.)

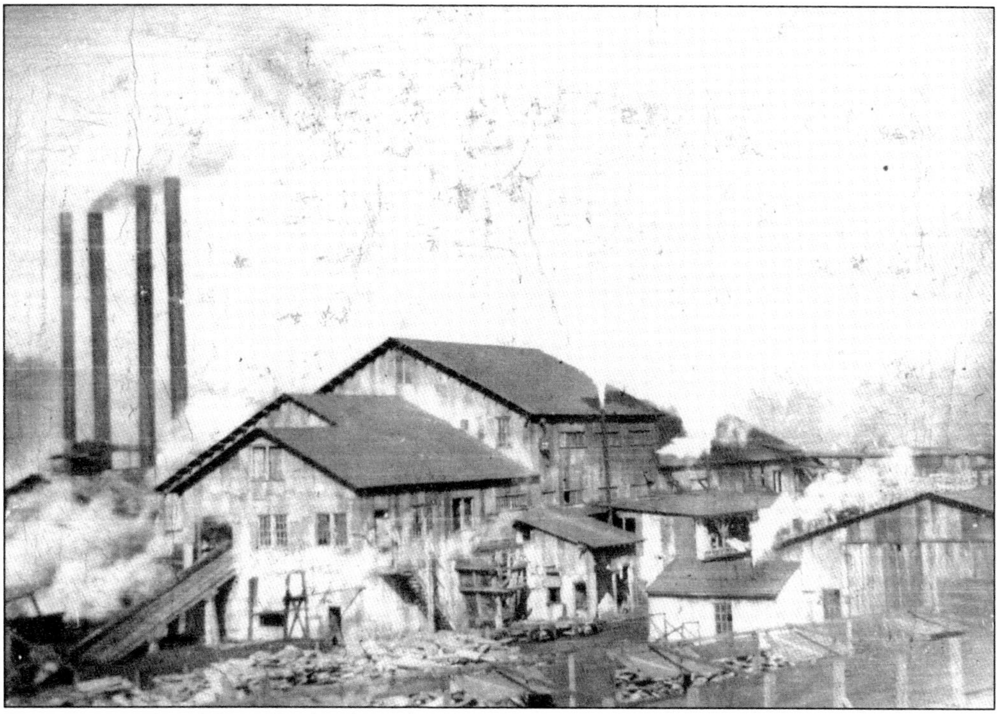

Down by the Old Mill. The hardwood mill in Suiter grew through the years. The company came to the Bastian area in 1927 and remained until the 1940s. (Courtesy of Georgia Stacy Havens.)

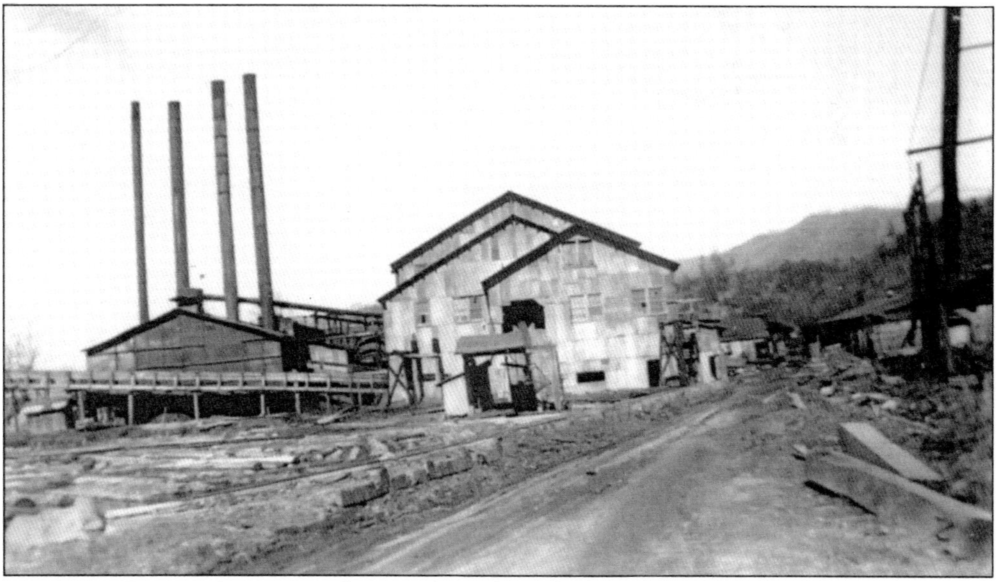

Boom and Bust. Like many industries that rely on harvesting natural resources, the Virginia Hardwood Lumber Company experienced good and lean times during its two-decade run in Bland County. (Courtesy of Georgia Stacy Havens.)

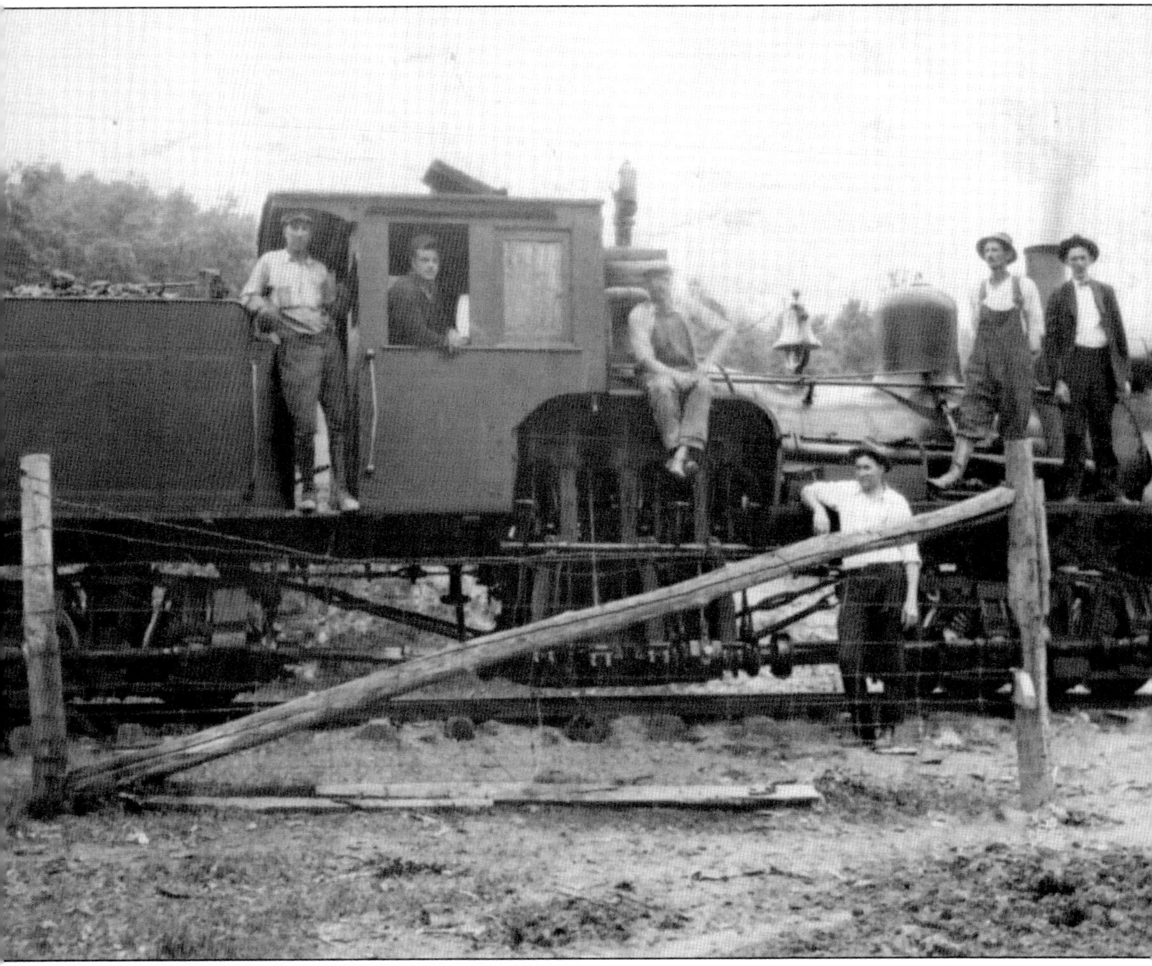

Room to Move. Rails played a huge roll in the operations of the Virginia Hardwood Lumber Company. In addition to moving logs to the mill and cut timber to Bruce Field for storage, workers used a shifter steam locomotive to transport company housing to the lumber camps. The men shown here on the shifter locomotive in Suiter are, from left to right, Mahlon Stacy, Frank Hall, Red Overstreet, Marion Presley, Noah Hagy, and Jahile Breeding. (Courtesy of Georgia Stacy Havens.)

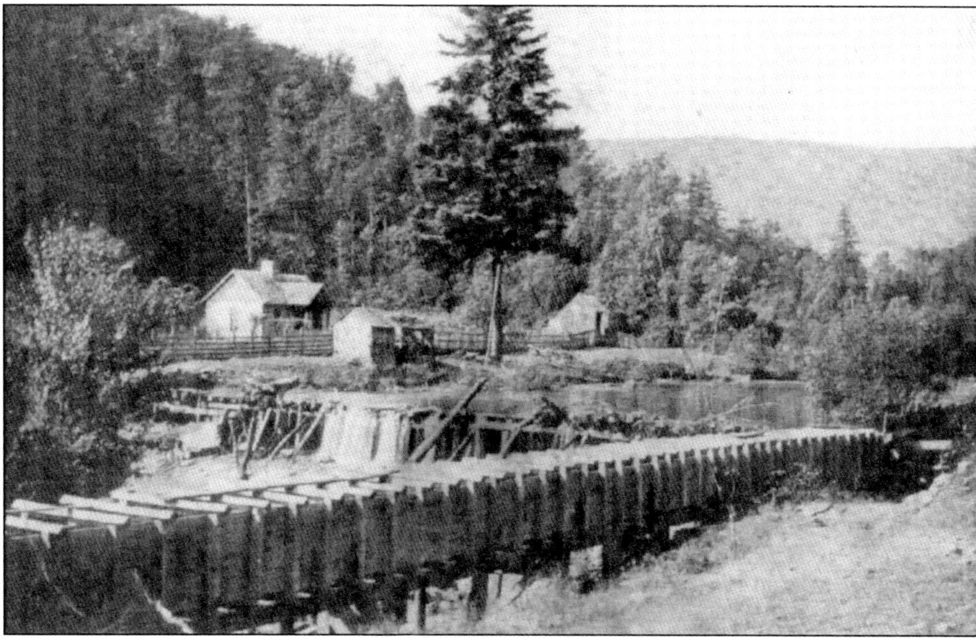

The Race. The Rocky Gap Race is shown here. The race was located at the old milldam on US Route 52 and was used to turn the water wheel for a gristmill. (Courtesy of Nannie Rose Tiller.)

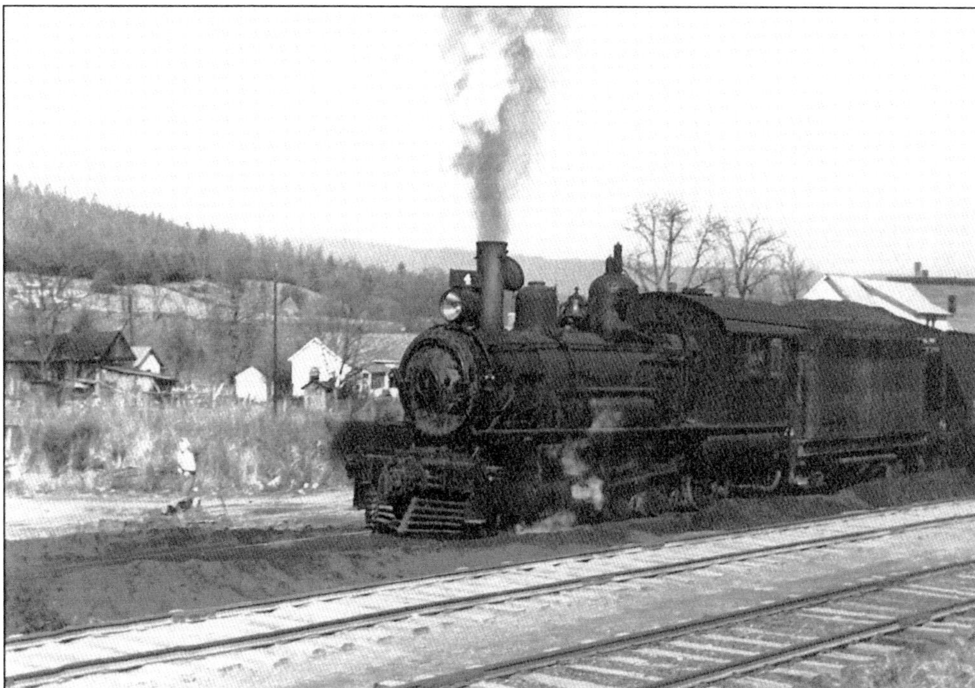

Training Day. In 1912, the New River, Holston & Western Railway built a line from its railhead in Narrows, Virginia, into Rocky Gap, Virginia. Two years later, steam locomotives, like the one shown here, started arriving in Bastian. (Courtesy of Georgia Stacy Havens.)

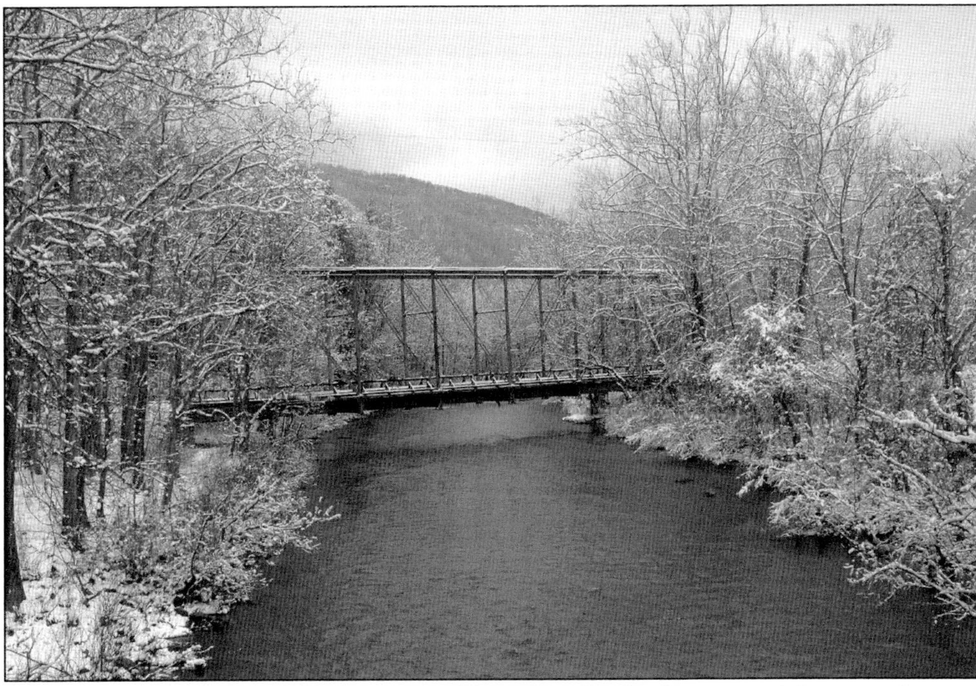

PICTURESQUE. The railroad bridge over Wolf Creek in Rocky Gap opened the central part of Bland County to passenger train service and provided a way to get goods to market. The bridge is on the Virginia Historical Registry. (Courtesy of Woody Bailey.)

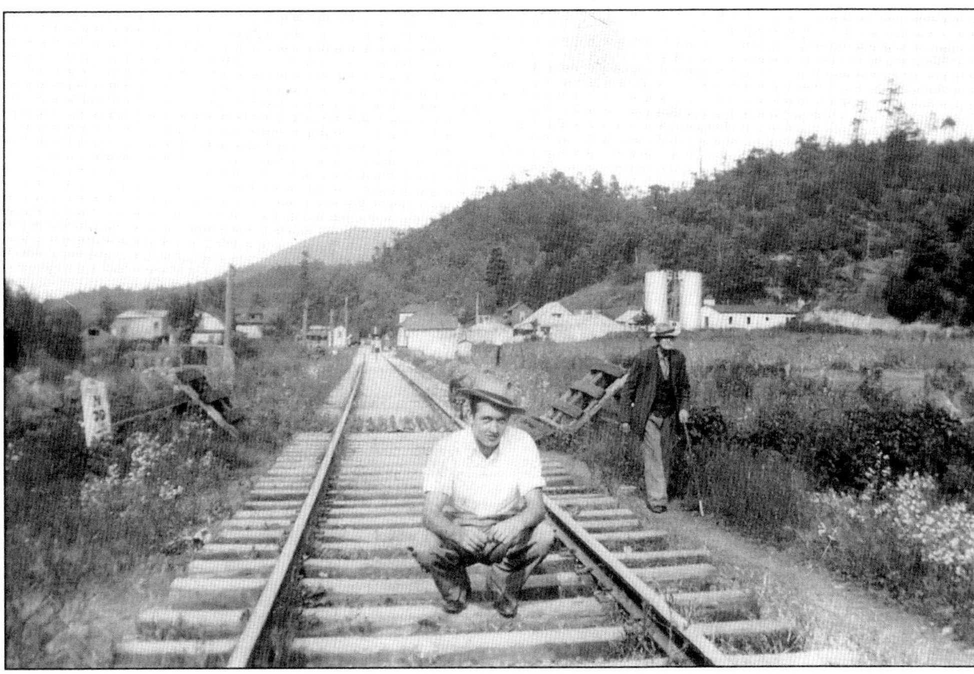

WORKING ON THE RAILROAD. An unidentified worker is shown here kneeling in the middle of the railroad tracks in Bastian. (Courtesy of Georgia Stacy Havens.)

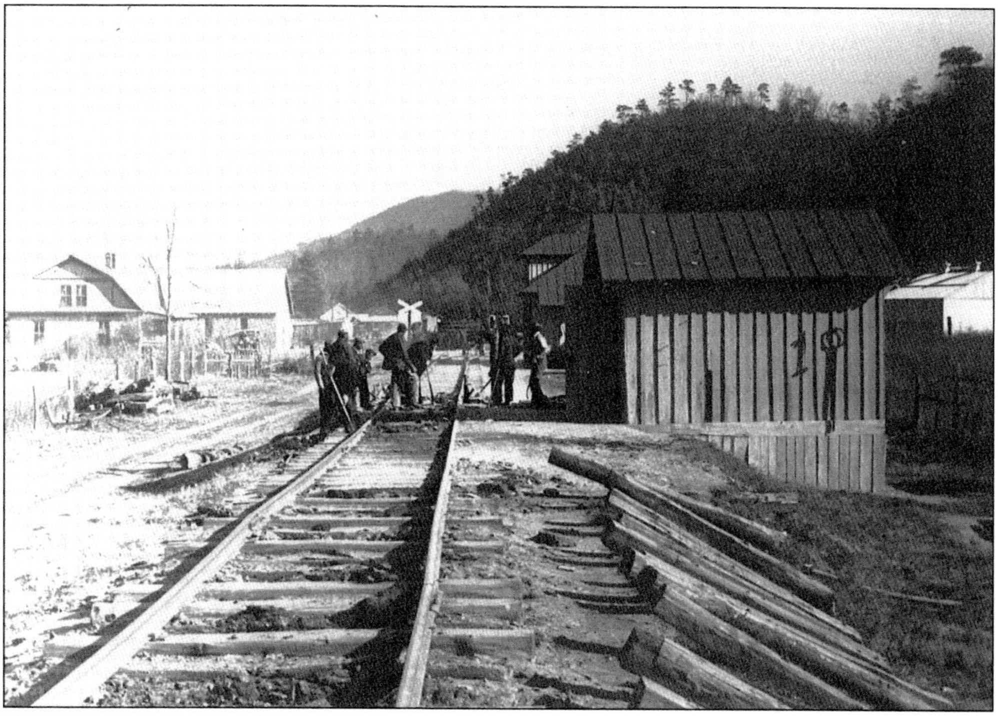

Track Removal. A railroad crew is shown here removing track in Bastian. The Norfolk & Western Railway took up tracks when the train was no longer used in various parts of the county. (Courtesy of Georgia Stacy Havens.)

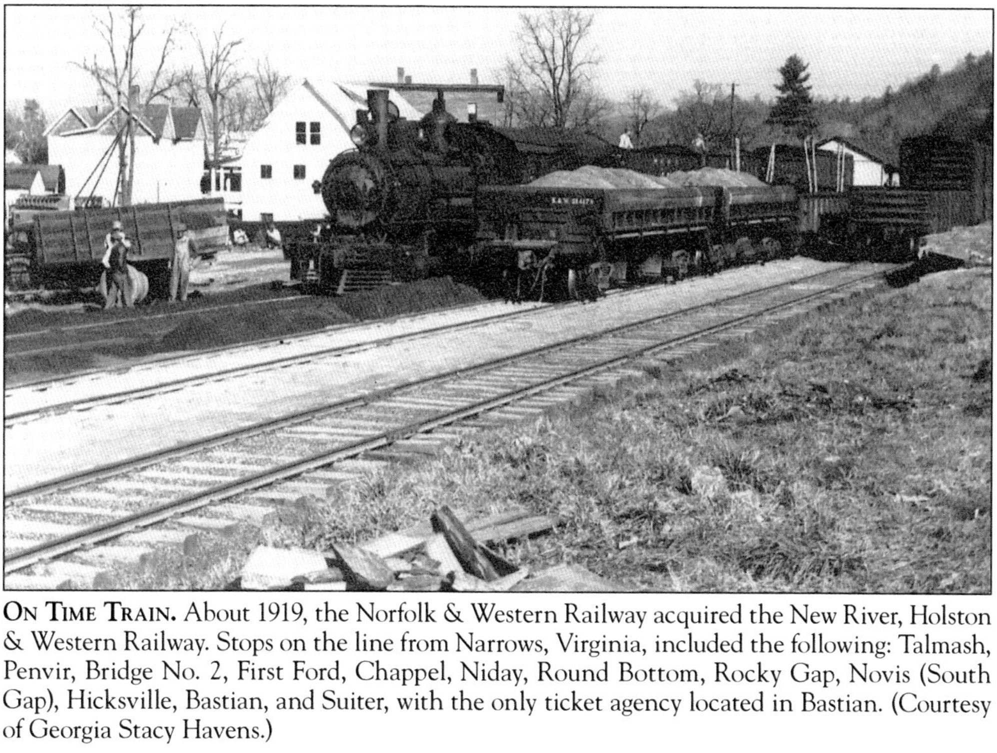

On Time Train. About 1919, the Norfolk & Western Railway acquired the New River, Holston & Western Railway. Stops on the line from Narrows, Virginia, included the following: Talmash, Penvir, Bridge No. 2, First Ford, Chappel, Niday, Round Bottom, Rocky Gap, Novis (South Gap), Hicksville, Bastian, and Suiter, with the only ticket agency located in Bastian. (Courtesy of Georgia Stacy Havens.)

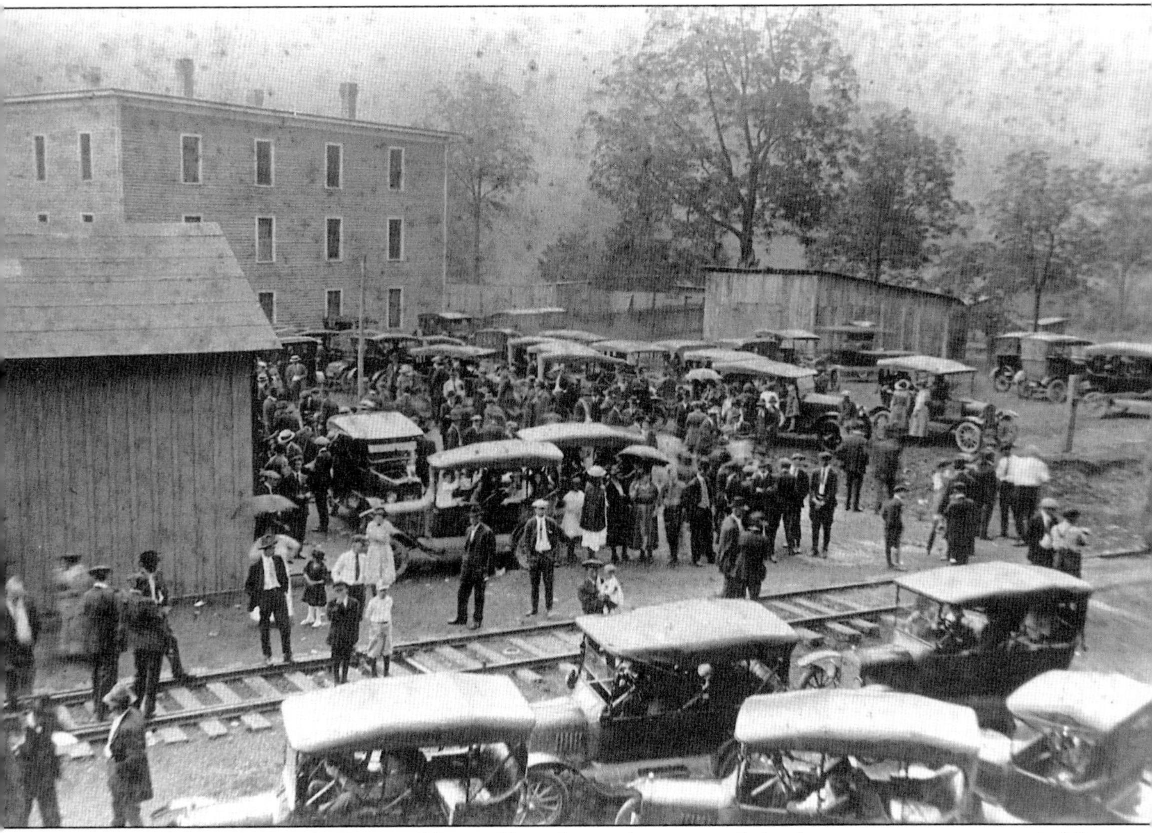

All Ye Faithful. The Bastian Union Church was the scene of a big homecoming event, probably in the 1930s, according to Georgia Stacy Havens. People came by rail and by car to attend the service. (Courtesy of Georgia Stacy Havens.)

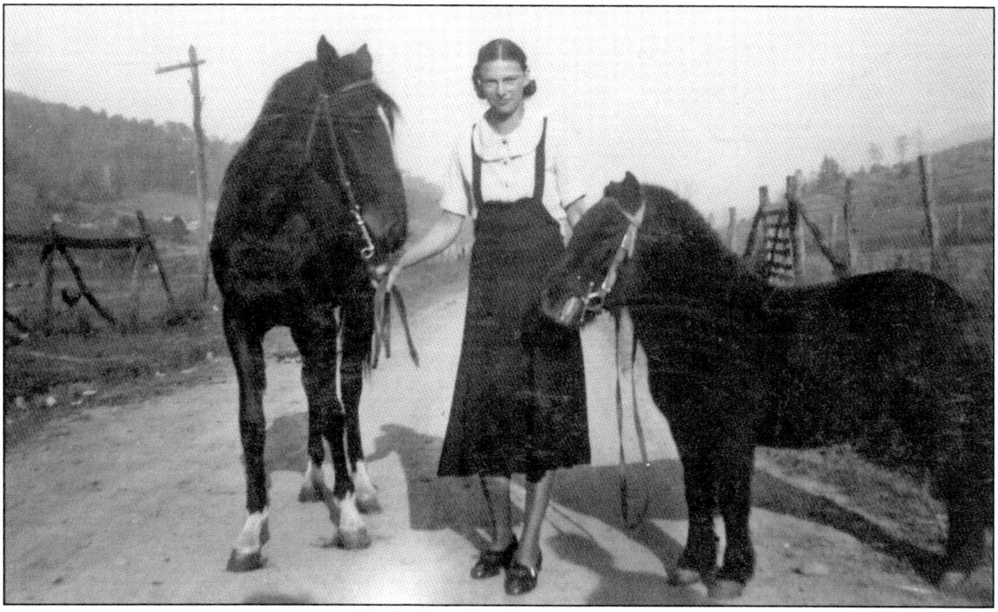

Big and Small. Nannie Rose Tiller is shown here with a full-size horse and a Shetland pony in this October 30, 1938, photograph. (Courtesy of Nannie Rose Tiller.)

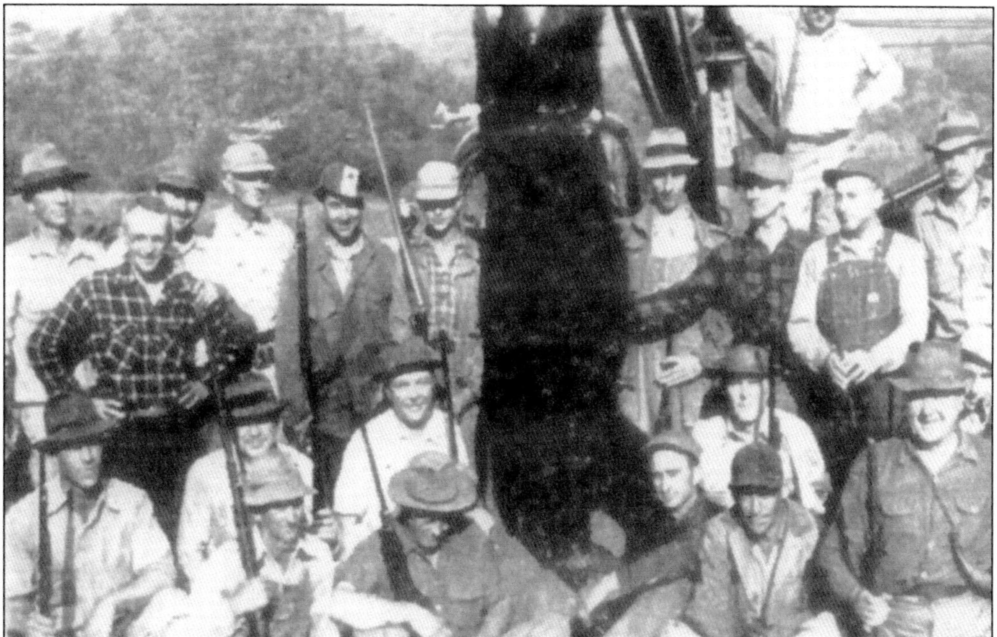

Bland County Bears. Several hunters went out to kill a sheep-killing bear that was roaming through Bland County. The hunters include, from left to right, (sitting or kneeling) C.W. Weeks Jr., Mason Claytor, H.A. Brunk, Chalmers Bailey, Chip Harvey, Grover Wiseman C.H. Litz (who killed the bear), Wilbur W. Hancock, Lum Brooks, and Charlie Carson; (standing) C.W. Weeks Sr., C.W. Wiseman, W.C. Shelburne, Ben C. Bird, Willard Hancock, Kenneth Hancock, J.J. Hancock, A.G. Updyke, C.C. King, Paul Umbarger, and Bill Compton standing in the truck. (Courtesy of the Bland County Historical Society.)

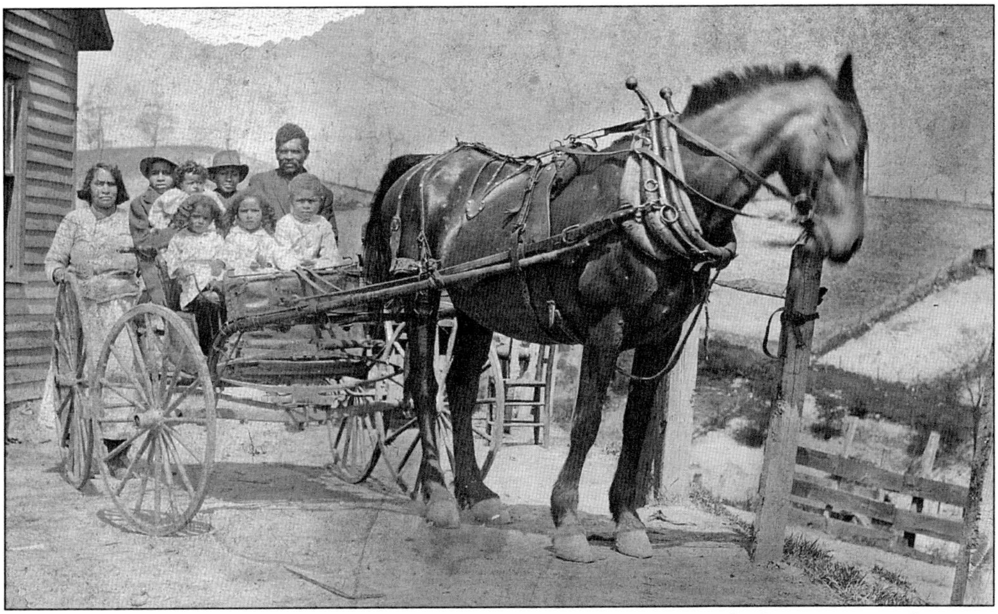

No Place Like Home. McDaniel "Mack" Ferguson and his wife, Cornelia Ferguson, are shown at their home on Dry Fork riding in a buggy with six of their 11 children, Priscilla, Estella, Brizzillia, Roosevelt, Andrew, and Woodrow. (Courtesy of Mary Little.)

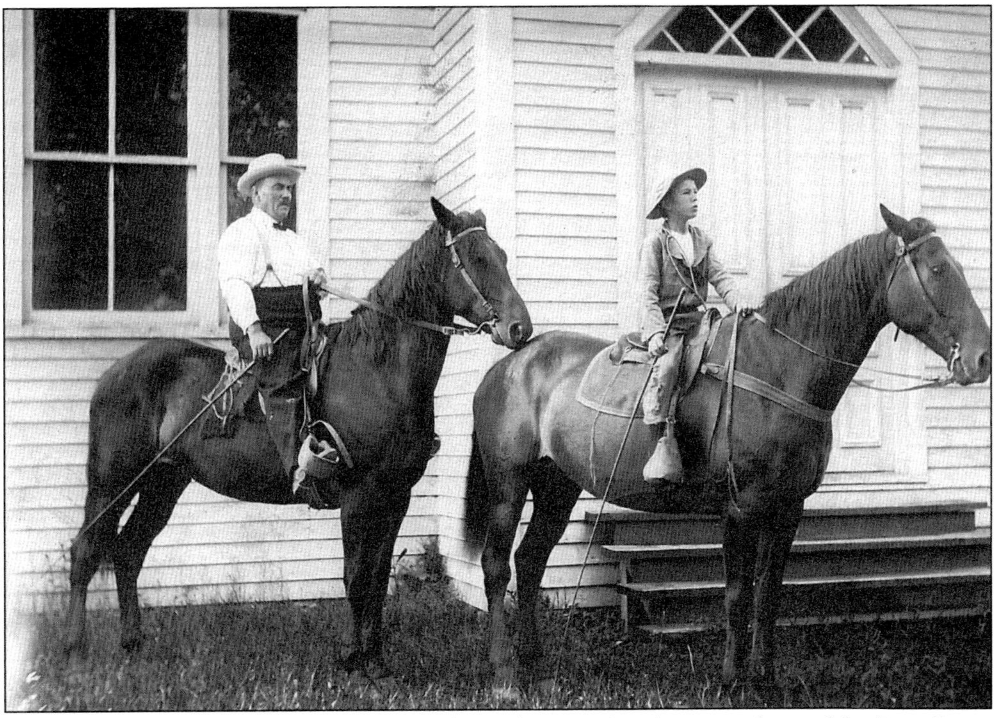

Horse Power. Two unidentified riders are shown here on their horses in front of the Pine Grove Methodist Church in Bastian, Virginia. (Courtesy of Billy Jean [Walters] Carty.)

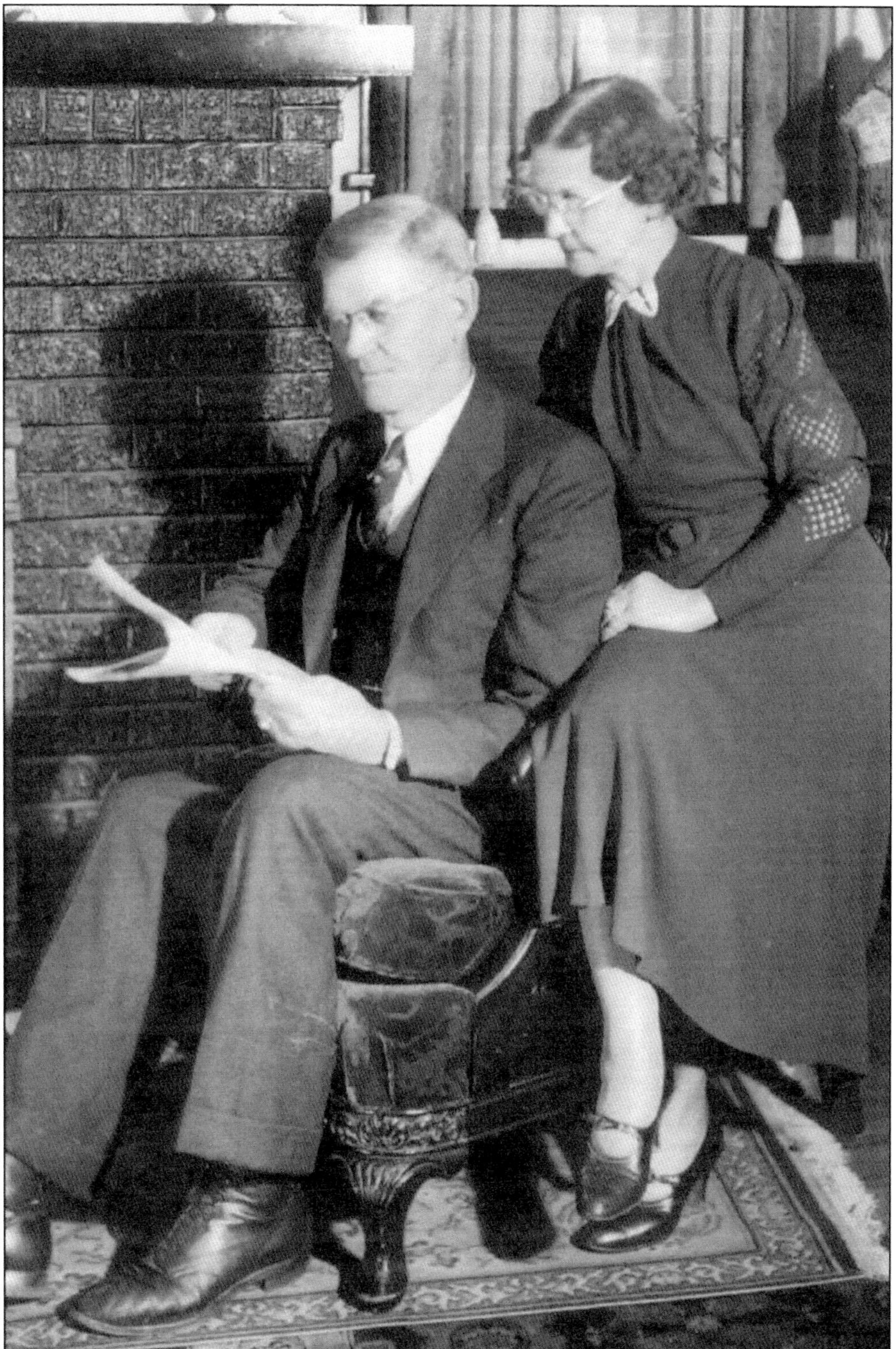

SPLICE OF LIFE. Here are John and Effie Newberry. John Allen Newberry was one of Southwest Virginia's most famous inventors. He invented a cable-splicing device that was used extensively on ships at sea. He later became a big game hunter in Alaska and British Columbia. One time while hunting, he became trapped in a snowstorm but was rescued from his predicament. He donated his extensive collection of mounted big game heads to the Bland Community Center. (Courtesy of Brenda King.)

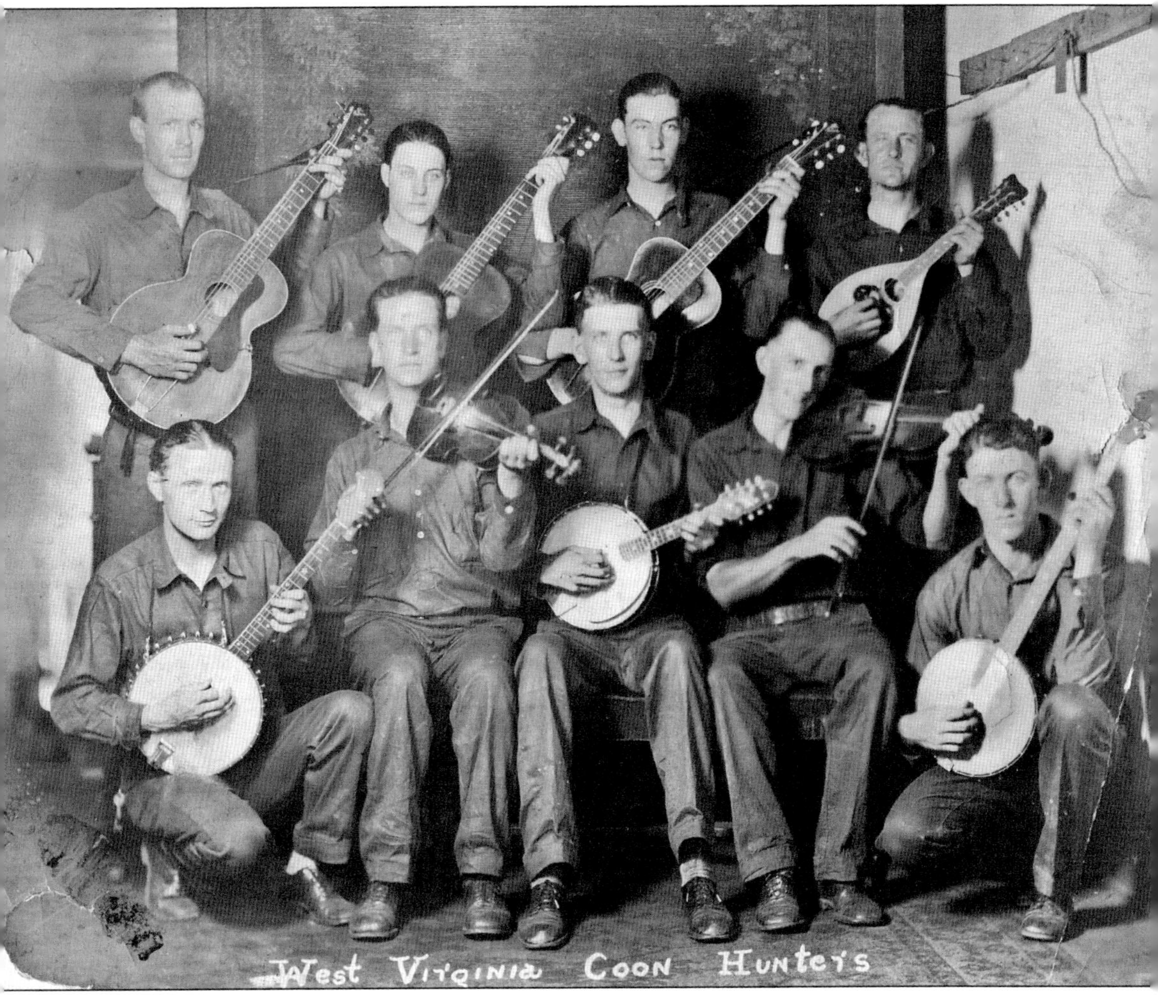

BRISTOL BOUND. Although the group hailed from Bland County, the West Virginia Coon Hunters were invited to the famous Bristol Recording Sessions of July and August 1927 that launched the careers of the Carter Family, Jimmie Rodgers, Alfred Reed, and many others. The Coon Hunters recorded "Greasy String" and "Your Blue Eyes Run Me Crazy" as well as two additional instrumentals on August 5, 1927, but according to Ivan Tribe, the group never recorded again. Shown here are from left to right, (first row) Dutch Stewart, W.B. Bane Boyles, Regal Mooney, Fred Pendleton, and Joe Stephens; (second row) Fred Belcher, Clyde S. Meadows, Jim Brown, and Vernal Vest. (Courtesy of Denise Smith.)

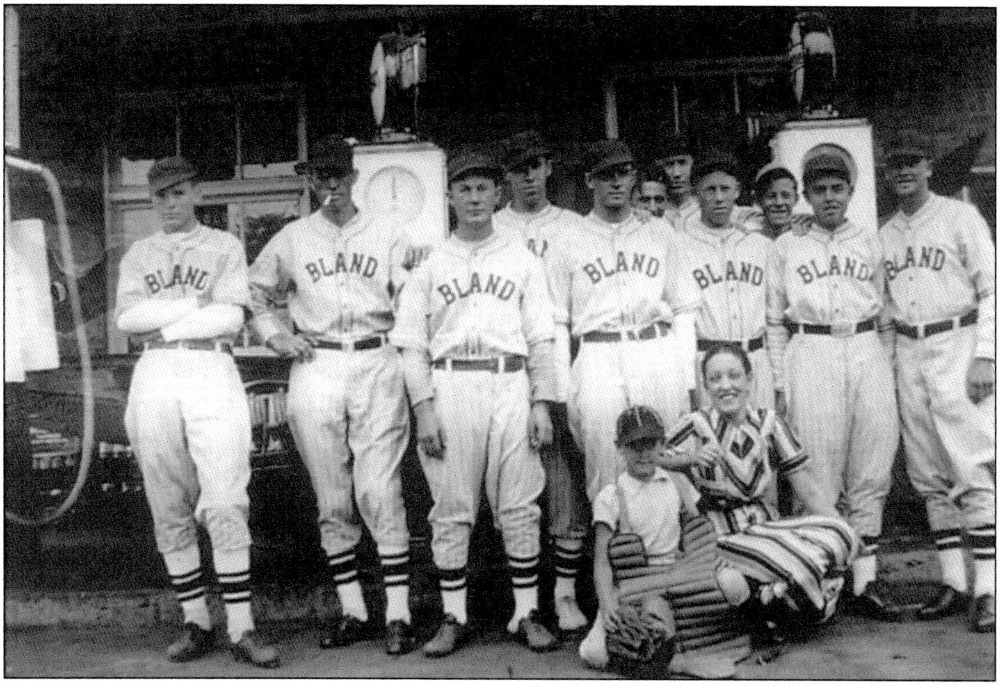

GAS HOUSE GANG. Baseball was Bland County's favorite national pastime, as these unidentified ballplayers would likely agree. (Courtesy of the Bland County Historical Society.)

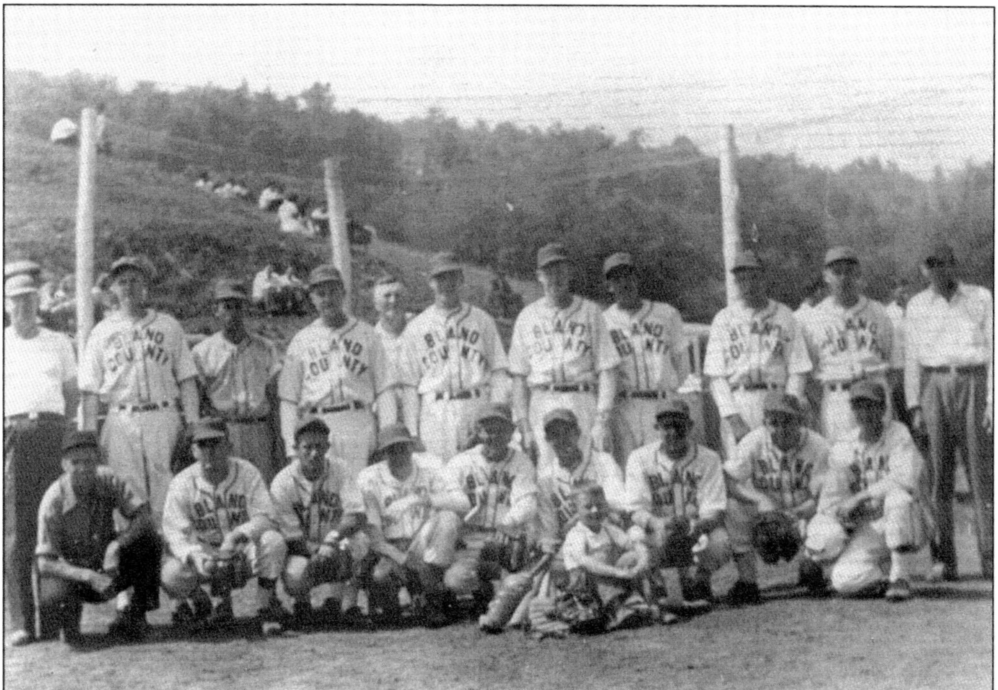

PLAY BALL. Bland County had a plethora of baseball teams like this one, which was created to give local fans a team to root for. (Courtesy of the Bland County Historical Society.)

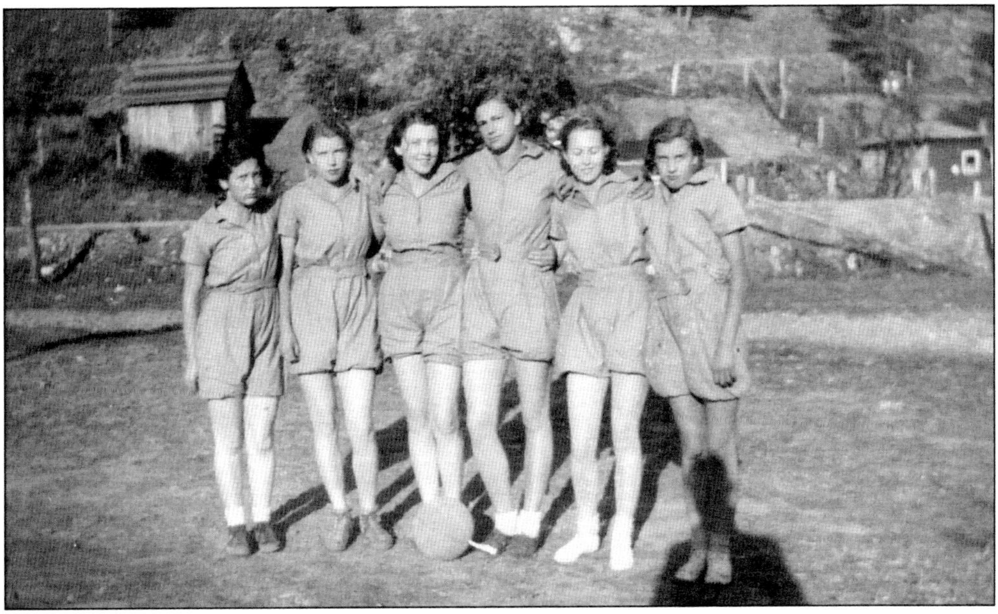

Go Girls! An early Rocky Gap High School girls' basketball team is shown here. Unfortunately, the identities of the girls on the team are not known. (Courtesy of the Bland County Historical Society.)

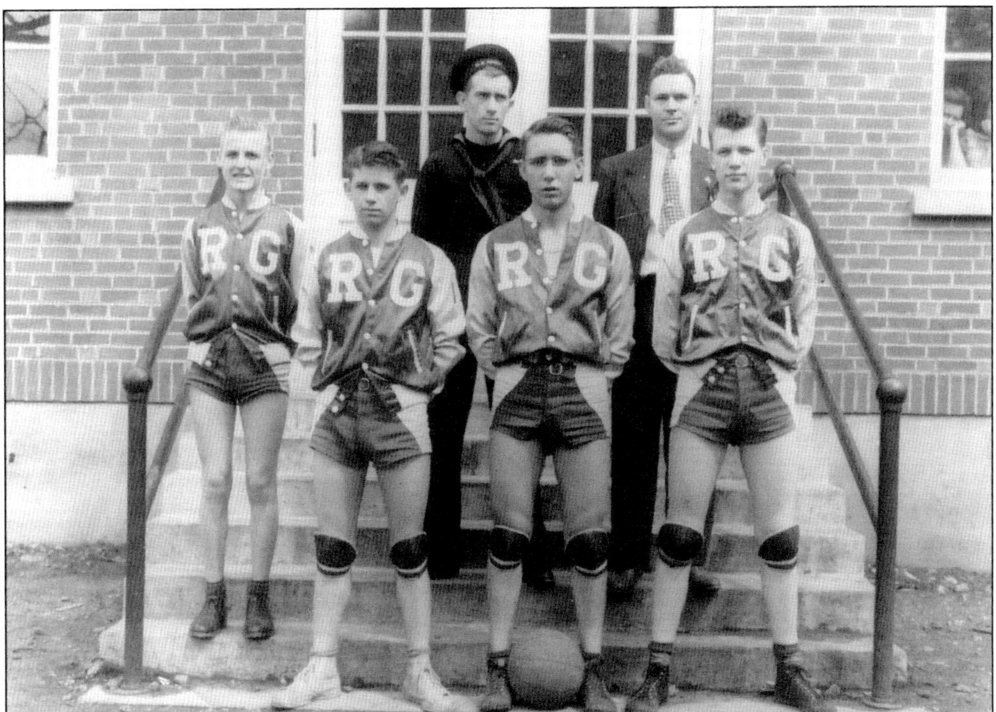

Basketball Skills. The 1946 Rocky Gap boys' basketball team is shown in this picture. Those picture are, from left to right, (first row) Manley Andrews, George Allen Thompson Jr., ? Stowers, and Harold Bivens; (second row) Jimmy Pemberton and Woodrow Stowers, principal. (Courtesy of the Bland County Historical Society.)

Four

OPENING THE WILDERNESS

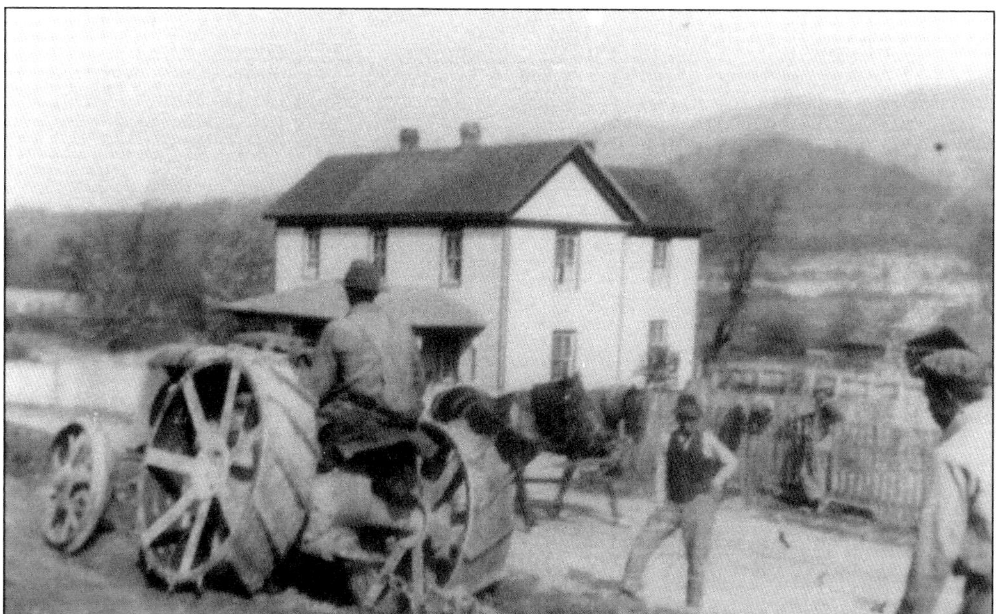

ROAD BUILDERS. The first paved highways in Bland County were built in 1930 and 1931 from Bland to the top of Big Walker Mountain in the south and then to East River Mountain in the north. (Courtesy of Billy Jean [Walters] Carty.)

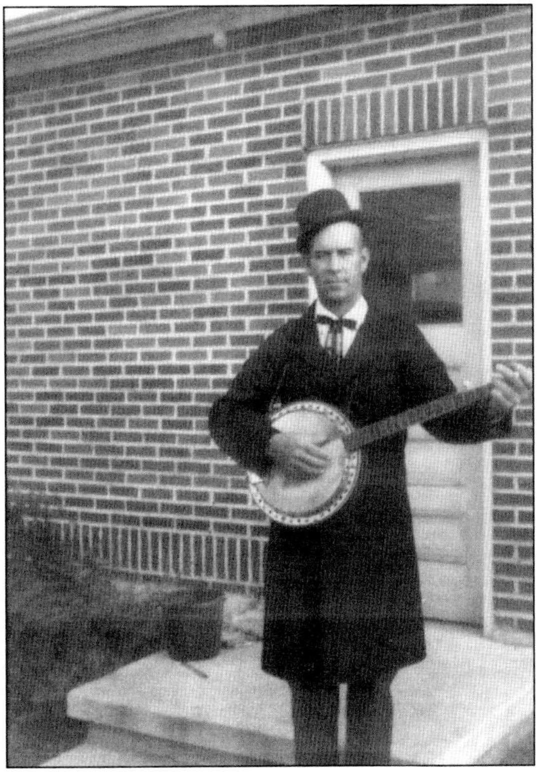

With a Banjo on My Knee. Buford Tiller is shown here demonstrating his musical talents as part of Bland County's centennial celebration in 1961. (Courtesy of Nannie Rose Tiller.)

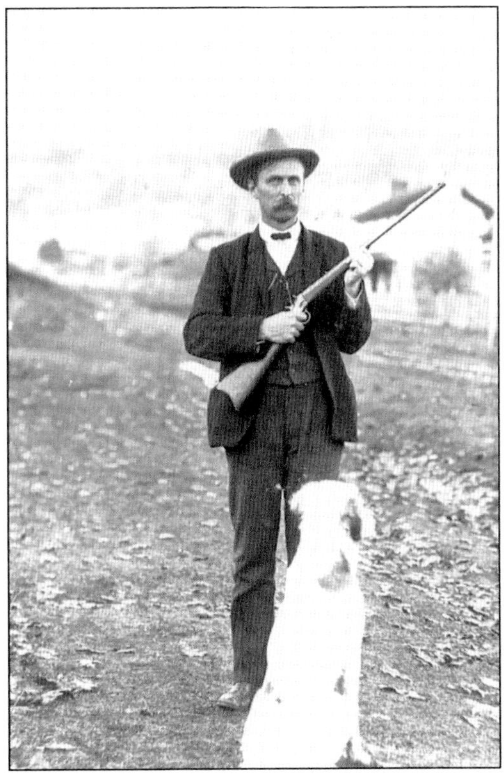

Doctor on the Hunt. Dr. Jasper Newton Walker of Bastian takes in a little hunting. He lived in Bland County in 1934. (Courtesy of Georgia Stacy Havens.)

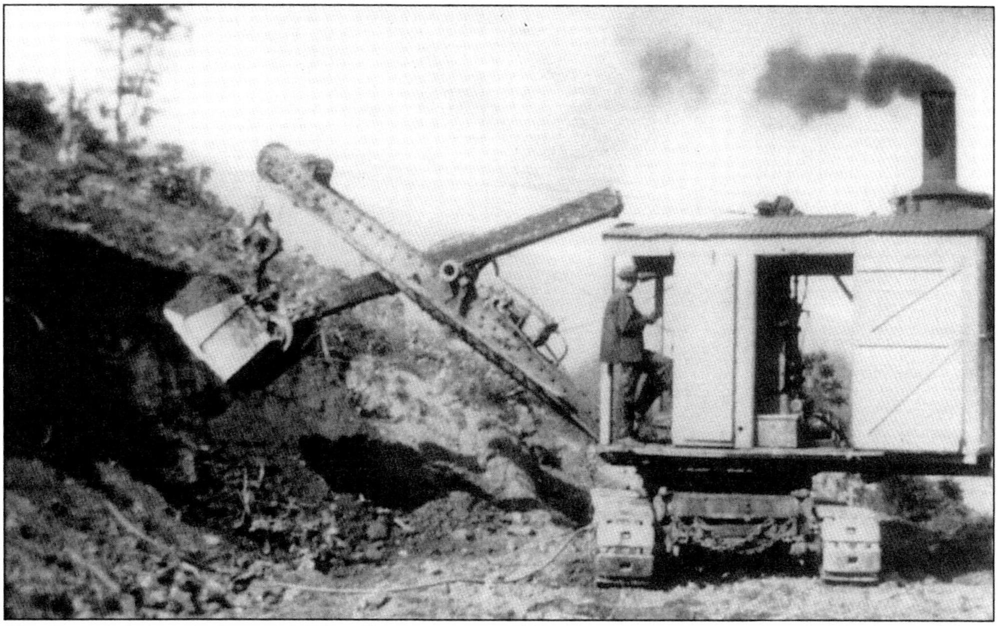

The Earth Moved. In 1926, Bland County issued bonds to buy a steam shovel to load rocks and dirt onto mule-drawn wagons during the construction of Bland County's 30-mile stretch of the Lakes-to-Florida Highway. There were 100 convicts assigned to dig the roadway with picks and shovels. (Courtesy of Billy Jean [Walters] Carty.)

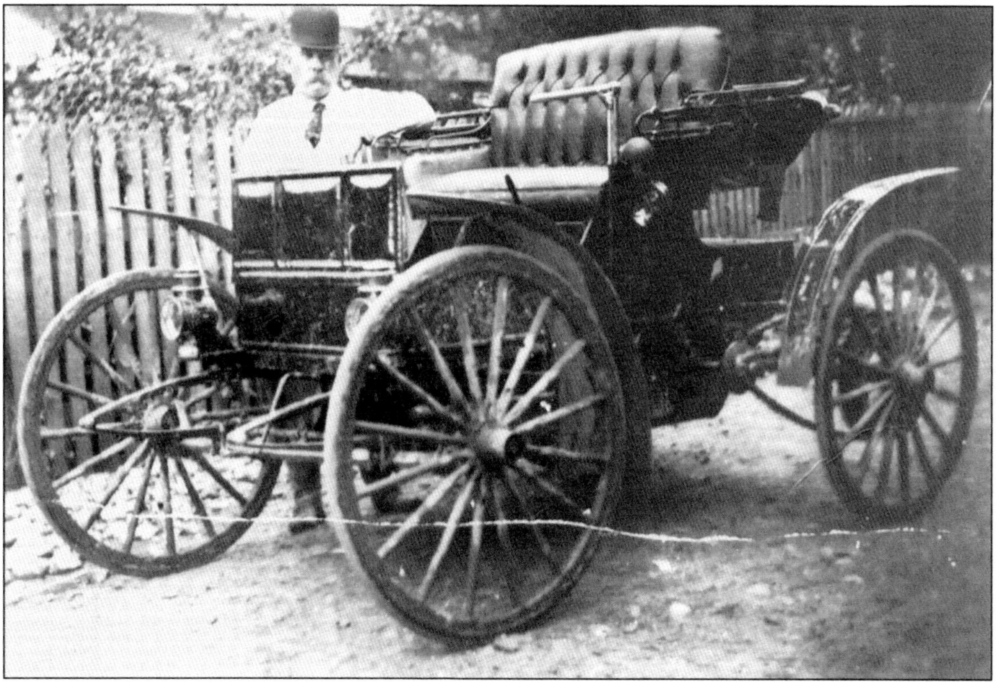

The Car. Dr. Jacob Adam Wagner purchased the first car in Bland County, Virginia, from Sears Roebuck. The car was shipped to Wytheville, Virginia, and assembled by Guy Dunn and Wagner, who later drove the car over Big Walker Mountain to his home in Bland, Virginia. (Courtesy of the Bland County Historical Society.)

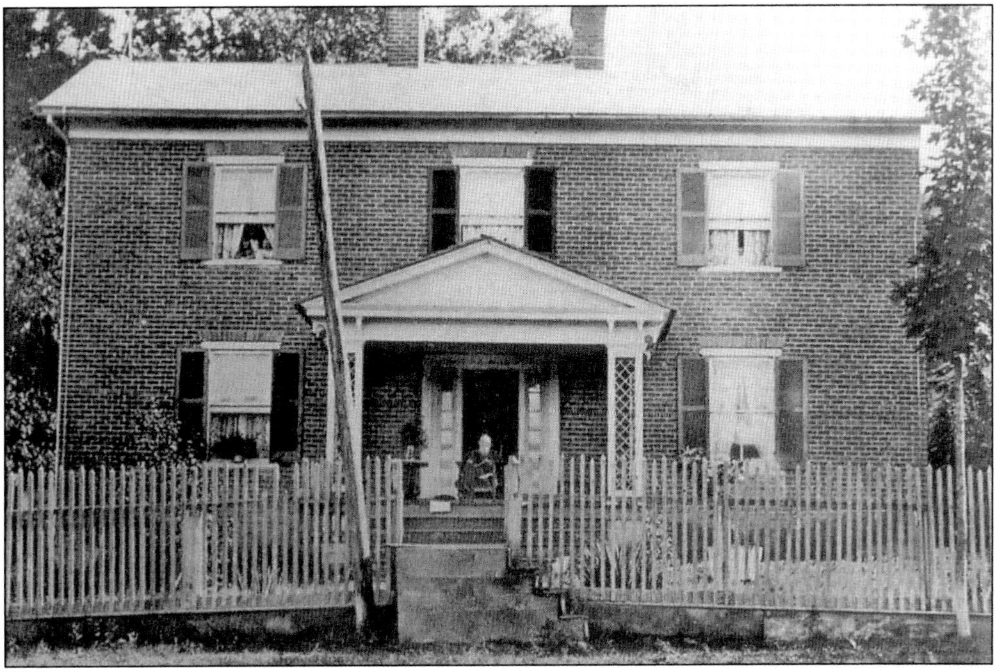

One Brick at a Time. The stately Albert Gallatin Updyke home in Mechanicsburg, Virginia, was erected in 1880 with bricks made from clay from the fields of the Mechanicsburg area. (Photograph from the Bogle Library Collection; courtesy of the Bland County Historical Society.)

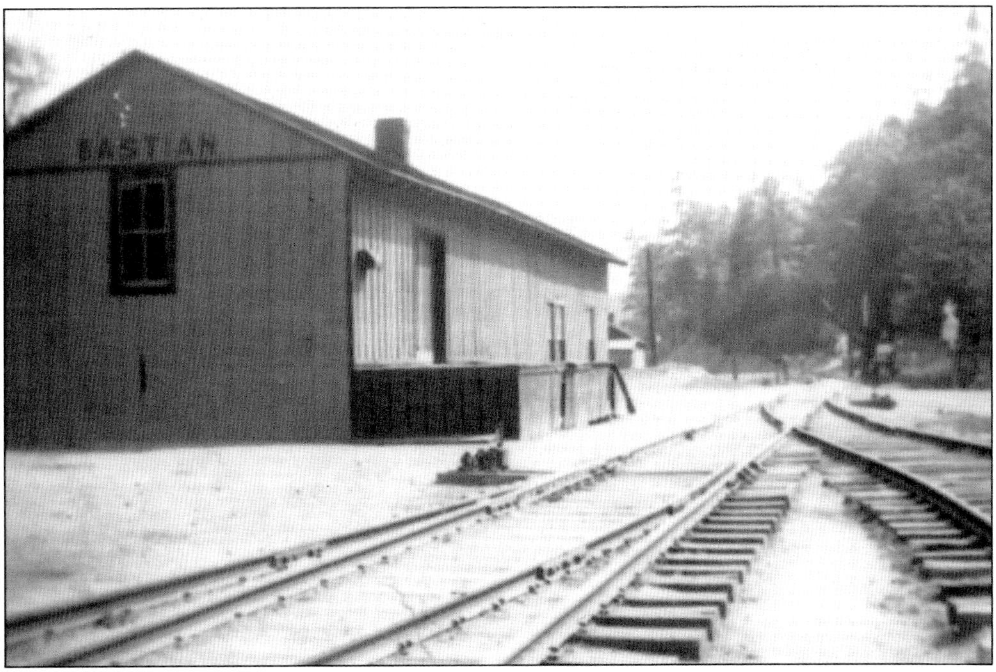

Making Tracks in the Snow. The Norfolk & Western station in Bastian was the only station on the N&W tracks operated in Bland County. (Courtesy of Georgia Stacy Havens.)

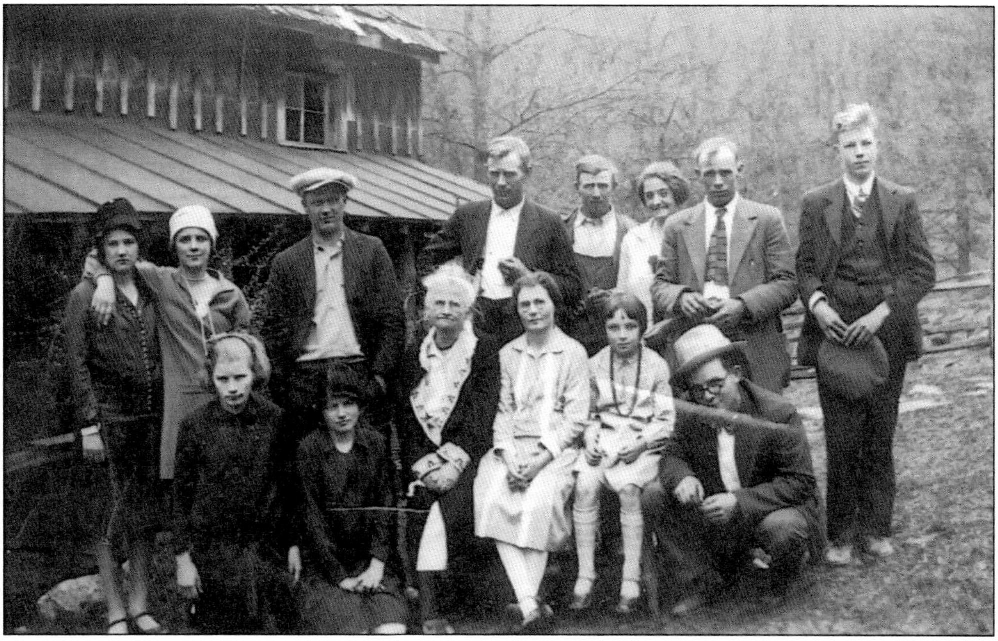

THE PAULEY FAMILY. The Pauley family is shown here at the home place, located near the Bogle School. The importance of family cannot be stated enough, as Bland County residents worked together to survive. (Courtesy of the Bland County Historical Society.)

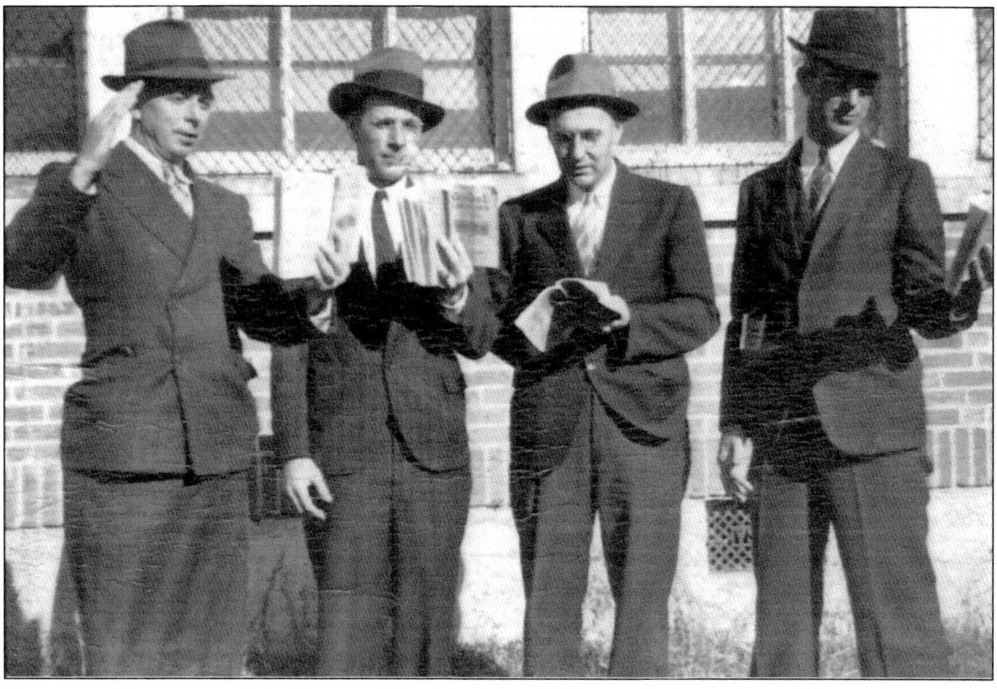

SONG AND TESTIMONY. The Bastian, Virginia, Gospel Quartet is shown here. Those pictured are, from left to right, Straley Kitts, George Weir, Hobert Ellswick, and Mark Blessing. (Courtesy of Georgia Stacy Havens.)

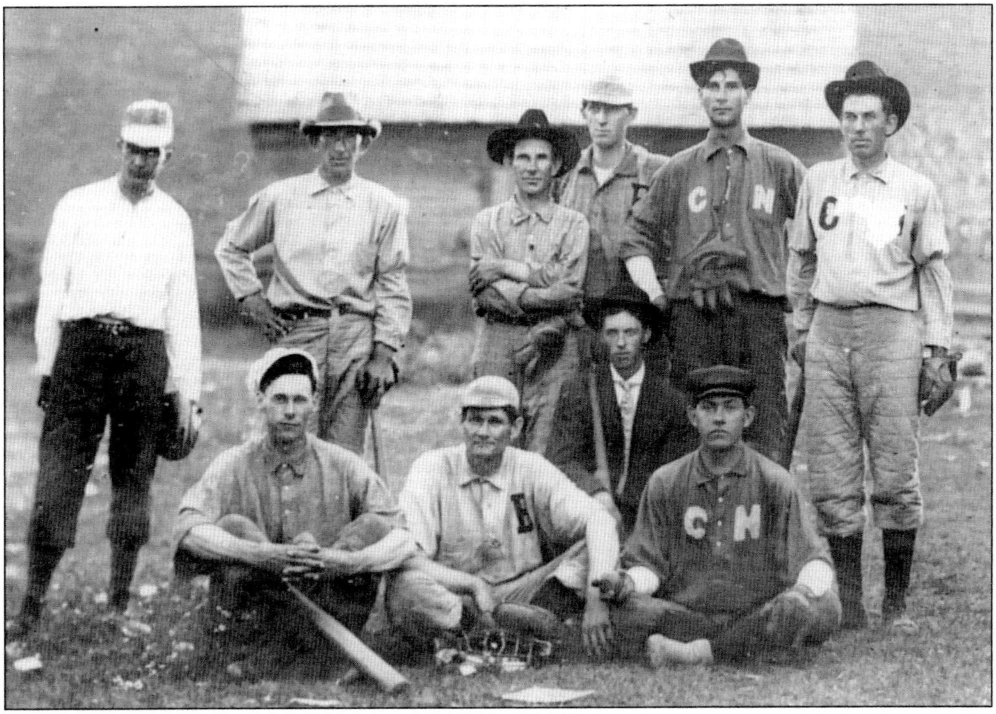

More Ball Players. Shown here in 1905, the baseball team from Cracker Neck looks ready for the game. (Courtesy of the Bland County Historical Society.)

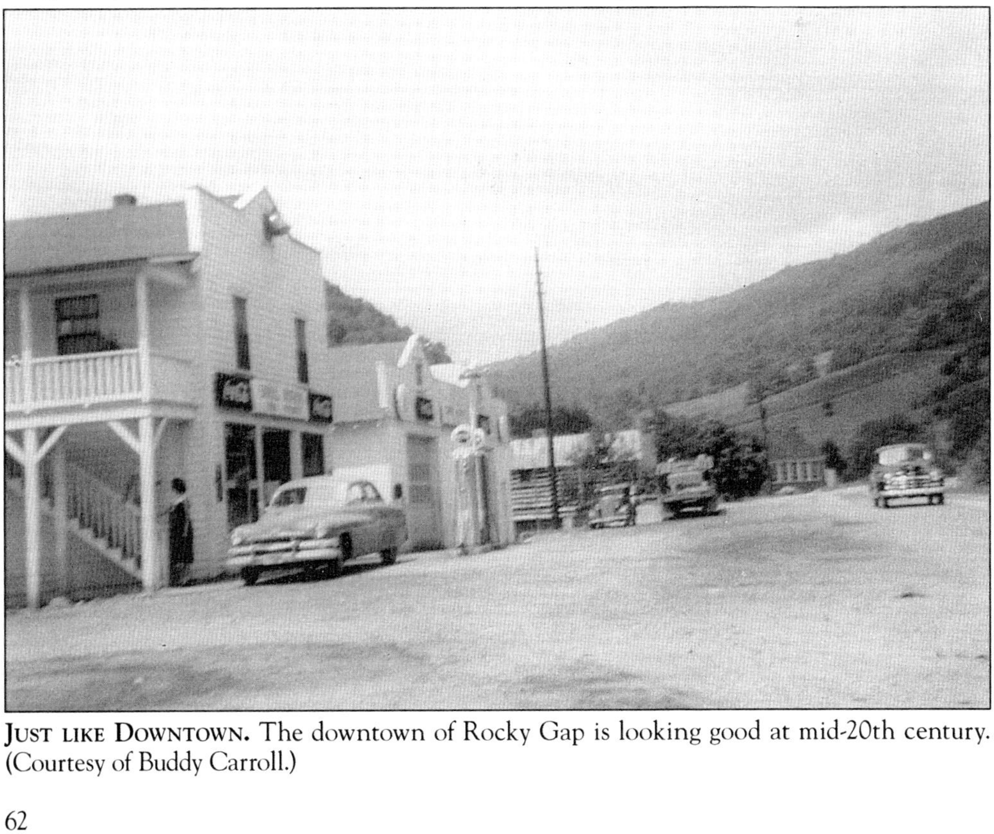

Just like Downtown. The downtown of Rocky Gap is looking good at mid-20th century. (Courtesy of Buddy Carroll.)

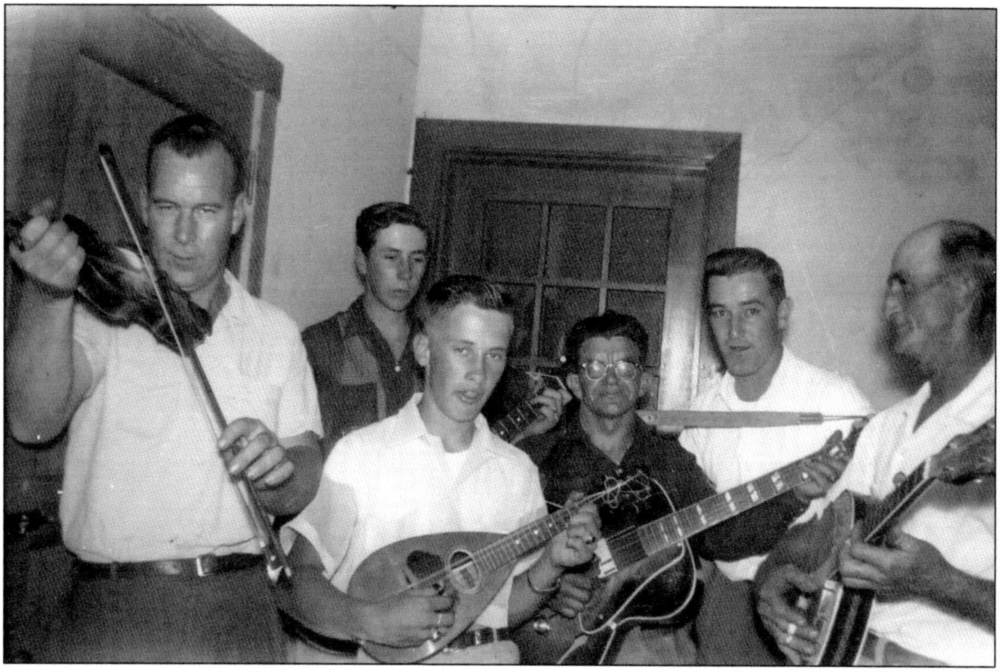

Pick It. Groups like the Bland County Ramblers, shown here, perform music inspired by life in the Western Virginia mountains. Three of the musicians in this 1954 photograph are, in no specific order, C.B. Telter, Henry Hounschell, and Claude Tickle. (Courtesy of Nannie Rose Tiller.)

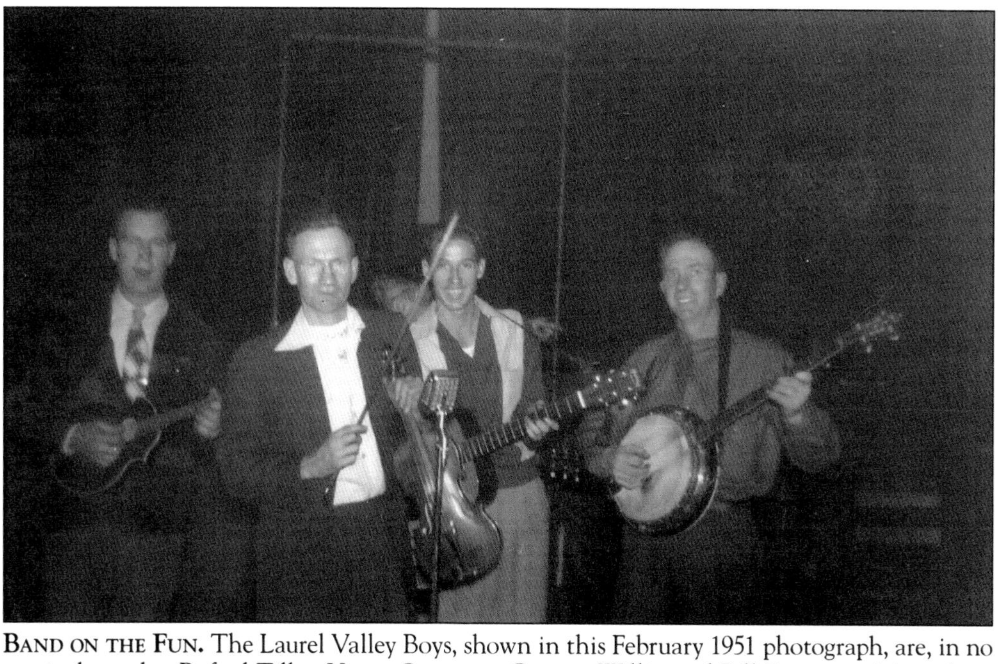

Band on the Fun. The Laurel Valley Boys, shown in this February 1951 photograph, are, in no particular order, Buford Tiller, Henry Summers, Sammy Willis, and Bill Summers. Music from the mountains became popular throughout the United States and beyond. (Courtesy of Nannie Rose Tiller.)

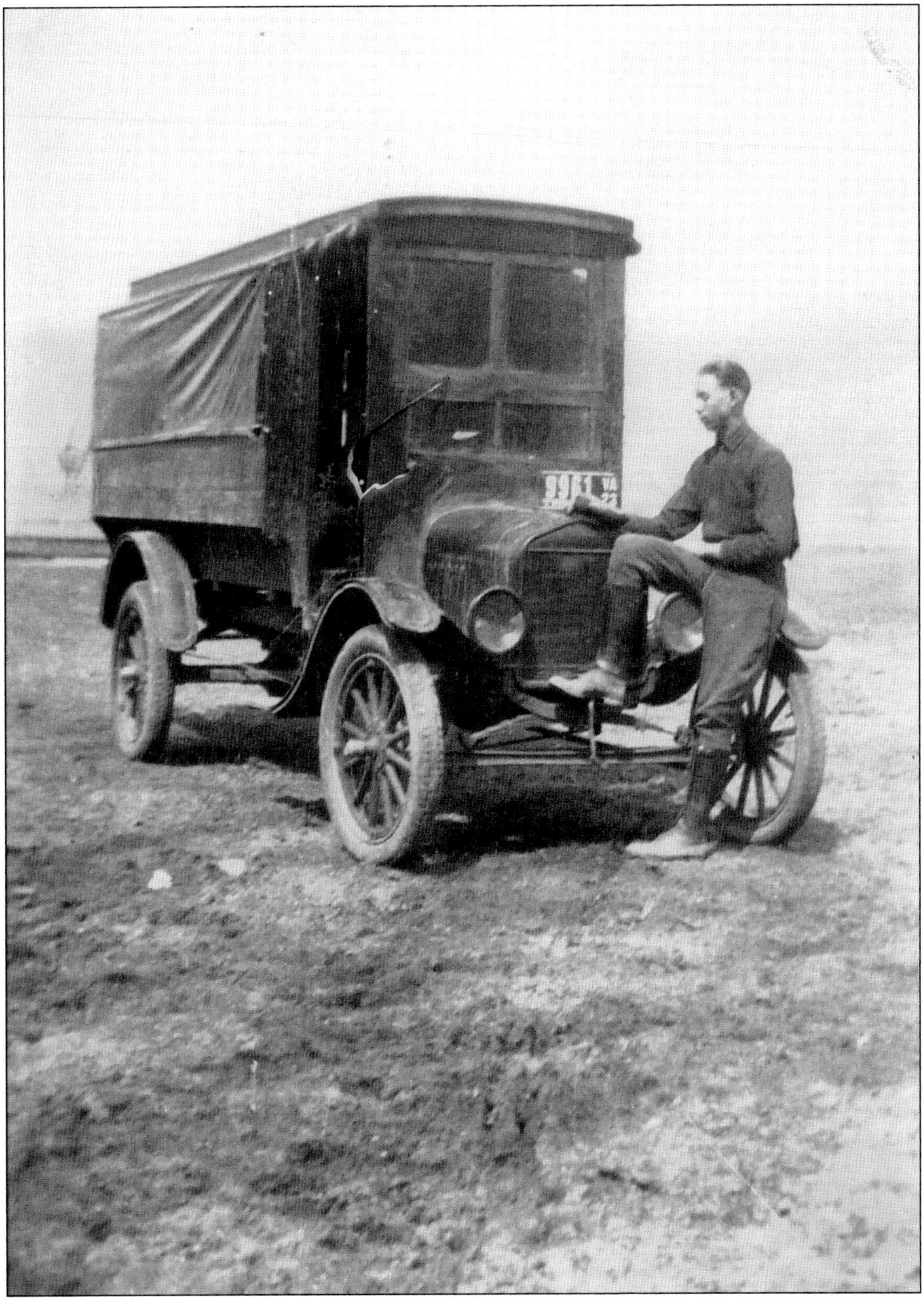

Bus Time. George Tickle is shown here standing in front of Bland County's first school bus. Tickle drove the bus in the 1922–1923 school year from the Slide area to Bland on Route 42, the old Holston Turnpike, which was later renamed the Blue Grass Trail. The bus was a Ford Model T that seated about 25 passengers. Jess Rudder painted the bus green. (Courtesy of Nannie Rose Tiller.)

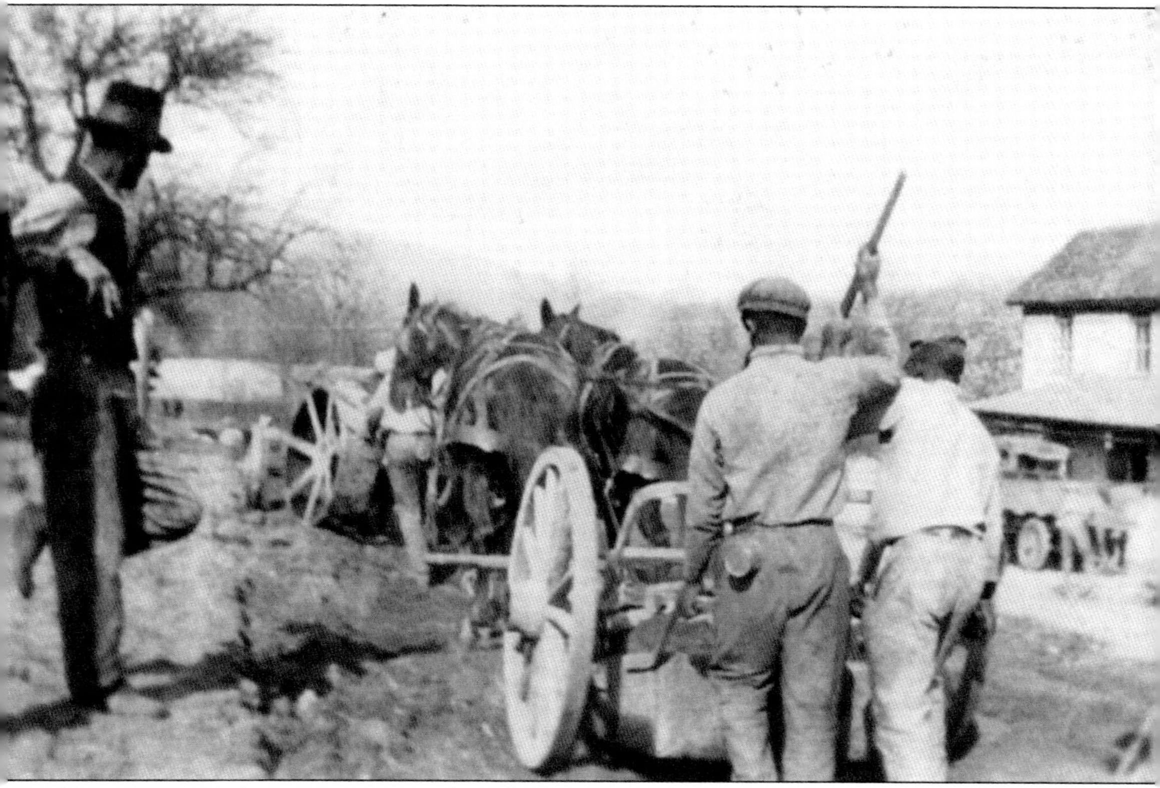

ROAD SHOW. Highway construction through the mountains of Bland County was a challenging endeavor with horse-drawn graders, shown here grading the roads. Farmers used the Holston Turnpike to transport salt from Saltville, Virginia, to the cities of eastern Virginia during the American Civil War. Other roads included the Raleigh-Grayson Turnpike, a wagon road that was built around 1830 for north-to-south travelers, and the Fincastle-and-Cumberland Turnpike, which dates to about 1840. (Courtesy of Billy Jean [Walters] Carty.)

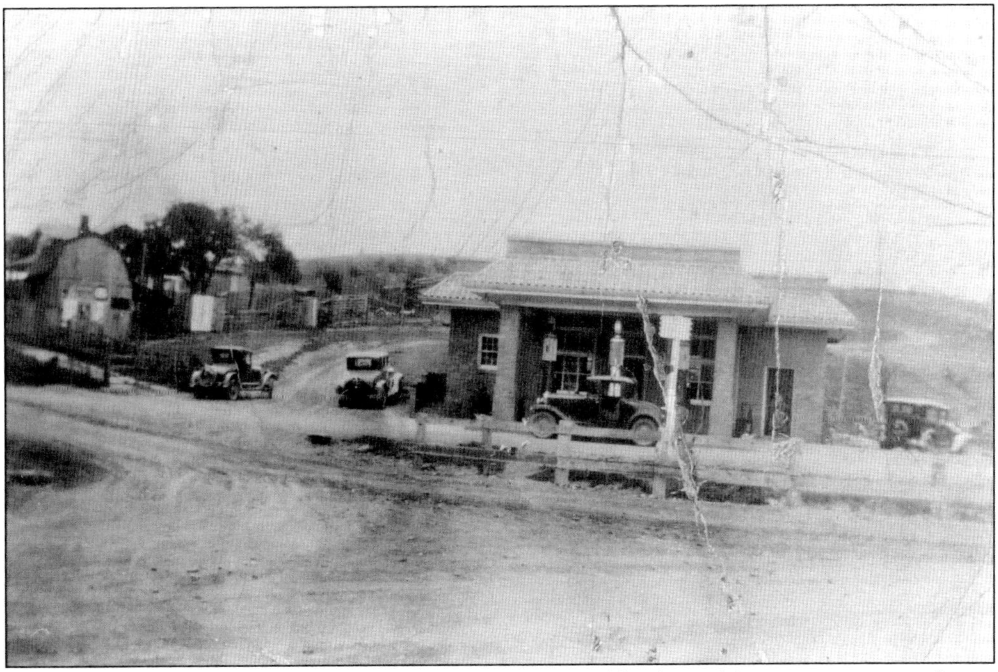

At the Station. With the coming of vehicles, gas stations like the Seddon service station, shown here, emerged in Bland County, Virginia. (Courtesy of the Bland County Historical Society.)

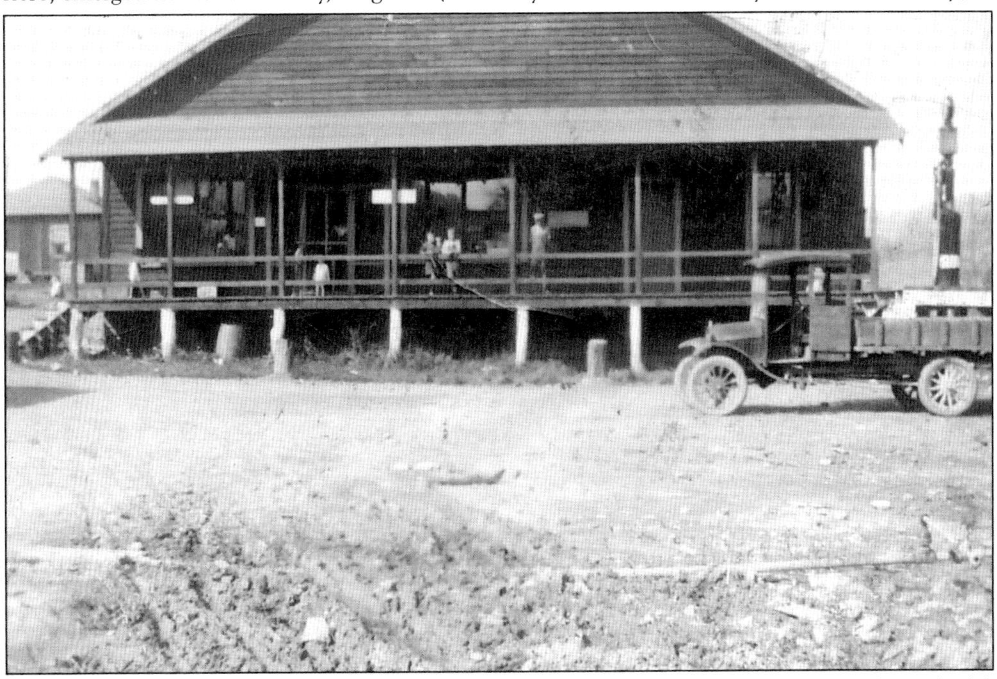

To the Rescue. After a prolonged period of economic depression, the nation started to rebuild, and one of the first steps in the rebuilding process was the formation of the Civilian Conservation Corps. CCC Camp 1388 P-53-VA, established in the late spring of 1933 in Bastian, was the second camp built in Virginia. The camp workers did a great deal to change the region in terms of road, infrastructure, and communications improvements. (Courtesy of Georgia Stacy Havens.)

Five

Down on the Farm

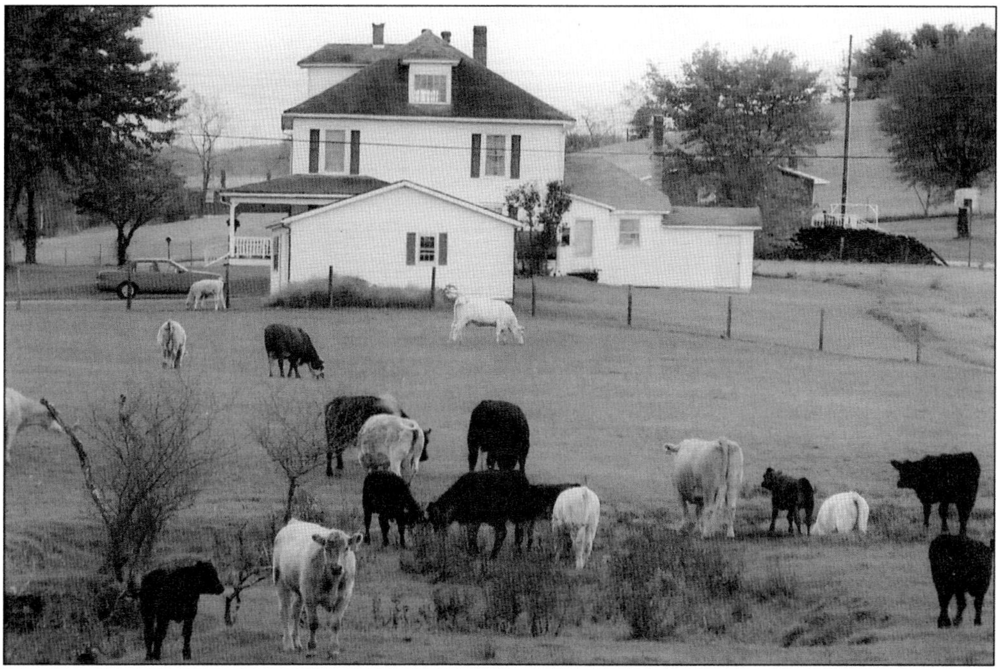

Home on the Farm. Outside of Bland, Virginia, livestock graze near the home of the late Henry Groseclose, the father of the Future Farmers of America. People and domestic animals live in harmony in Bland County's farm country. (Author's.)

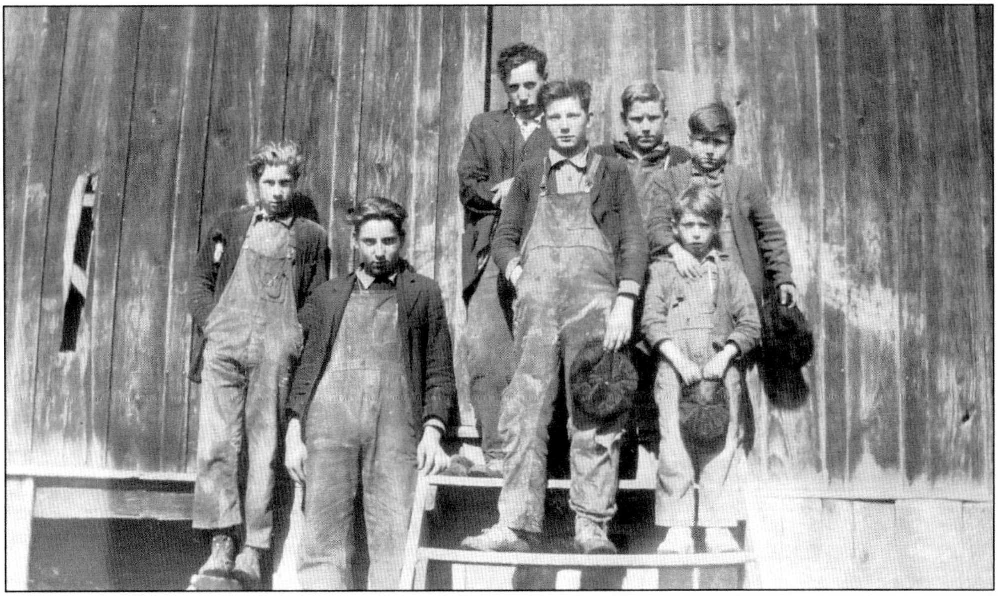

Backbone of the Future. Several students of the Bogle School are shown outside the school. The school opened in 1858 and eventually served children as well as young men and women. (Courtesy of Billy Jean [Walters] Carty.)

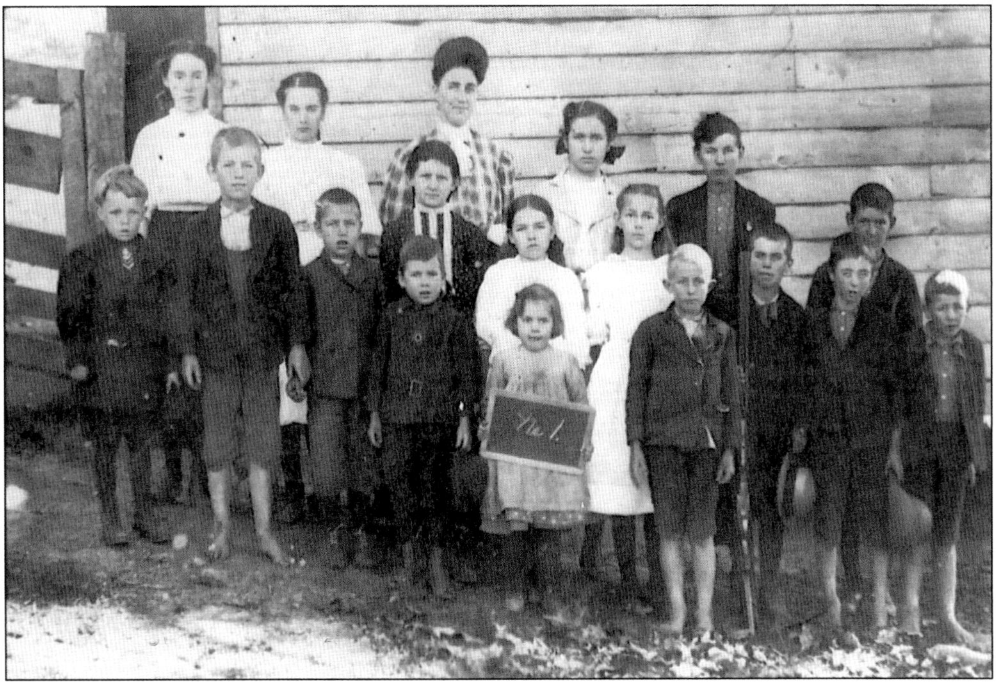

School Days. Students of the Hicksville School are shown here in 1913. Those pictured include Alderson Shufflebarger, Carla Deavers, Earl Kidd, Otis Shufflebarger, Vance Dunn, Robert Linkous, Oakie Kidd, Guy Bruce, Elmer White, Jasper Dunn, Nannie Lilly, Elizabeth Bruce, and Annie Starks, Clara Gross, Sena Linkous, teacher Lucille Shufflebarger, Bessie Gross, Mary Gross, and Monroe White. (Courtesy of the Bland County Historical Society.)

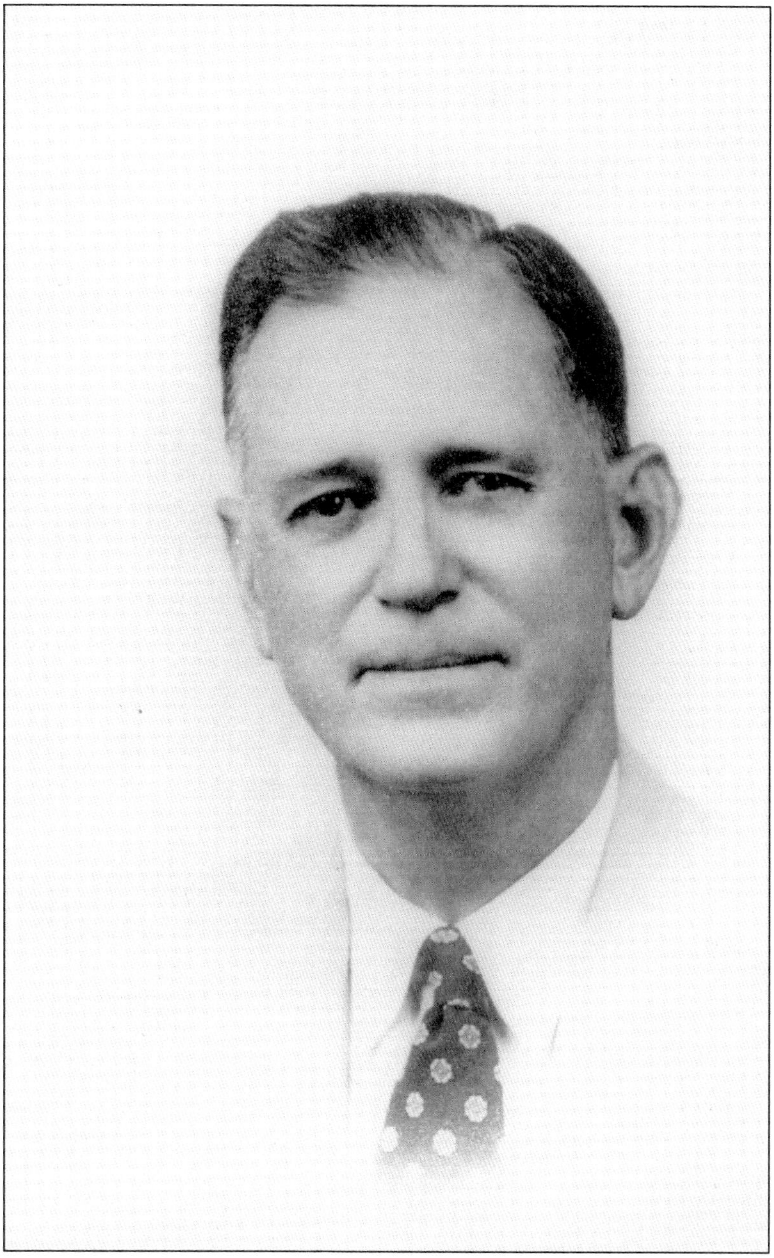

VISIONARY EDUCATOR. In the early 1920s, Henry C. Groseclose, the father of the Future Farmers of America, was teaching in Buckingham County, Virginia, when he realized that the industrialization of the United States was drawing some of the top academic students from the rural farming country to become the professionals and civic leaders of the nation's urban centers. Still, Groseclose realized that many bright and talented young men would stay at home to operate the family farms. According to his widow, Marie Groseclose, Henry Groseclose established the Future Farmers of Virginia to provide high school students with a basic understanding of parliamentary procedure and Robert's Rules of Order, as well as the farming philosophies of two Virginia farmers, George Washington and Thomas Jefferson, who both extolled the virtues of good farming practices. (Courtesy of Marie Groseclose.)

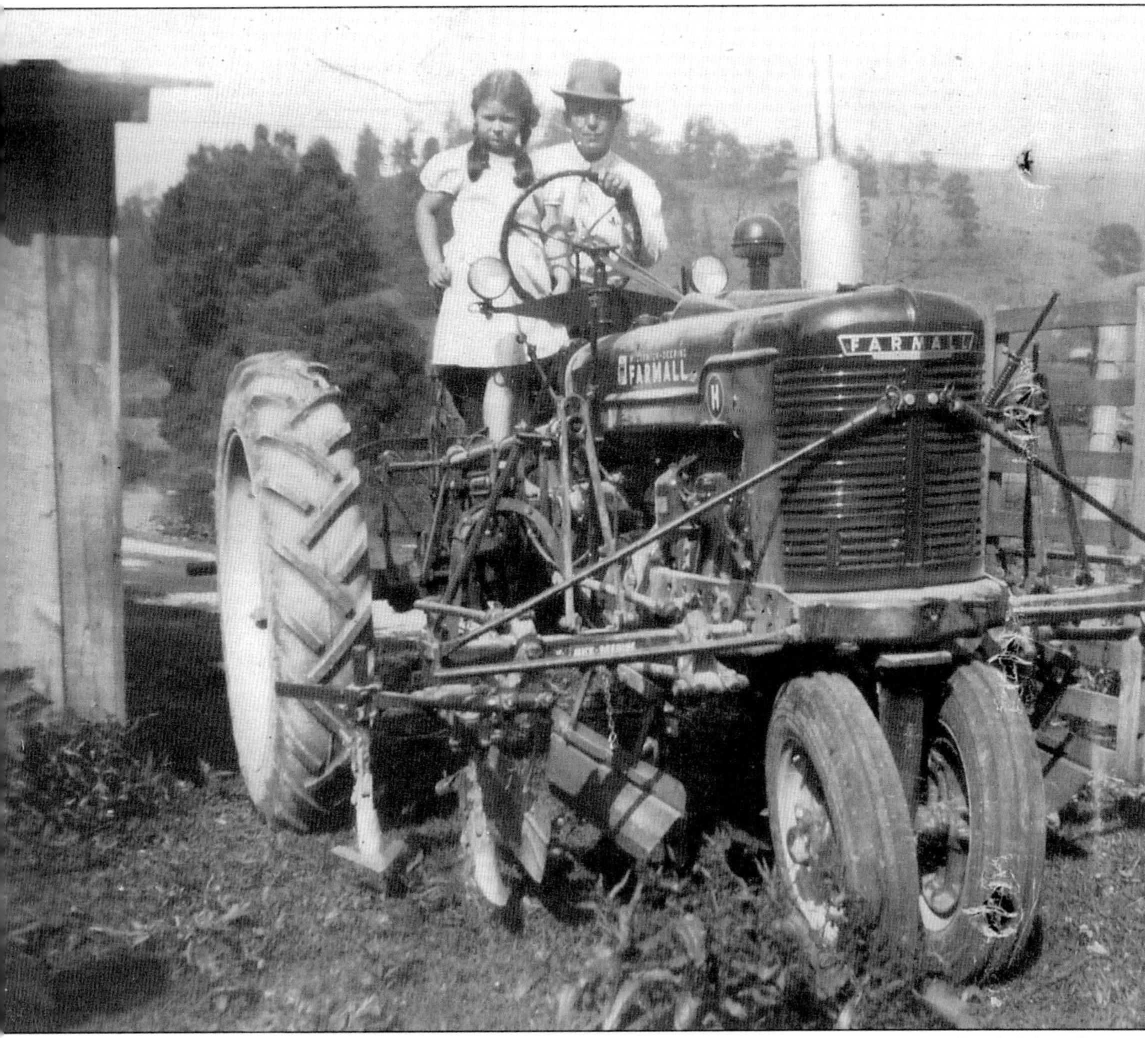

Tradition of Farming. A Bland County uncle and his niece are preparing to till a field with their Farmall tractor. JoAnn Tickle Scott is shown here getting a tractor's-eye view of farming, courtesy of her uncle Ellis Morehead. Although Henry Groseclose envisioned a Future Farmers of America to help young men, both male and female students are now allowed in the FFA, an organization that helps young people—with or without a farming background. (Courtesy of JoAnn Tickle Scott.)

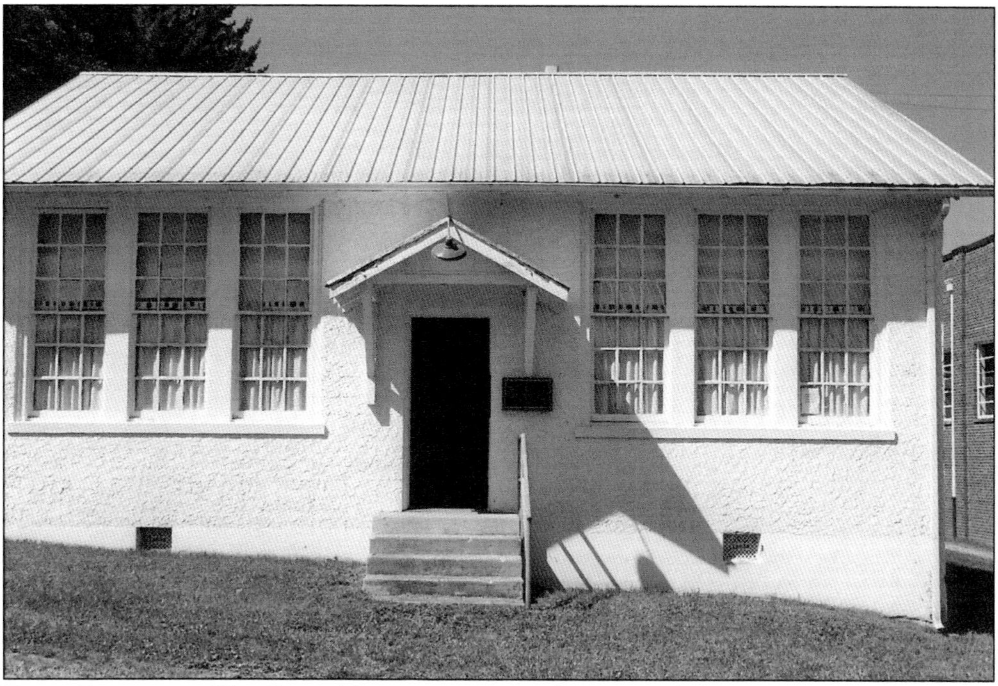

EARLY EDUCATION. The Ceres Alumni Association has restored the old vocational education building at the Ceres High School complex. The building now houses a museum. (Author's.)

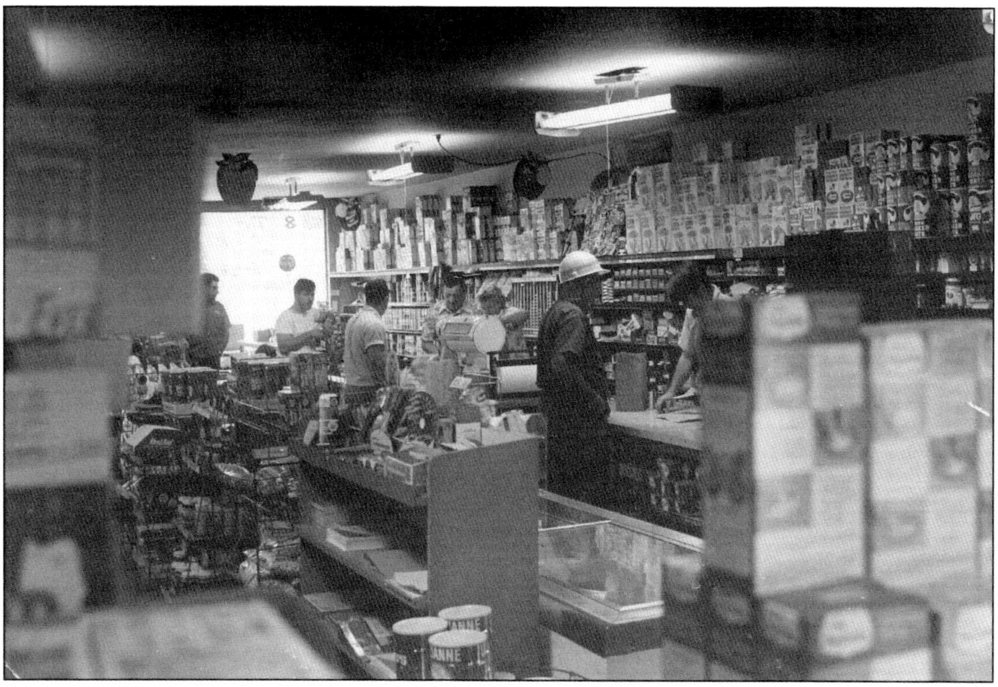

CHANGING TIMES. Prior to the dawn of the 20th century, most Americans were more aware of the role farmers played in manufacturing food. However, with the advent of modern grocery stores like the Carroll Brothers' Grocery Store in Rocky Gap, Virginia, people have less direct contact with farmers. (Courtesy of Buddy Carroll.)

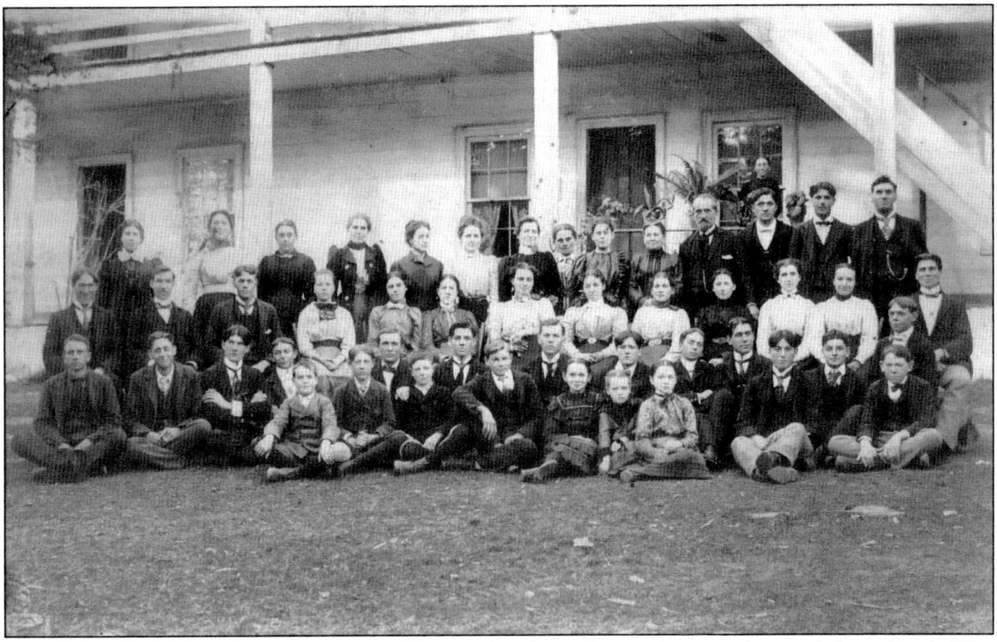

College Prep. Students of Sharon College School are shown here in front of the school. The school was founded in 1892 and served students until it closed in 1901. Students attending the school took courses aimed at preparing them for college work. The school was located in a former health resort that was built when Ceres was known as Effna, Virginia. (Photograph from the Harry Thompson Collection; courtesy of the Bland County Historical Society.)

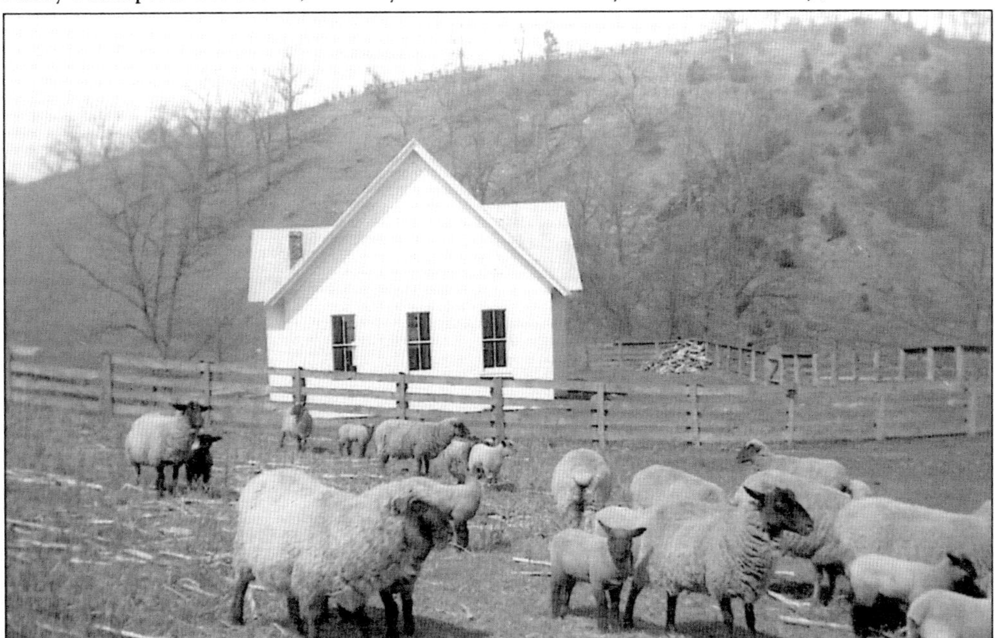

At One with Nature. Sheep are shown grazing in a Bland County field beside the Walkers Creek Methodist Church. People and livestock live in close proximity throughout the county. (Courtesy of Wanda Burton Reynolds.)

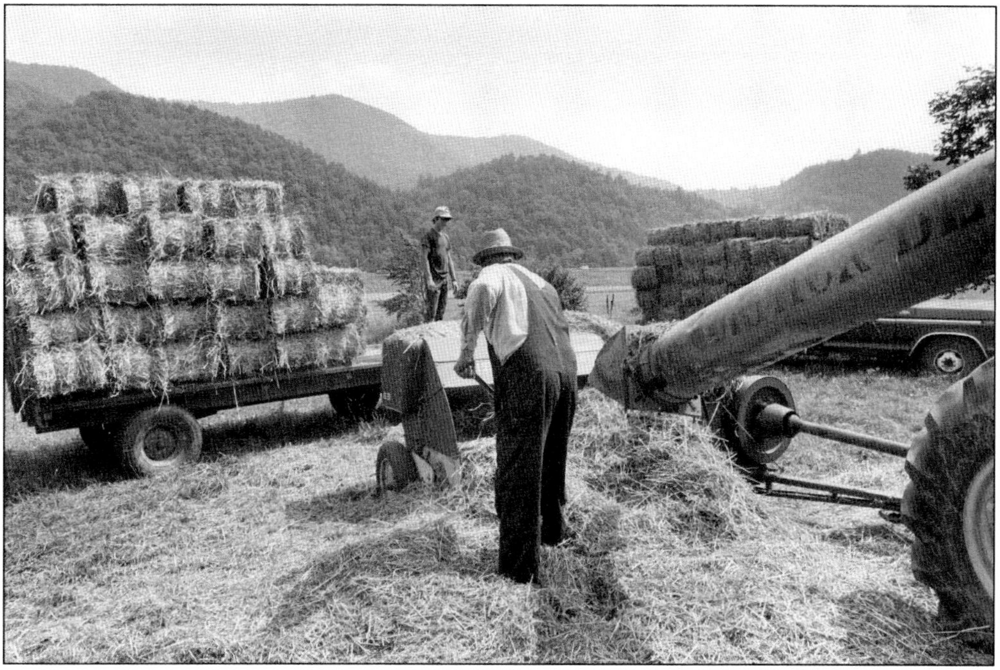

FARM LIFE. A Bland County farmer is loading wheat into a stationary threshing machine that separates the straw and the chaff from the stalk. (Courtesy of Billy Jean [Walters] Carty.)

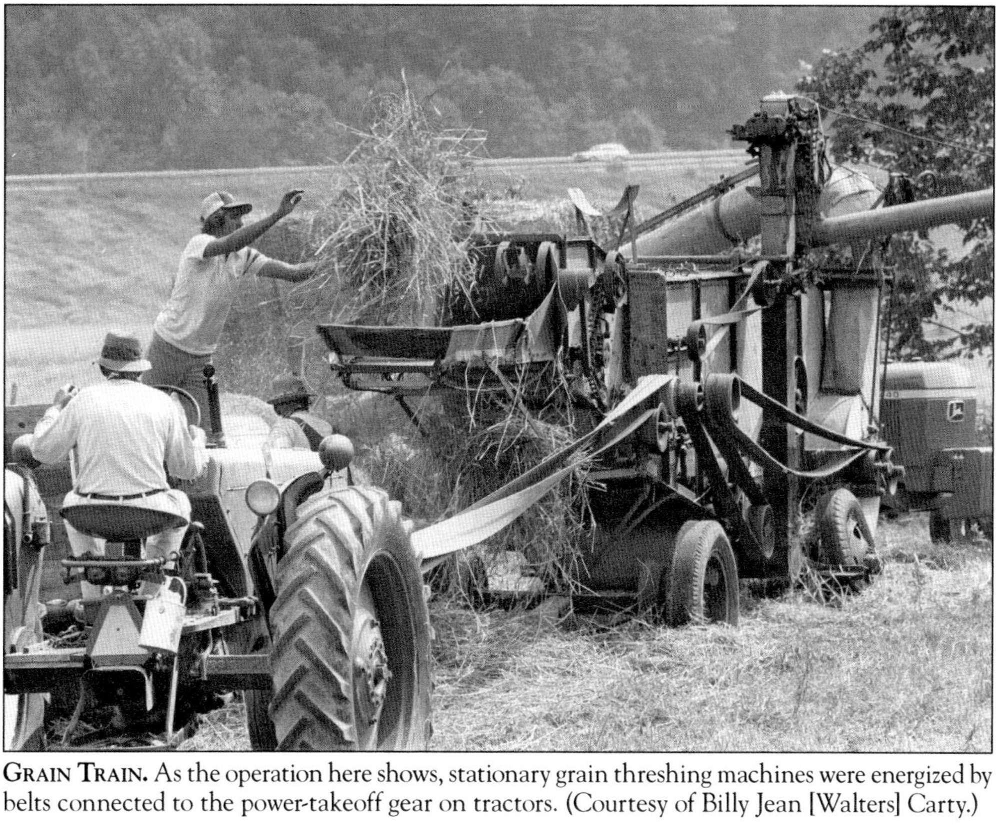

GRAIN TRAIN. As the operation here shows, stationary grain threshing machines were energized by belts connected to the power-takeoff gear on tractors. (Courtesy of Billy Jean [Walters] Carty.)

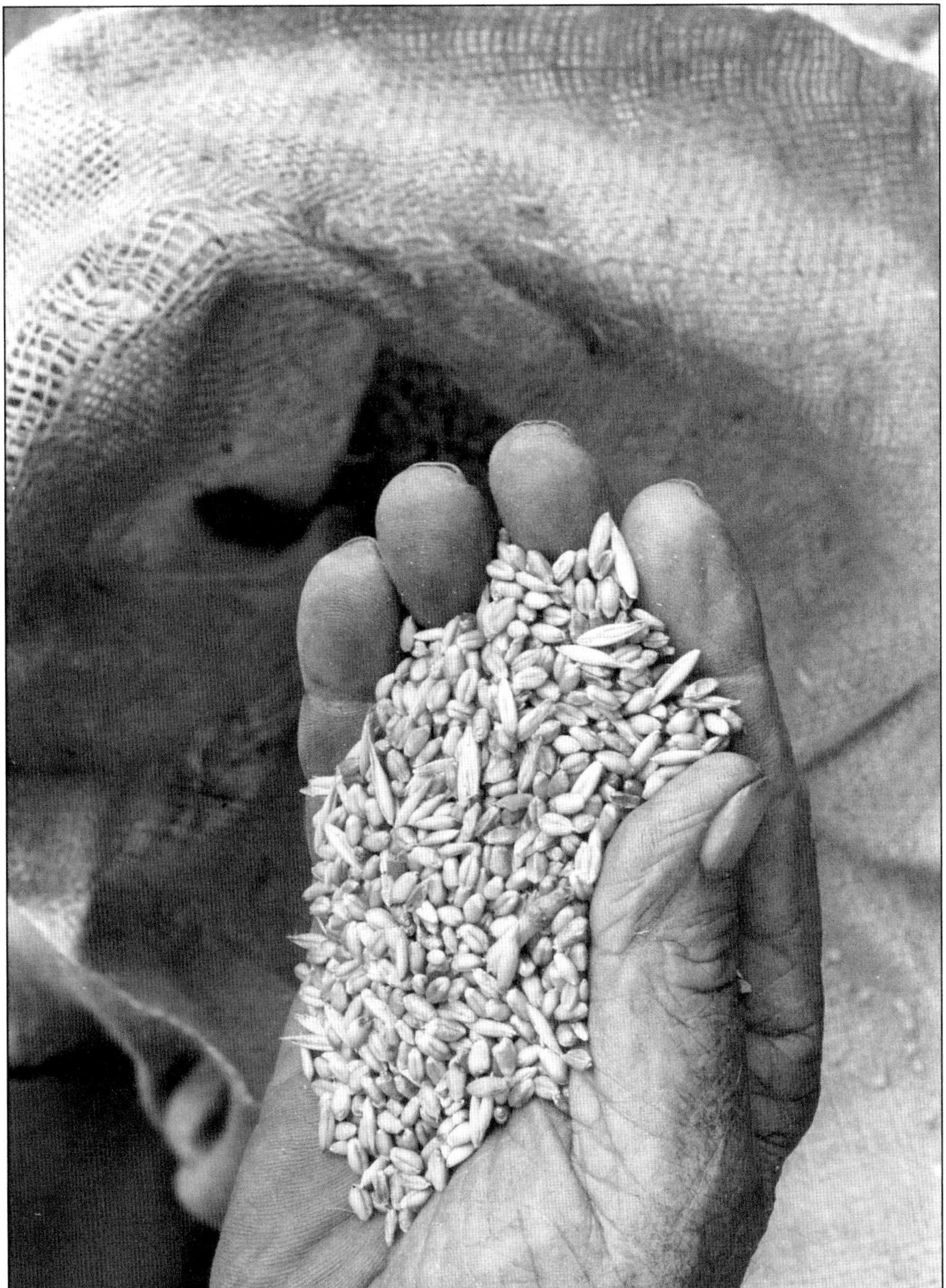

In the American Grain Feed. A farmer is examining a handful of wheat that was freshly harvested through the use of a threshing machine on his Bastian-area farm. European farmers brought the art of growing wheat with them when they settled the North American continent. Native Americans cultivated corn. The New World soil was fertile, so both crops performed well. (Courtesy of Billy Jean [Walters] Carty.)

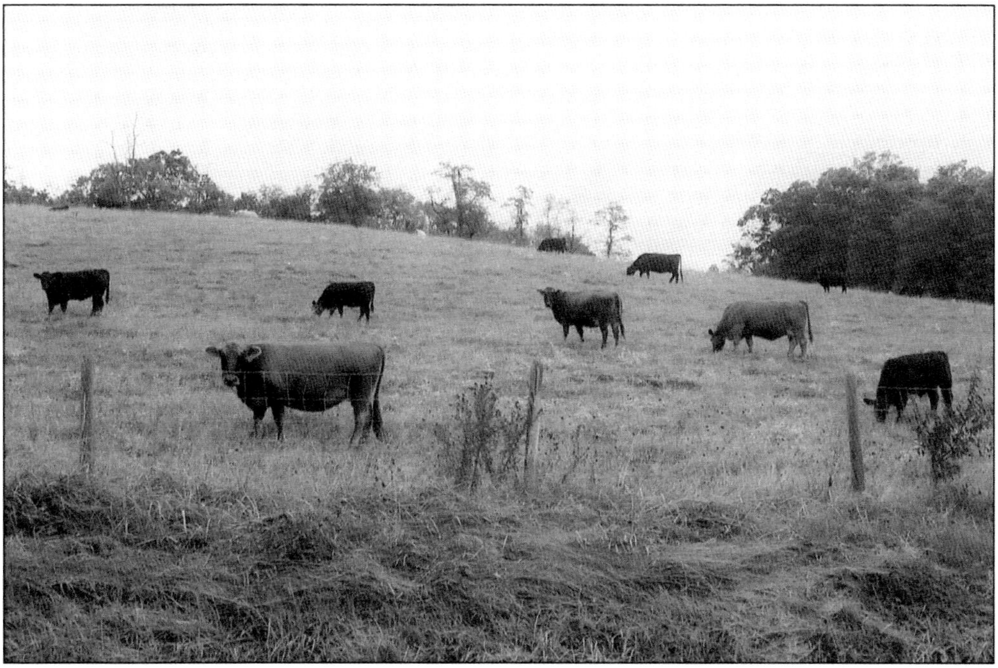

Cow Tech. Bland County farmers continue to graze their cattle in pastures during the summer and feed them grain in the winter. (Author's.)

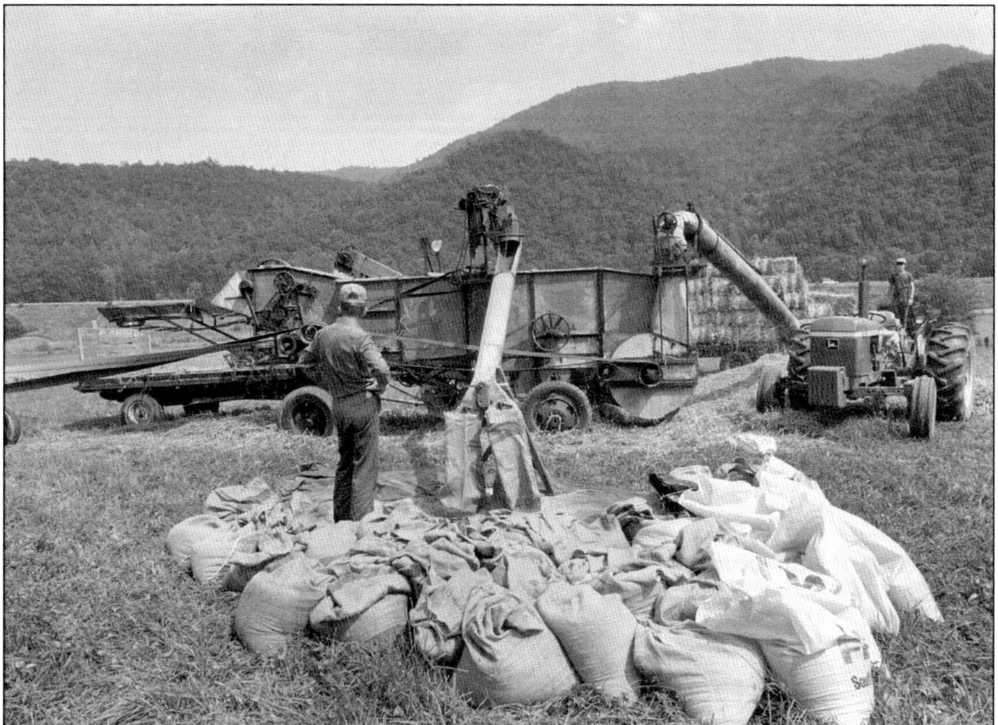

Bag Age. Harvesting grain with a threshing machine is a dusty job, but the bags of wheat are manageable when filled. (Courtesy of Billy Jean [Walters] Carty.)

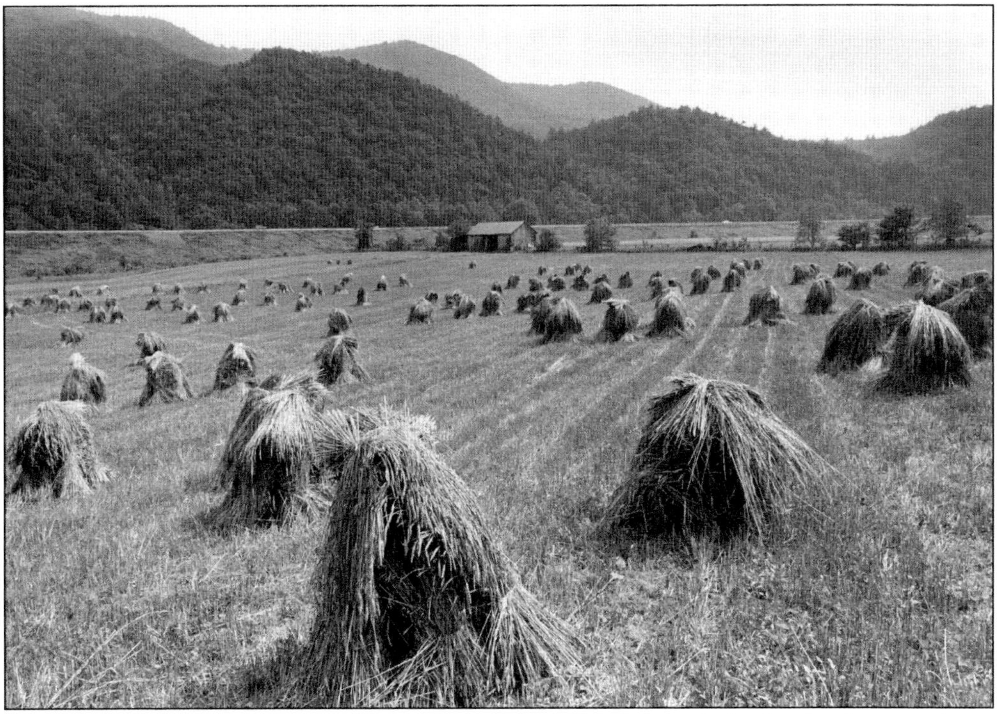

Wheat Shocks. Farmers cut the wheat into stacks to make them ready for the threshing machine. (Courtesy of Billy Jean [Walters] Carty.)

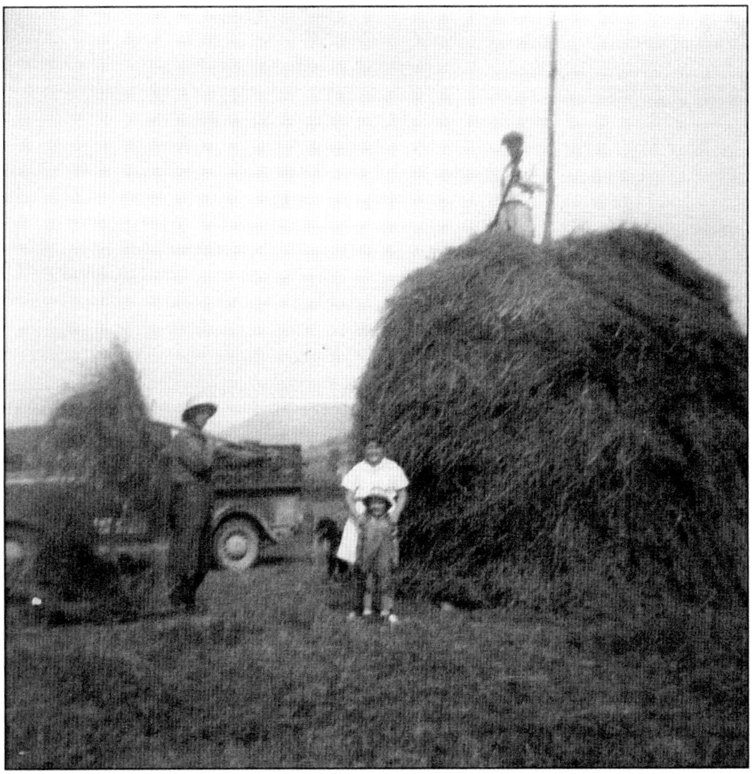

Stacked. Farmers put wheat straw and/or hay into haystacks one forkful at a time. Experienced farmers are able to recall that each fork of hay or straw in a stack made for easy use when preparing bedding or feeding livestock. (Courtesy of Nannie Rose Tiller.)

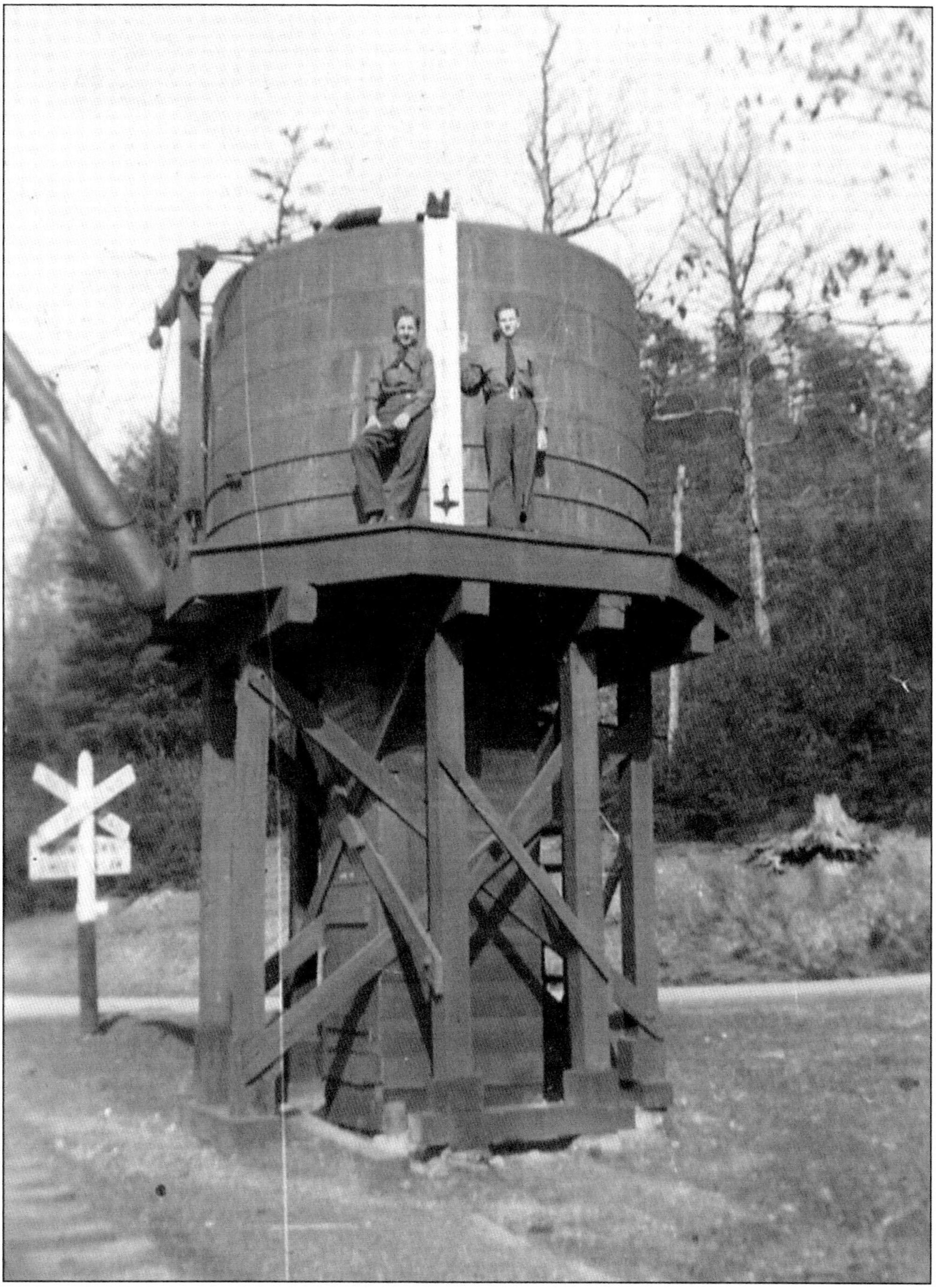

MUCH TO BE TANK FULL FOR. Two uniformed men serving with the Civilian Conservation Corps are shown here standing on the walkway surrounding the water tower near the Norfolk & Western Railway tracks in Bastian. Within a few weeks of Congress passing the bill that made the CCC possible, Bastian was chosen as the site for the second CCC camp in Virginia. The US War Department leased 10 acres from W.J. Bruce of Bastian for the camp. (Courtesy of Georgia Stacy Havens.)

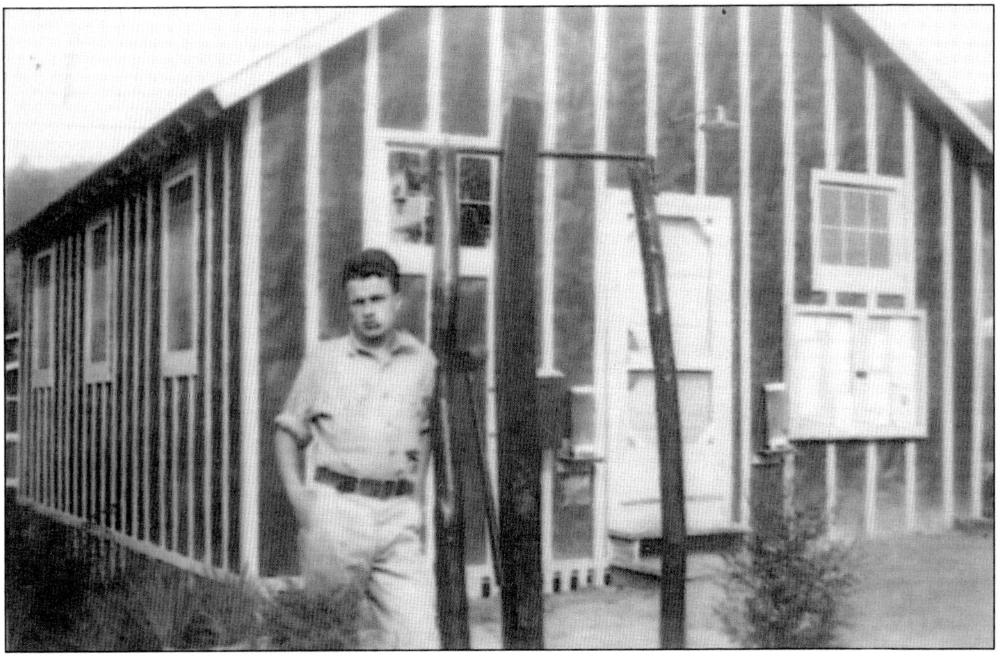

Depression Aftermath. The stock market collapse of 1929 hurled the United States into the Great Depression and left millions of Americans out of work. For many able-bodied young men, like the man shown above, life in a CCC camp represented an alternative to starvation. (Courtesy of Georgia Stacy Havens.)

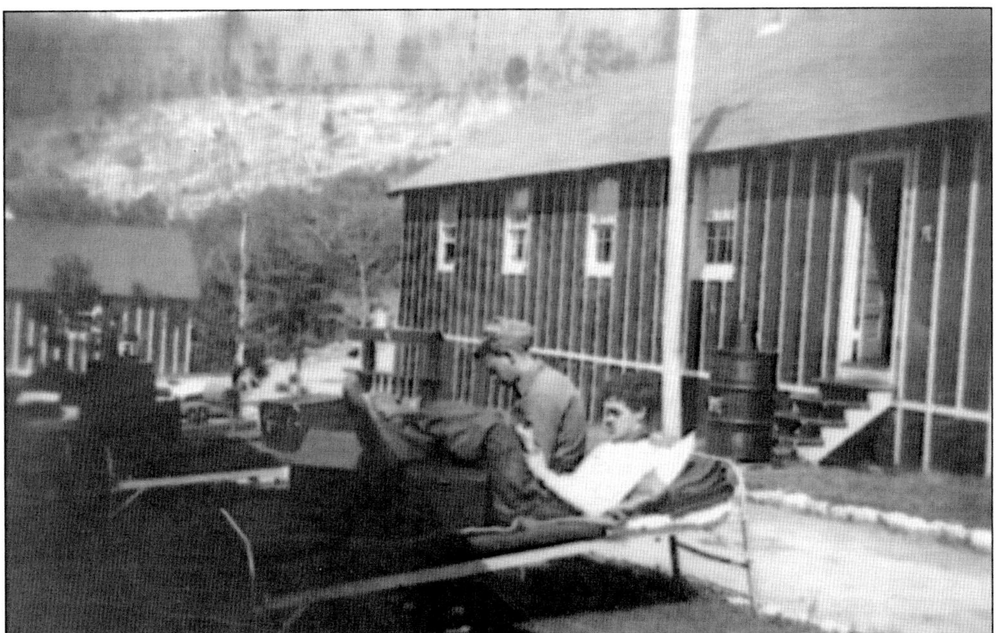

Three Hots and a Cot. Civilian Conservation Corps workers are shown here relaxing on cots outside of their barracks in Bastian, Virginia. (Courtesy of Georgia Stacy Havens.)

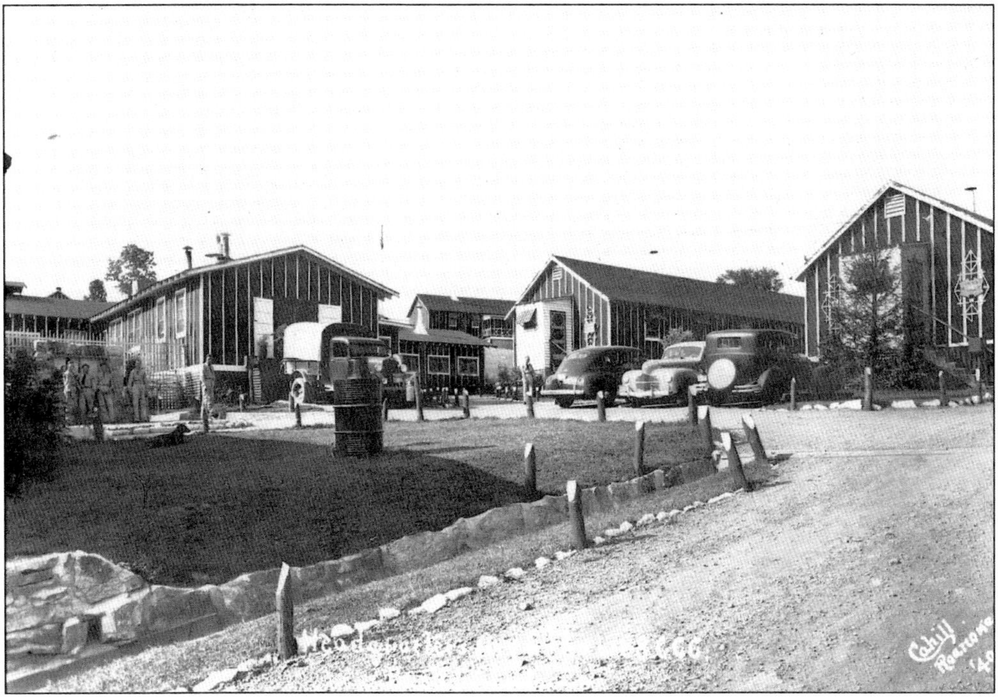

Government Issue. CCC Camp 1388 P-53-VA in Bastian was well maintained and kept clean from the arrival of its initial group of 212 officers and men from Fort Monroe, Virginia, on June 4, 1933, until the camp closed on December 9, 1942—just one year and two days after the Japanese attacked Pearl Harbor and the United States entered World War II. (Courtesy of Georgia Stacy Havens.)

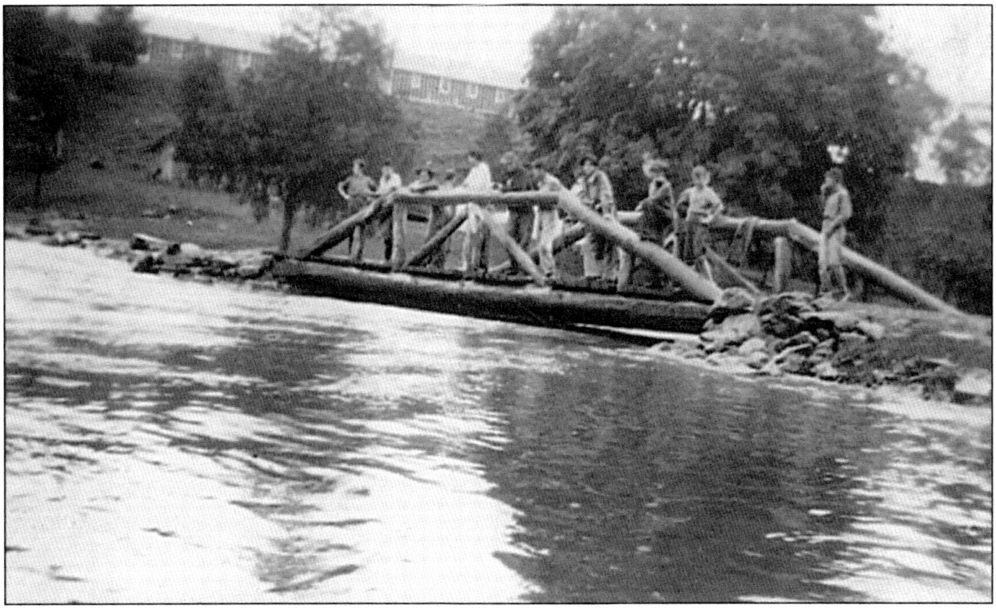

Bridge over Troubled Waters. Civilian Conservation Corps workers are shown here after building a bridge over Wolf Creek. The CCC provided a lifesaving bridge for many people swept up in the throes of the Great Depression. (Courtesy of Georgia Stacy Havens.)

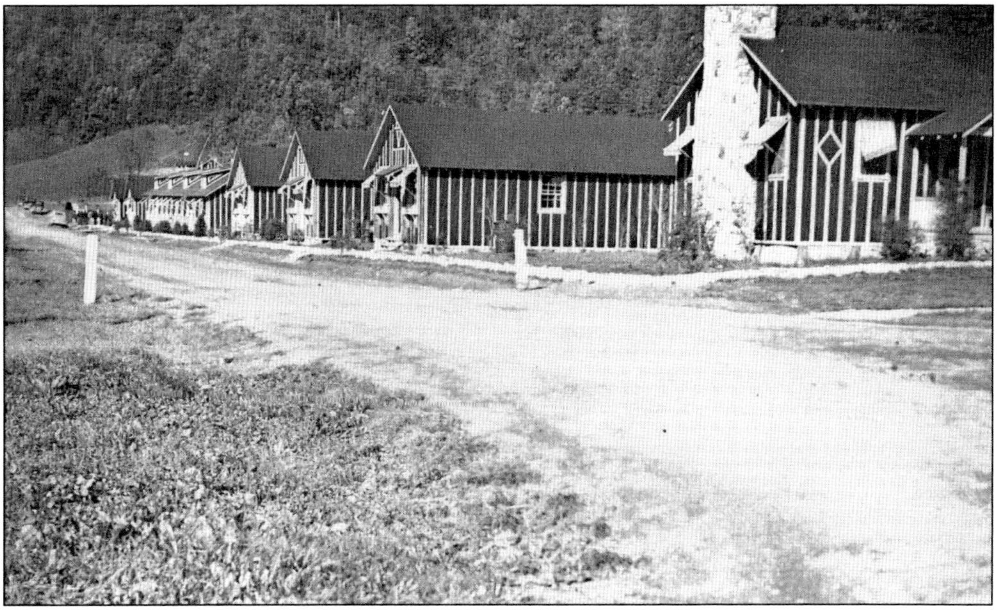

Row Houses. Workers of the Civilian Conservation Corps went out on jobs by day and returned to the relative comfort of their cabins at night. Company 1388 did truck-trail, tower, bridge, and telephone line construction and rendered superior fire-control services during the 1935 and 1936 fire seasons. (Courtesy of Georgia Stacy Havens.)

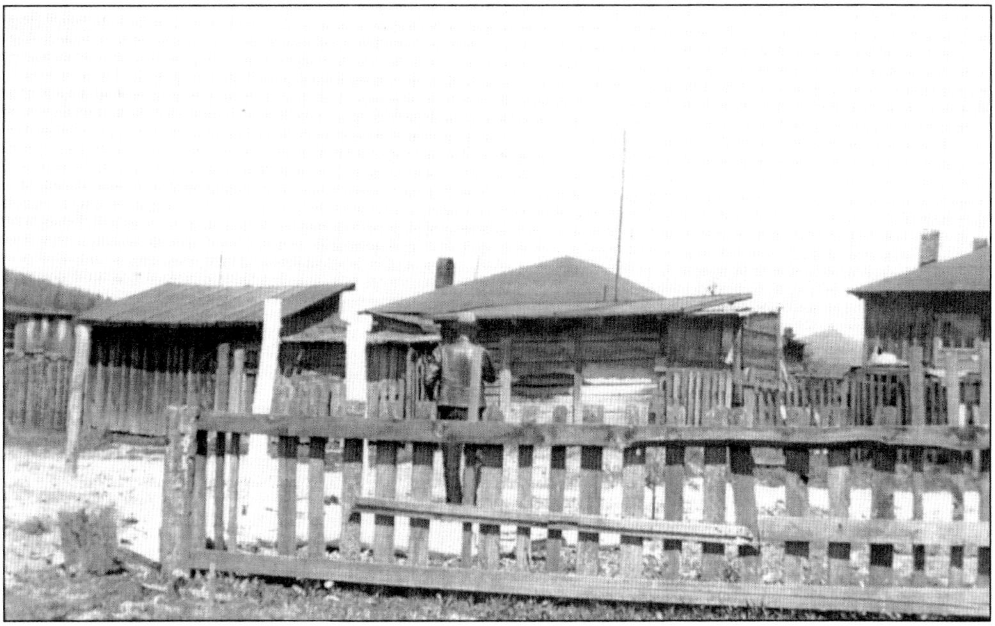

Timber Business. Workers with the Virginia Hardwood Lumber Company were living on another side of Bastian in company housing, located near the lumber mill. (Courtesy of Georgia Stacy Havens.)

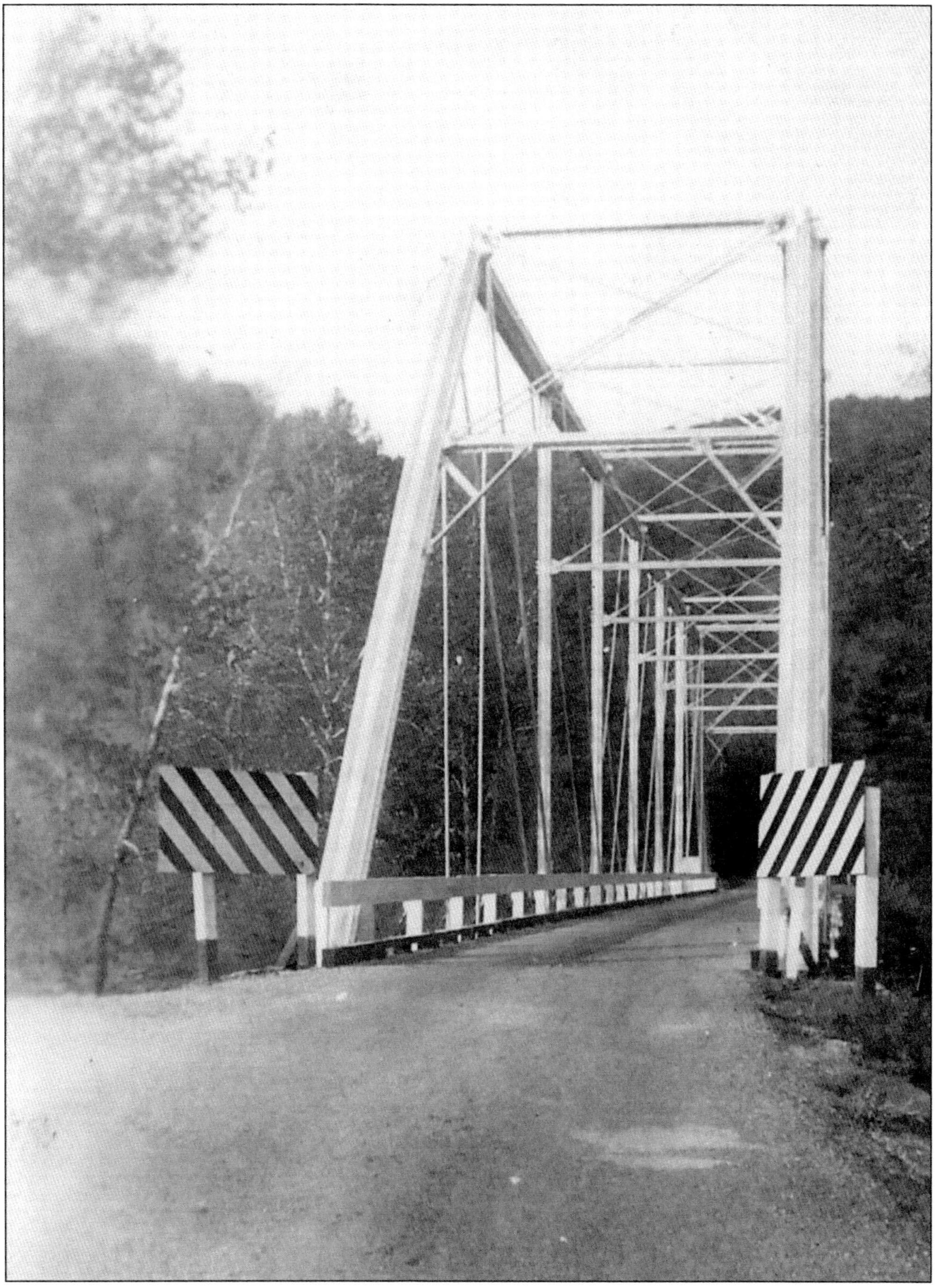

Bridging the Gap. When the Civilian Conservation Corps closed its Bland County operations in 1942, the highway improvement projects had already provided better access to the region for automobiles and trucks. The Norfolk & Western Railway stopped its Narrows-to-Bastian service in 1946, and the county soon converted Bridge No. 2, near Rocky Gap, into a vehicle bridge for motorists traveling State Route 61 along Wolf Creek into Giles County. (Courtesy of the Bland County Historical Society.)

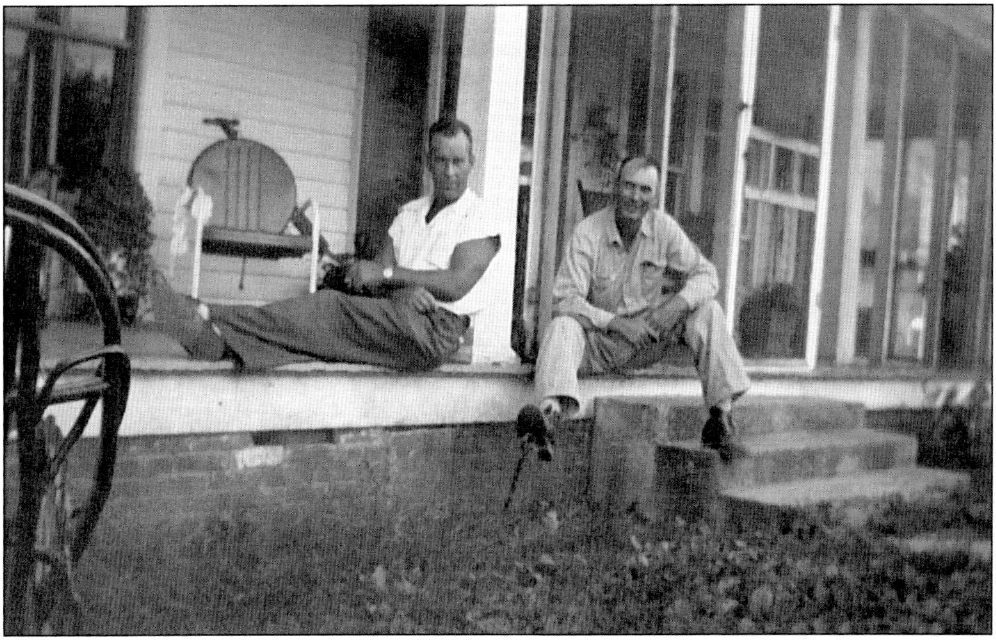

FRONT PORCH TIME. Bland County residents Buford Tiller (left) and Joe Compton are shown here at the Compton home taking a well-deserved break. (Courtesy of Nannie Rose Tiller.)

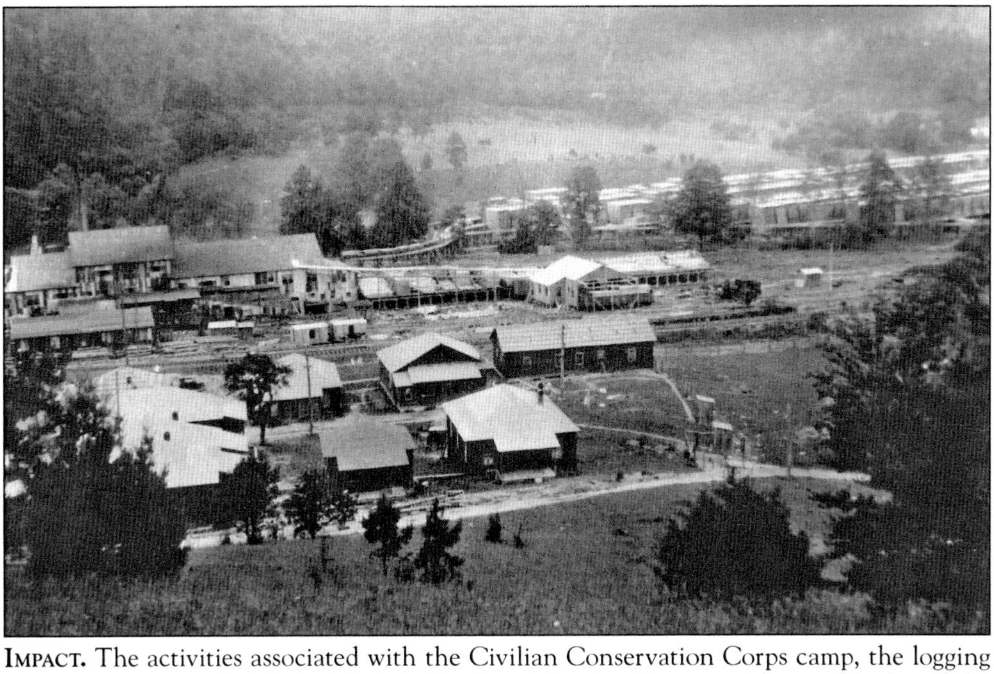

IMPACT. The activities associated with the Civilian Conservation Corps camp, the logging operations connected with the Virginia Hardwood Lumber Company (shown above), and the road construction projects provided by the government opened up the county for commerce and settlement but also had an impact on the people when the rains came. Logging in the 1930s contributed to the flooding in the 1950s. (Courtesy of Georgia Stacy Havens.)

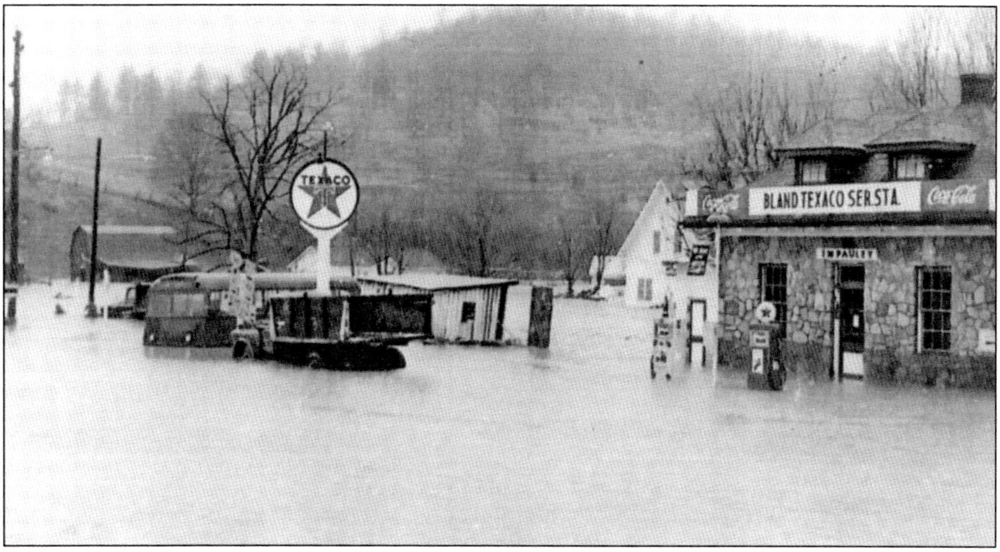

Water Everywhere. Three days of rain soaked Bland County in late January 1957, breached the 28-acre Crab Orchard Lake recreational project, and sent too much water into Bland, knocking homes from their foundations and swamping businesses like the Texaco station. (Photograph from the Robert Pike Collection; courtesy of the Bland County Historical Society.)

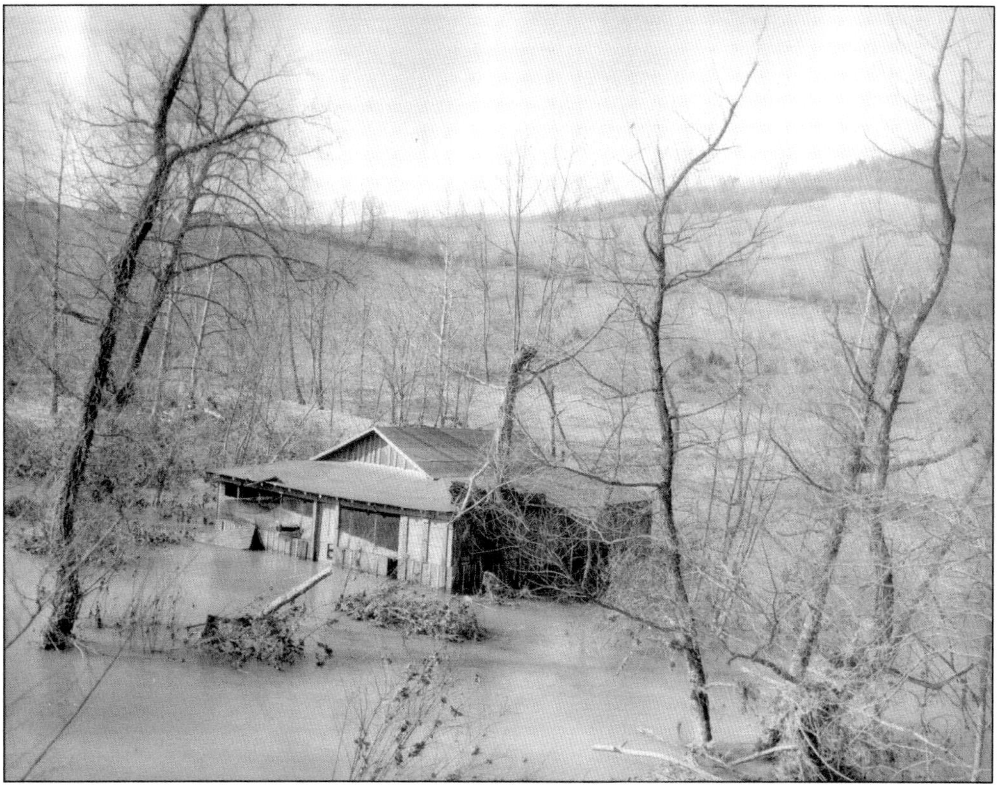

Under Water. Houses in Bland were inundated with water after the Crab Orchard Lake failed on January 29, 1957. (Photograph from the Robert Pike Collection; courtesy of the Bland County Historical Society.)

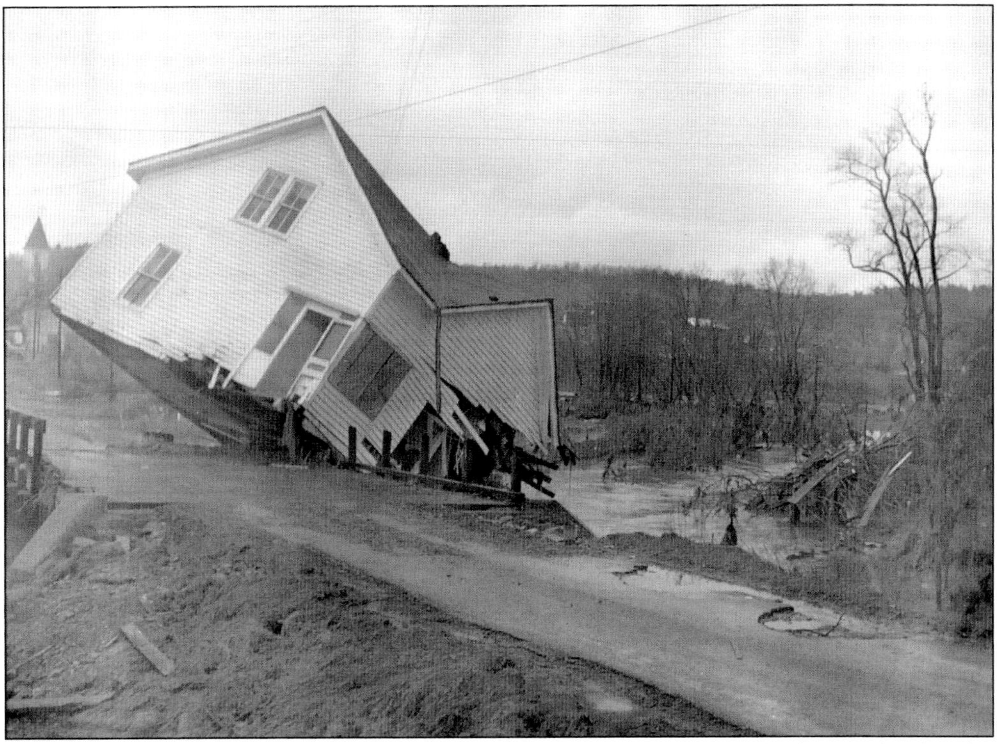

Low Bridge. Floodwaters swept the home of Ray and Roxie Neal over a bridge in Bland in the January 29, 1957, flood. (Photograph from the Robert Pike Collection; courtesy of the Bland County Historical Society.)

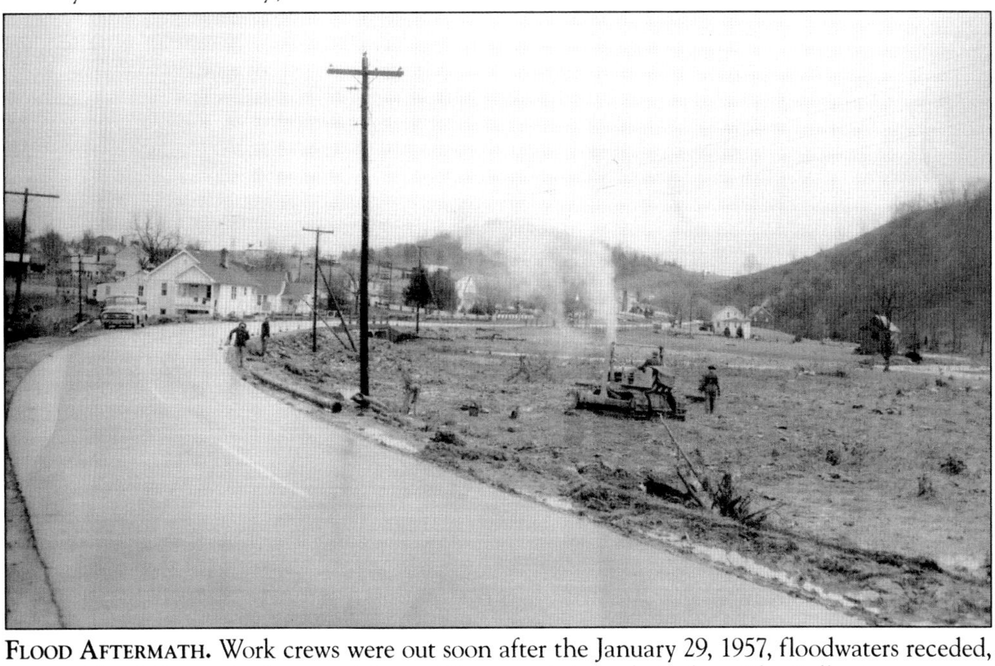

Flood Aftermath. Work crews were out soon after the January 29, 1957, floodwaters receded, putting Bland County back in good shape. (Photograph from the Robert Pike Collection; courtesy of the Bland County Historical Society.)

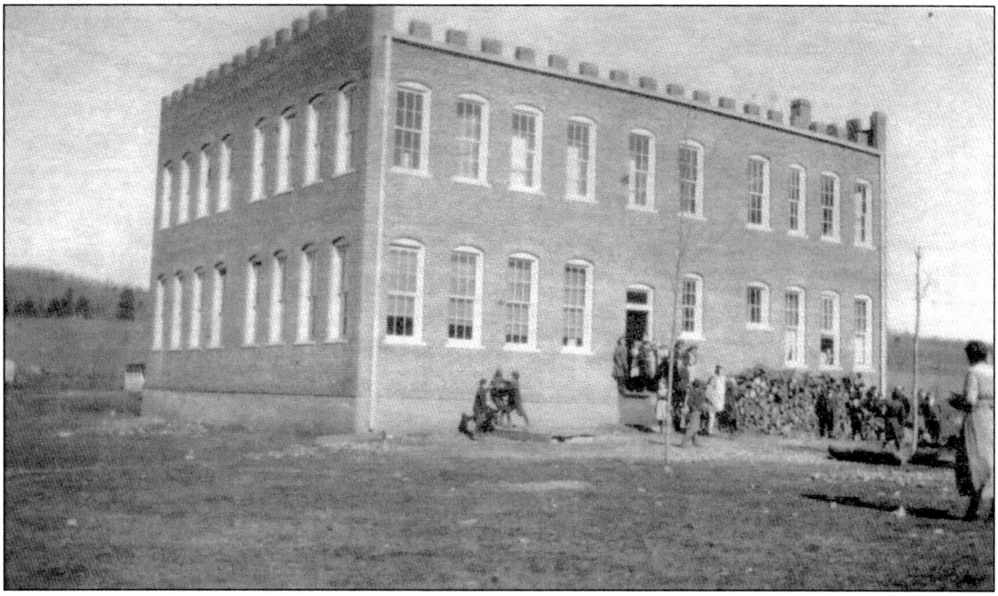

BHS. From its location overlooking Bland, Bland High School began serving students in 1922. The building shown here is still part of the BHS complex. (Courtesy of the Bland County Historical Society.)

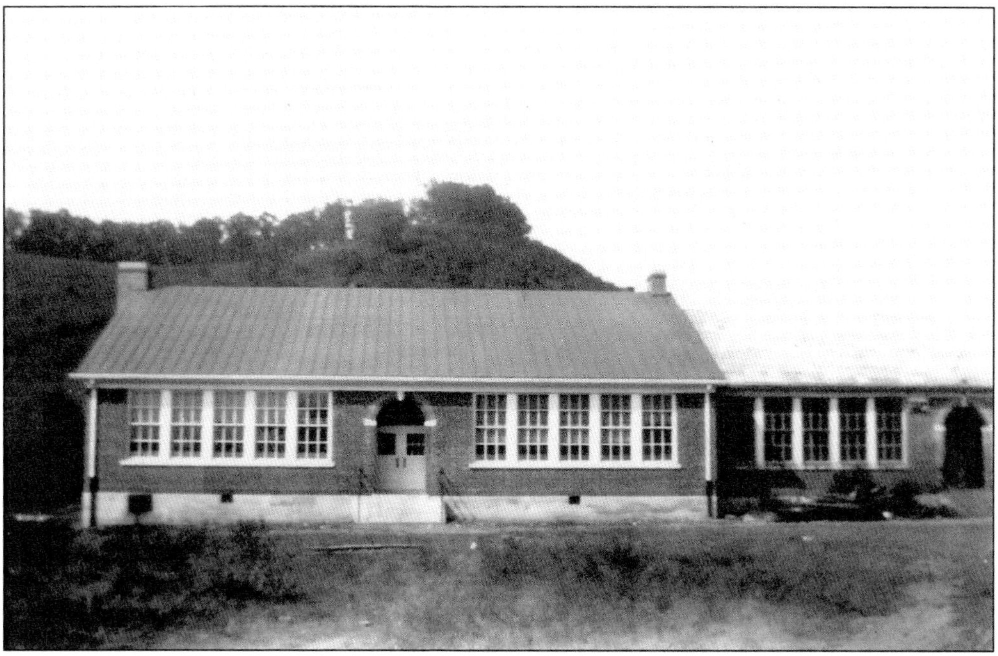

RGHS. Rocky Gap High School is Bland County's only other high school. Although the two county schools are rivals on the hardwoods, they come together in football and perform as the Bland County Bears. The building shown here is still part of the Rocky Gap high and elementary school complex. (Courtesy of the Bland County Historical Society.)

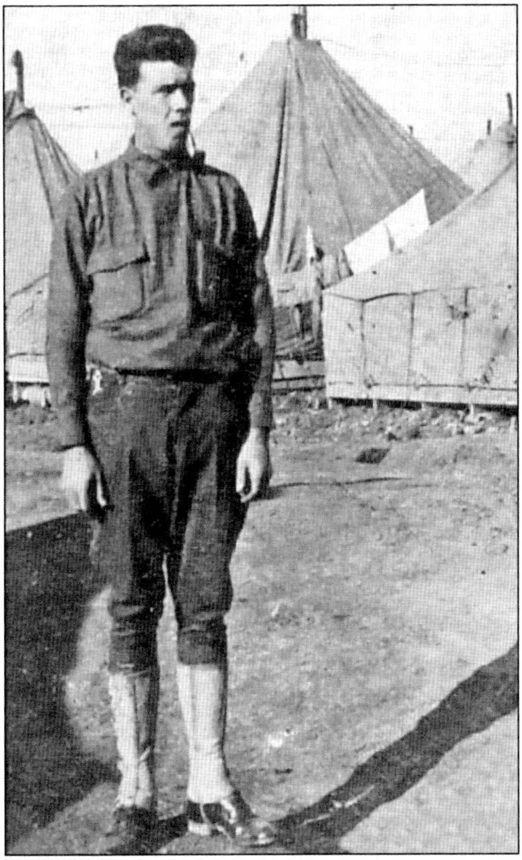

High Sheriff. Minor M. Muncy, shown here in his military uniform, served as Bland County sheriff from 1932 to 1936. (Photograph from the Bogle Library Collection; courtesy of the Bland County Historical Society.)

Stamp Act. Bruce Shufflebarger, postmaster at Bastian, Virginia, is shown here standing in the doorway of the old post office. (Courtesy of Georgia Stacy Havens.)

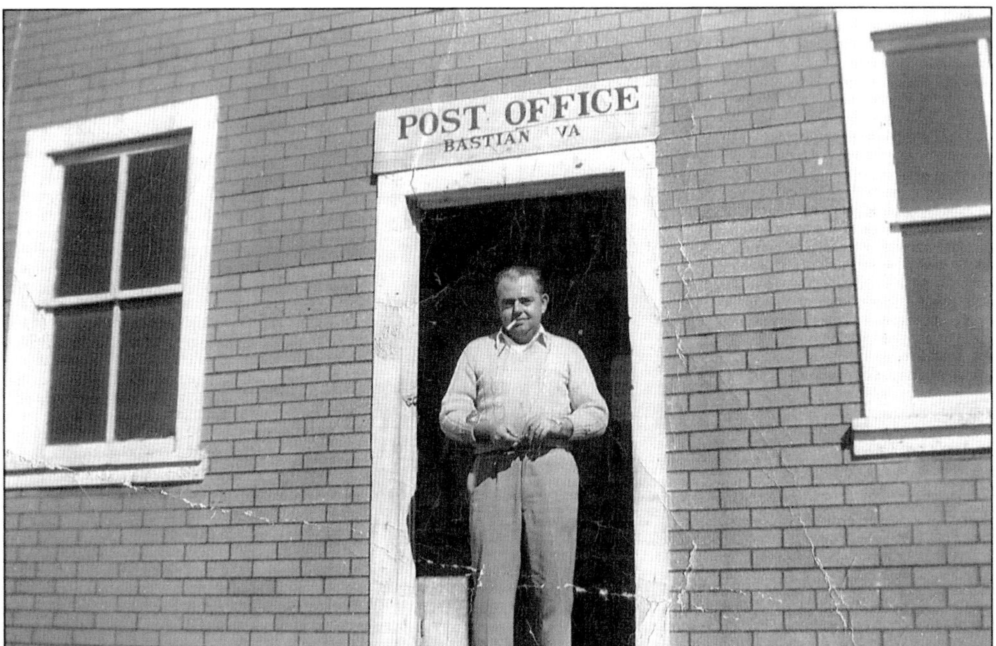

Six

ON THE LOOKOUT

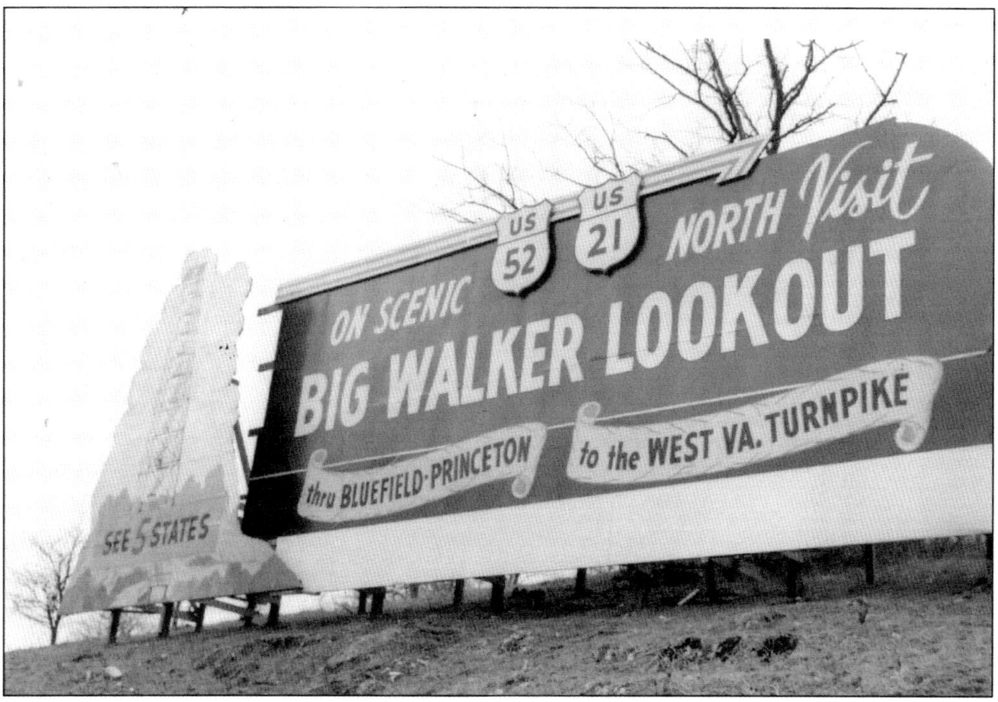

ON THE MAP. Big Walker Lookout is one of Southwest Virginia's most enduring tourist attractions. The lookout is located on the county line of Wythe and Bland on top of Big Walker Mountain. The attraction has drawn tourists to the region for more than six decades. (Courtesy of Ron Kime.)

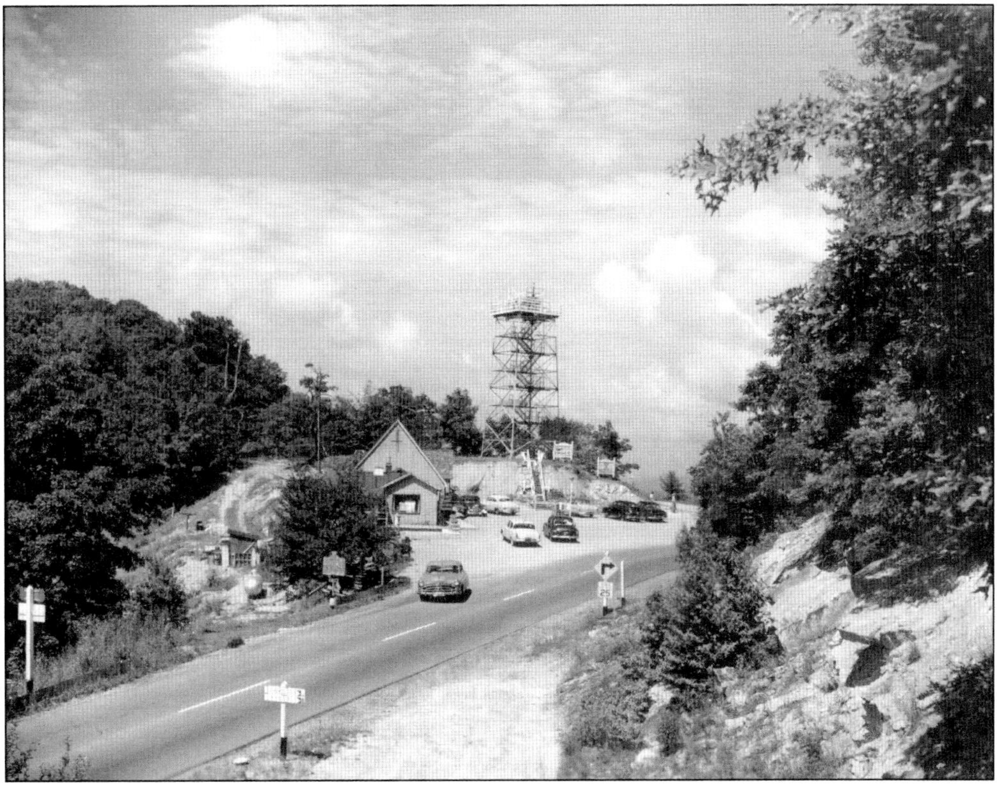

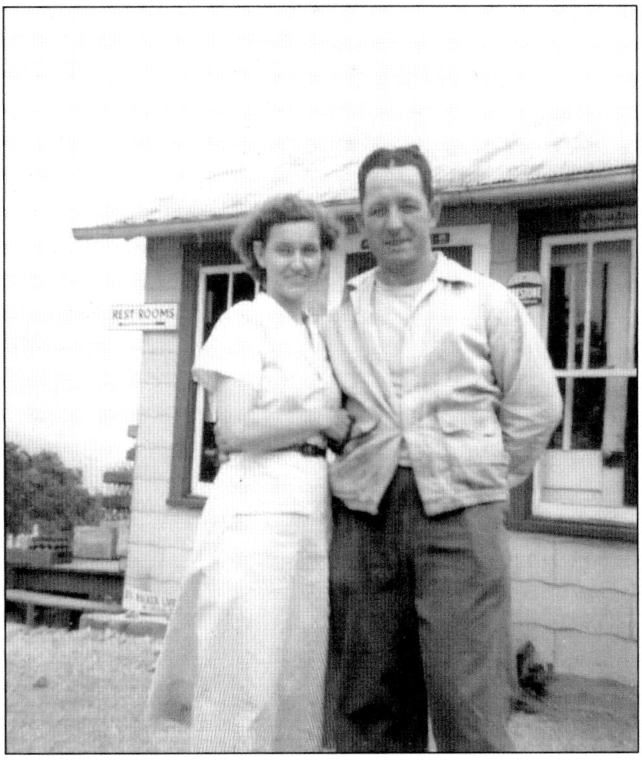

TOP SIDE OF THE MOUNTAIN. Big Walker Lookout holds both a historic and an important scenic position in Southwest Virginia. Union colonel John T. Toland came through the mountain pass in July 1863, when he attacked Wytheville, Virginia, and on clear days, visitors can see Virginia, North Carolina, Kentucky, West Virginia, and Tennessee from the 3,787-foot summit. (Courtesy of Ron Kime.)

DREAM SEQUENCE. The Big Walker Lookout was the dream creation of Abbie and Stuart Kime, shown here in front of the mountaintop business that occupied the site before the Kime family bought it in the late 1940s. (Courtesy of Ron Kime.)

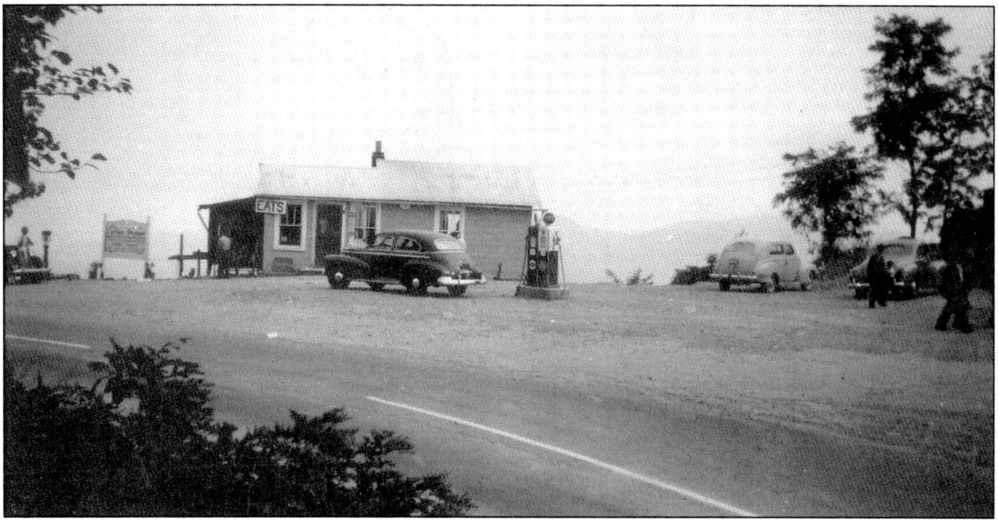

Good Spirits. Bland County was a dry county when highways started opening up the area to visitors. The previous owners of the mountaintop opened a tavern on the hill across the county line into non-dry Wythe County to serve Bland County residents or visitors who might like a taste of distilled spirits. (Courtesy of Ron Kime.)

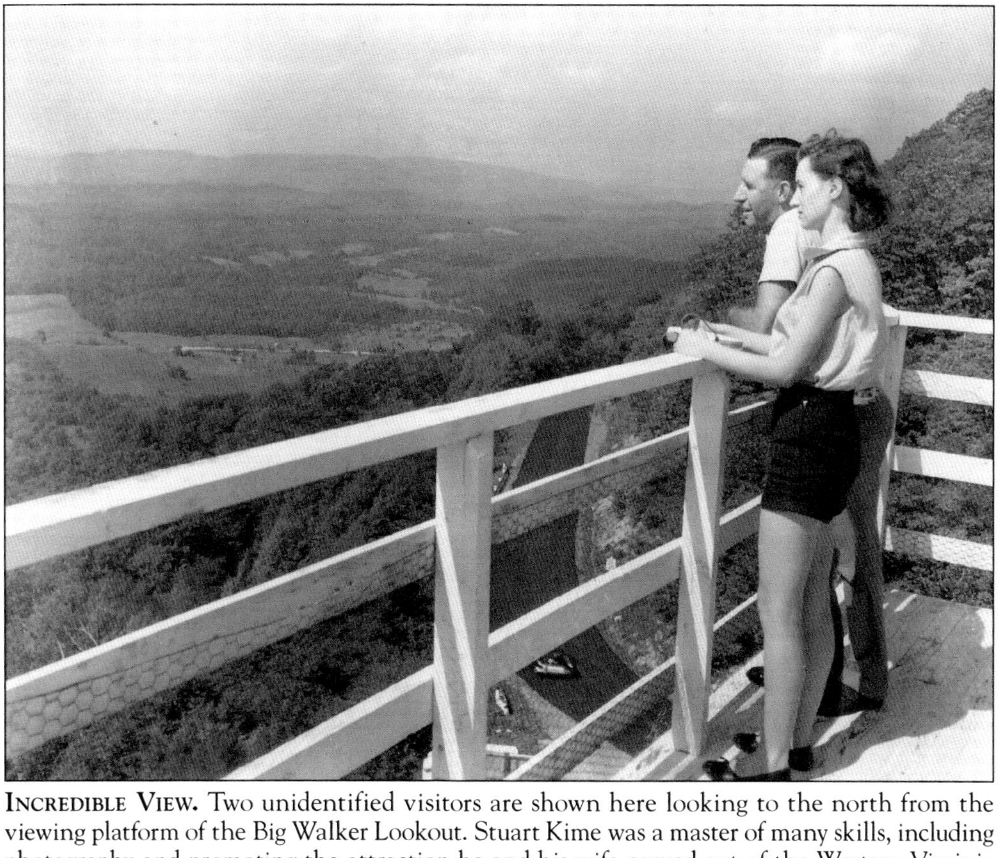

Incredible View. Two unidentified visitors are shown here looking to the north from the viewing platform of the Big Walker Lookout. Stuart Kime was a master of many skills, including photography and promoting the attraction he and his wife carved out of the Western Virginia wilderness. (Courtesy of Ron Kime.)

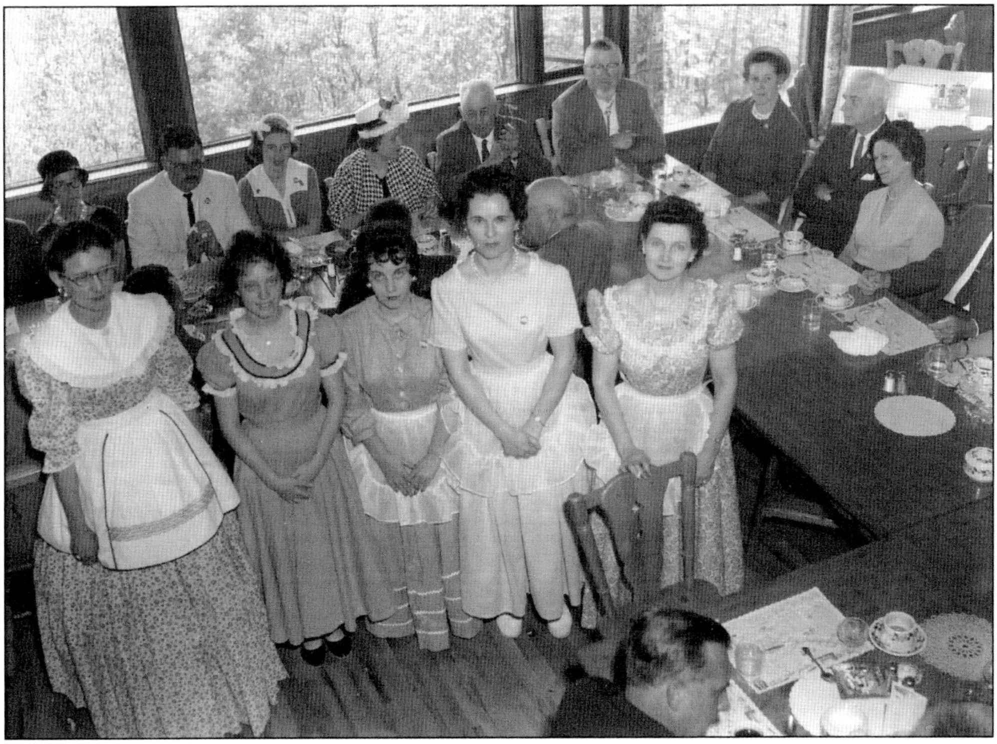

High Altitude Menu. The Big Walker Lookout Restaurant was itself a popular attraction, and after more than a decade of operations, waitresses at the restaurant got into the Bland County centennial spirit in 1961 and came to work in old-time attire. (Courtesy of Ron Kime.)

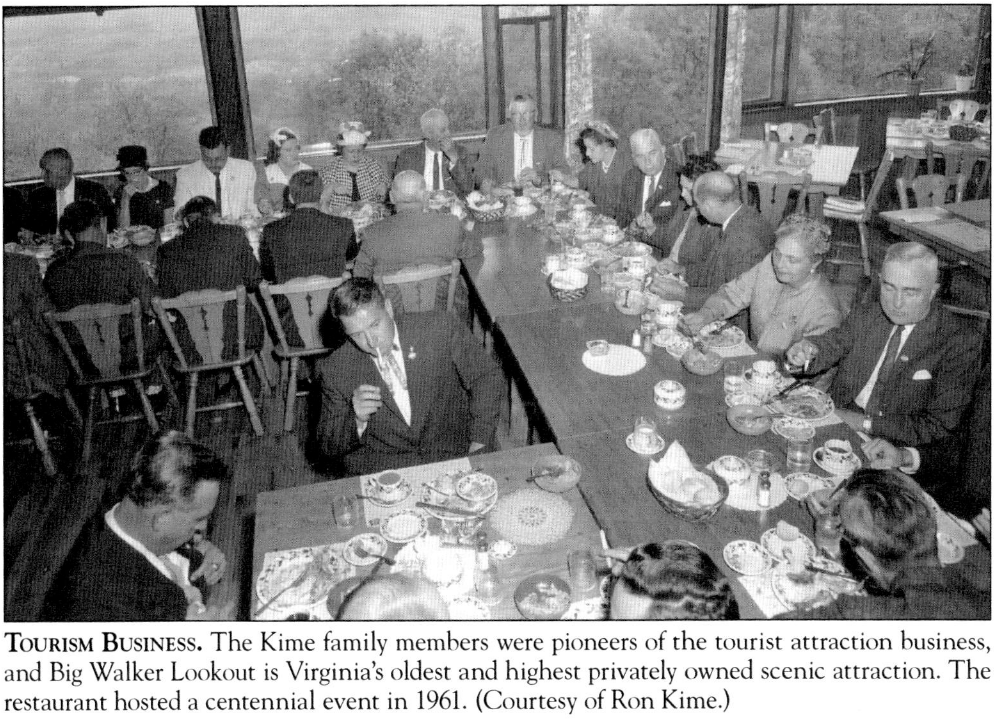

Tourism Business. The Kime family members were pioneers of the tourist attraction business, and Big Walker Lookout is Virginia's oldest and highest privately owned scenic attraction. The restaurant hosted a centennial event in 1961. (Courtesy of Ron Kime.)

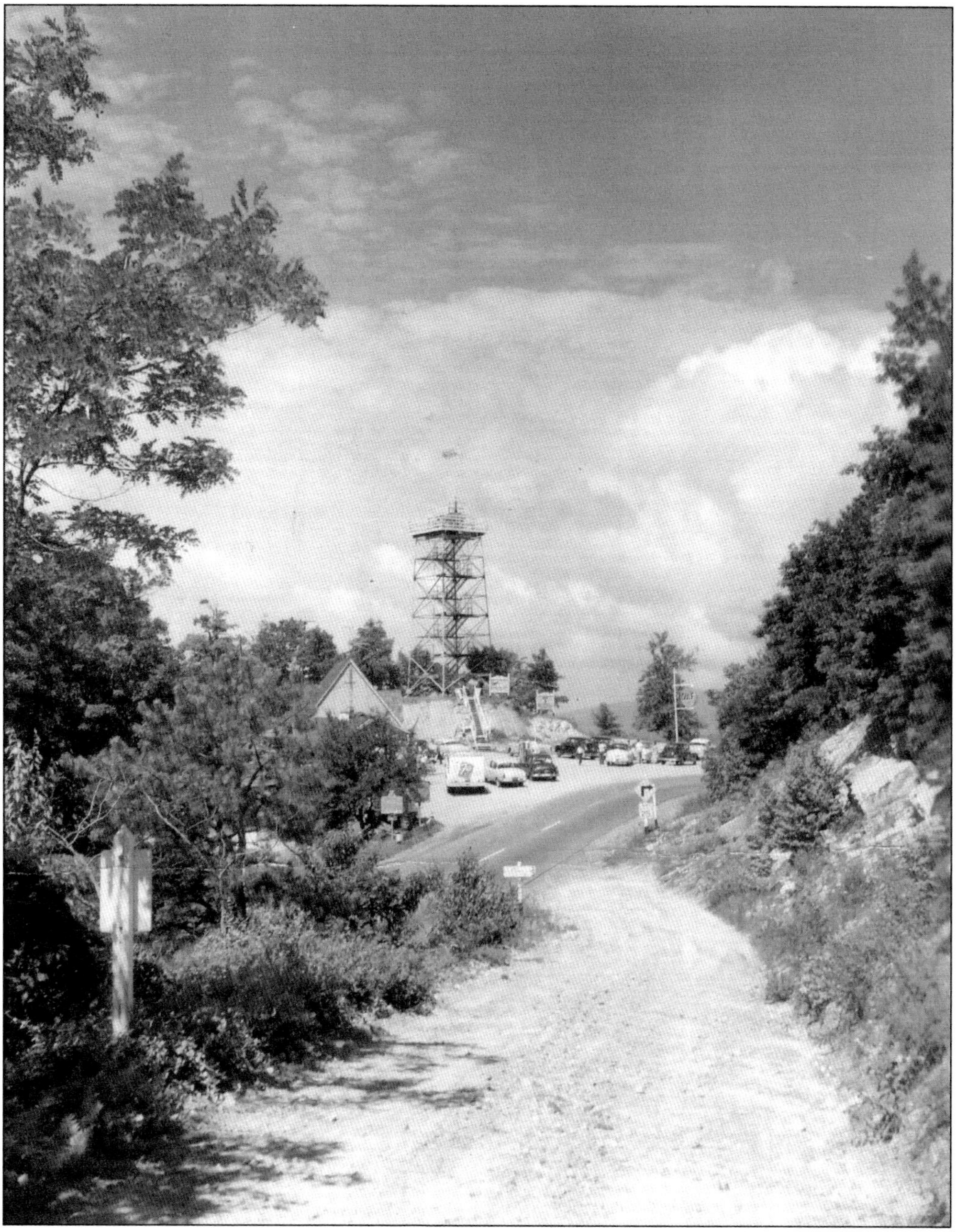

EUREKA. Stuart Kime visited a mountaintop scenic overlook in Arkansas when he was serving in the military during World War II and decided he wanted to build his own attraction when the war ended. Kime was stationed stateside for the duration and flew frequently over the eastern United States. On one trip, he spotted the Walker Mountain clearing and set his sights on making it his life's work. Stuart and Abbie Kime were a team for work. He was a builder, an exceptional carpenter, an artist and photographer, and a dreamer. He and Abbie dreamed big together, saw the potential for the region, and joined with others, including the late H. Edward "Eddie" Steel and Dr. Carl Stark, on the Lakes-to-Florida Highway Association to improve regional highway conditions. (Courtesy of Ron Kime.)

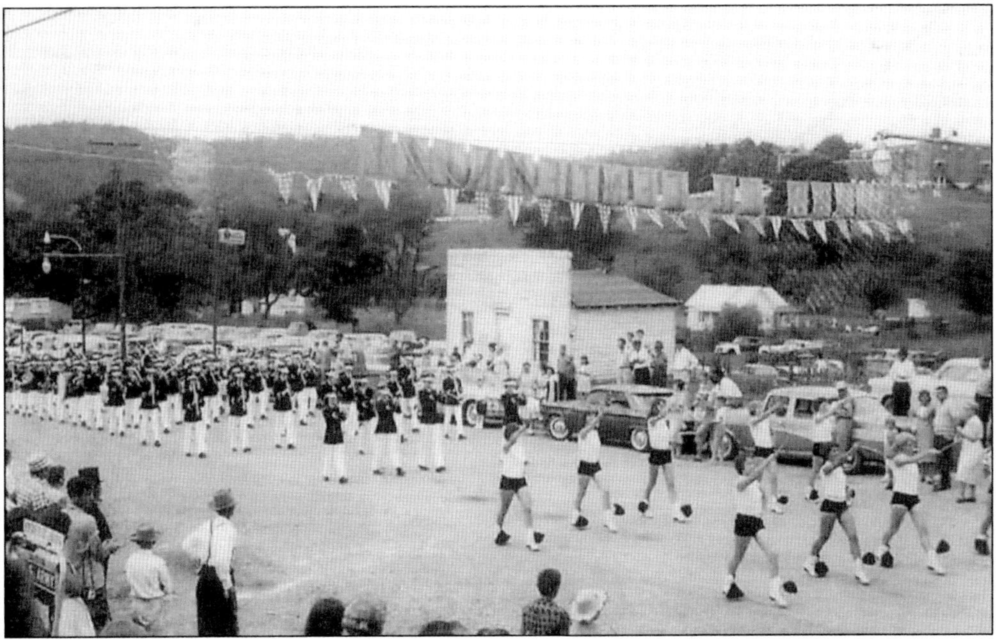

Celebrating One Century. Bland County residents turned out to see the county's centennial parade through the heart of Bland in 1961. (Photograph from the Bogle Library Collection; courtesy of the Bland County Historical Society.)

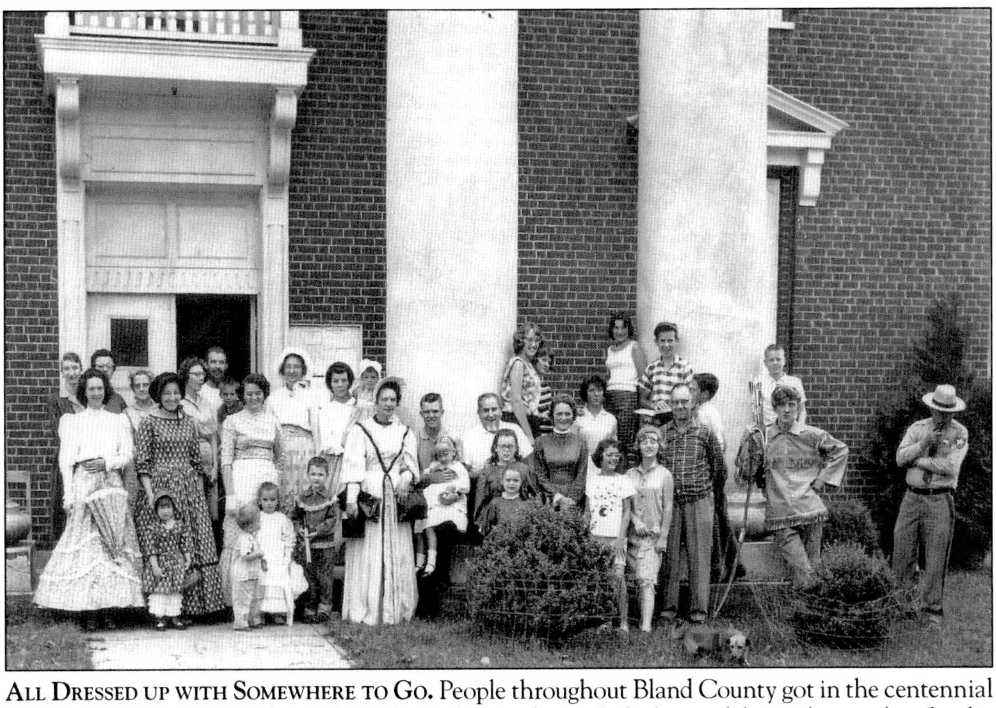

All Dressed up with Somewhere to Go. People throughout Bland County got in the centennial spirit. Several people are shown here dressed in traditional clothing of the earlier settlers for the 1961 celebration. (Photograph from the Bogle Library Collection; courtesy of the Bland County Historical Society.)

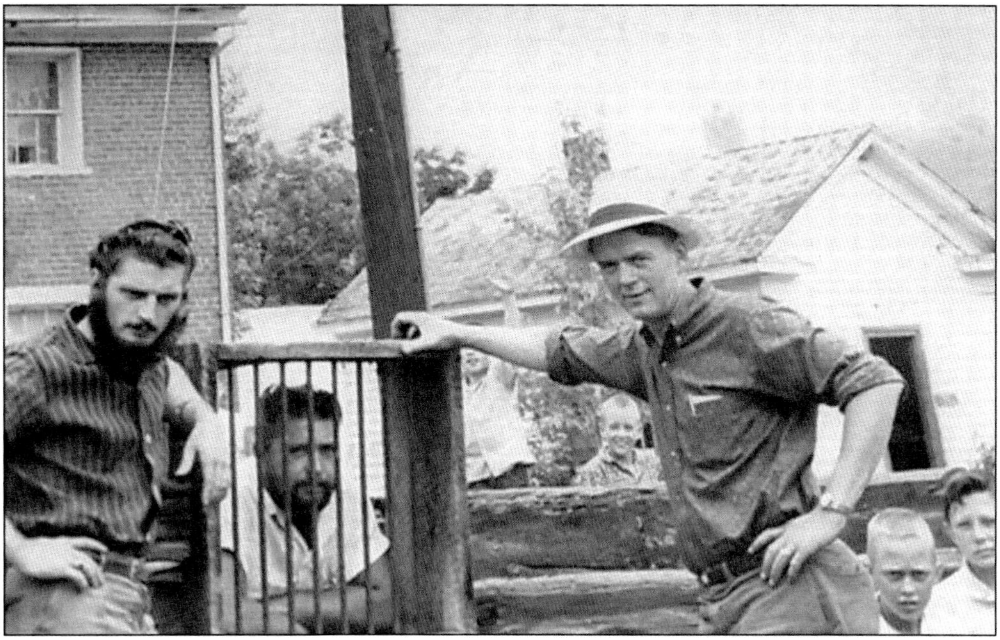

Bearded Gentlemen. Several Bland County men grew beards as part of the county's 1961 centennial celebration. Those pictured are, from left to right, Donnie Clark, Jack Repass, Pete Newberry, Virgil Six, Freddie Gabbert, and Mike Wimmer with Gary Dillow in the background. (Photograph from the Bogle Library Collection; courtesy of the Bland County Historical Society.)

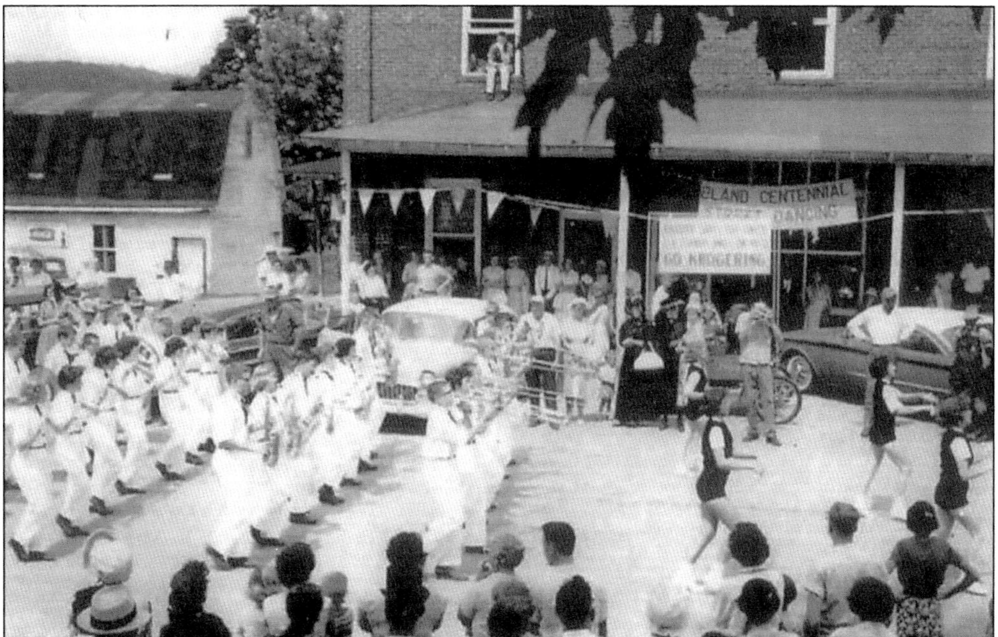

Marching Proud. Several marching units, floats, and motorized units participated in the centennial parade in Bland in 1961. (Photograph from the Bogle Library Collection; courtesy of the Bland County Historical Society.)

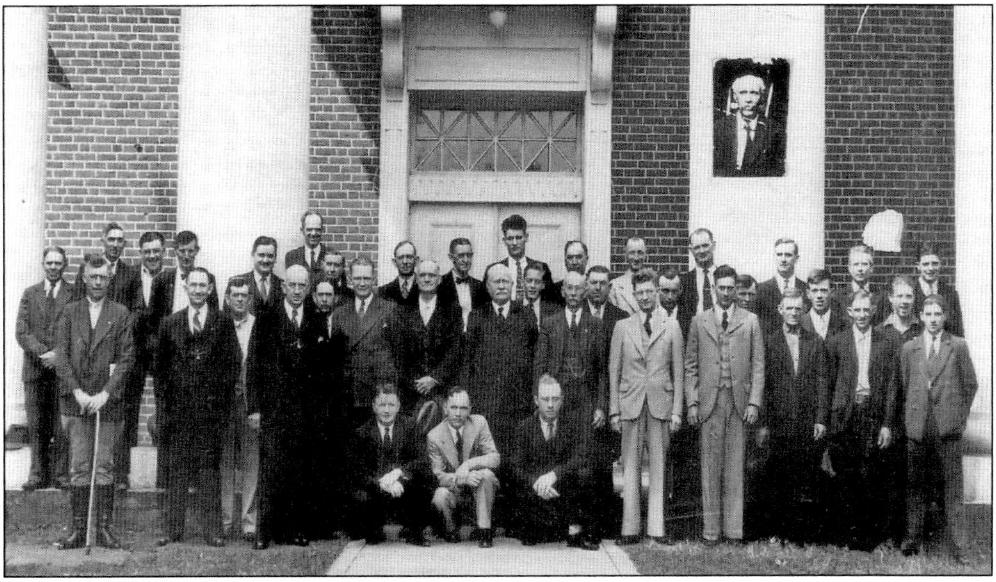

The Word. The Bland County Men's Bible Class is shown here around 1935 in front of the Bland County Courthouse. Included are (first row) Raymond Booze, the Reverend ? Newton, and Andrew Kitts; (second row) Minor Muncy, W.S. Dunn, H.B. Hubble, Jim Gollehou, Hubert Robinette, Dr. J.A. Wagner, Fred Richardson, Claude Richardson, Dewey Ashworth, John Stafford, Roy Repass, Bud Richardson, Bill Dillow, Jake Dillow, Peery Pauley, Darst Hall, Minor Muncy Jr., and J.T. Dunn; (third row) ? Hall, Ben Bird, Charles Muncy, John Dillow, James Muncy, M.L. Greever, H. Painter, Frank Dunn, Tilden Lambert, Harve Pauley, Sherill Newberry, B. Repass, Frank Wright, and Jeff Richardson. Bascom Mustard's portrait is on the wall behind the men gathered. (Courtesy of the Bland County Historical Society.)

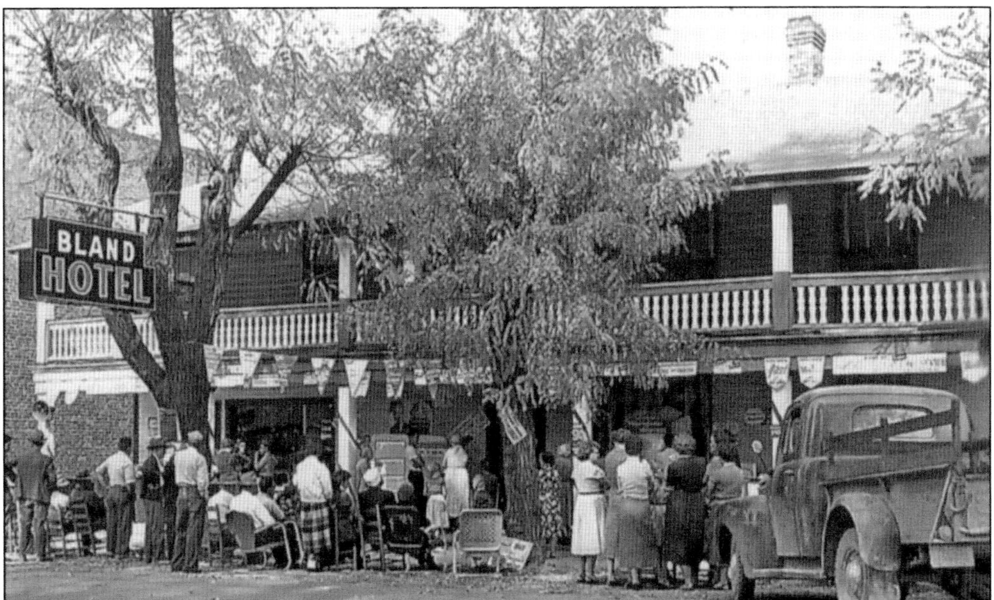

Hotel. By mid-20th century, the Bland Hotel had become a popular stop. It was one of the few hotels in Bland County. (Courtesy of Wanda Burton Reynolds.)

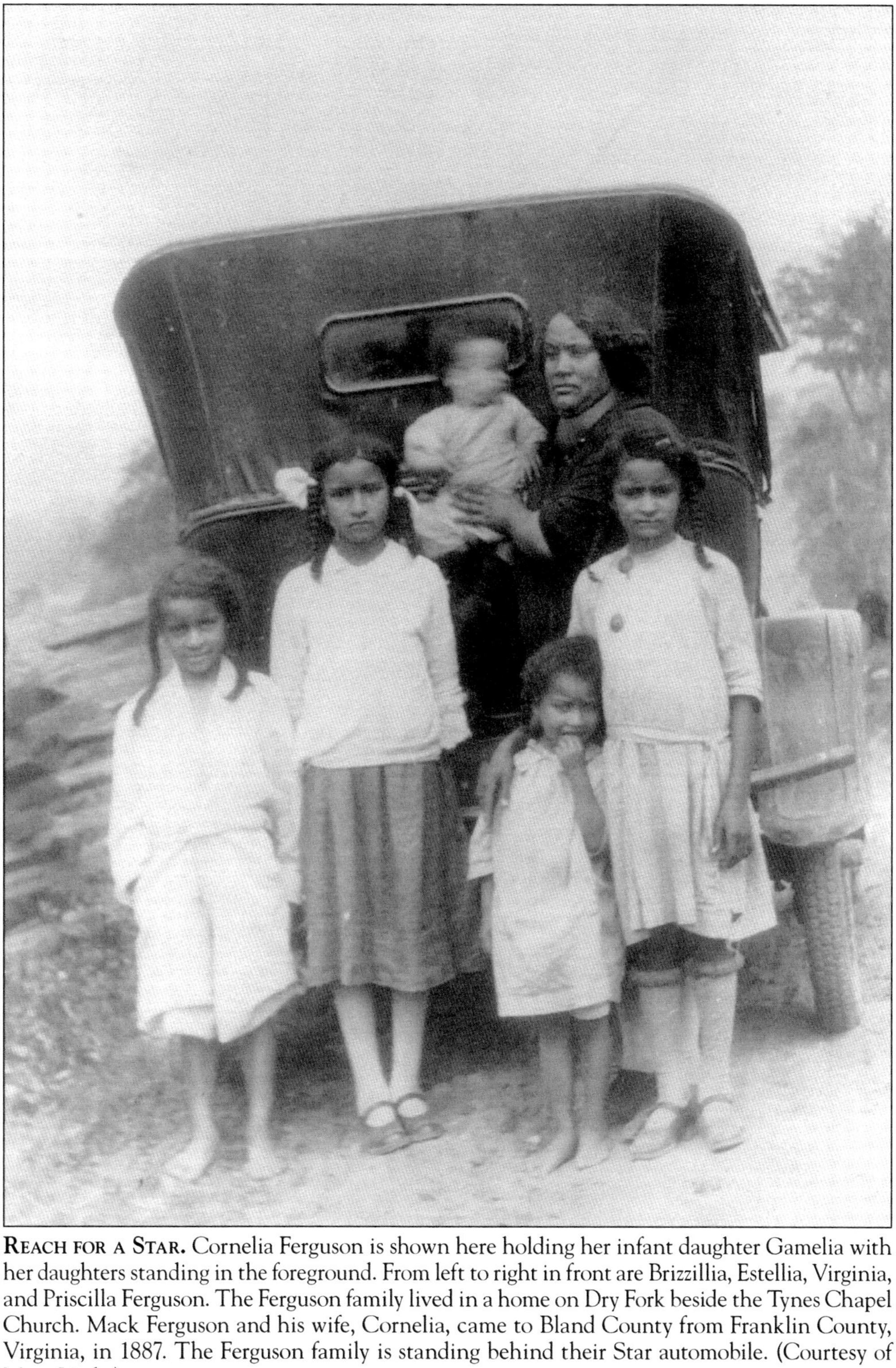

REACH FOR A STAR. Cornelia Ferguson is shown here holding her infant daughter Gamelia with her daughters standing in the foreground. From left to right in front are Brizzillia, Estellia, Virginia, and Priscilla Ferguson. The Ferguson family lived in a home on Dry Fork beside the Tynes Chapel Church. Mack Ferguson and his wife, Cornelia, came to Bland County from Franklin County, Virginia, in 1887. The Ferguson family is standing behind their Star automobile. (Courtesy of Mary Little.)

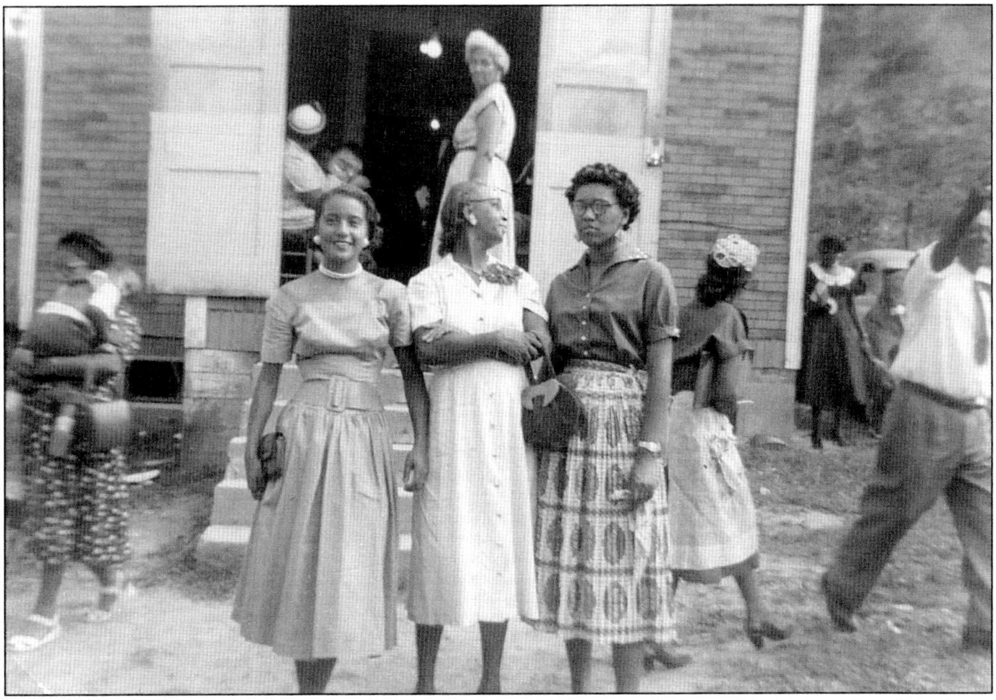

Church Meeting. Patty Saunders (left) and Jane Robinson (right) are shown standing beside an unidentified woman who may have been Jane's aunt. The women are at a 1955 church meeting at Tynes Chapel Church on Dry Fork. (Courtesy of Mary Little.)

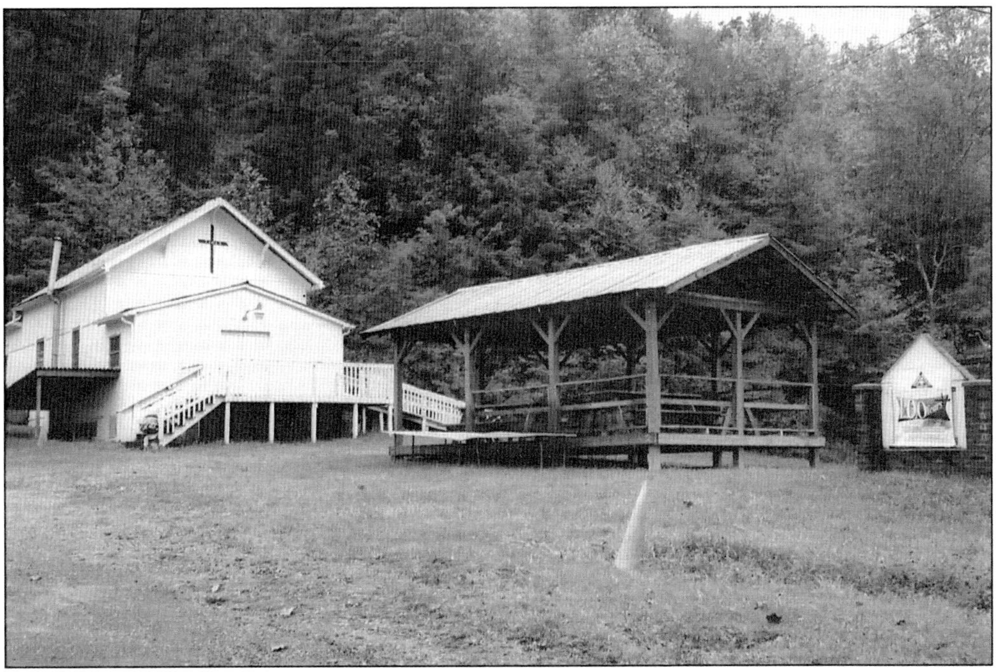

Century of Services. Tynes Chapel Church celebrated its first 100 years of service to the region in 2010. (Author's.)

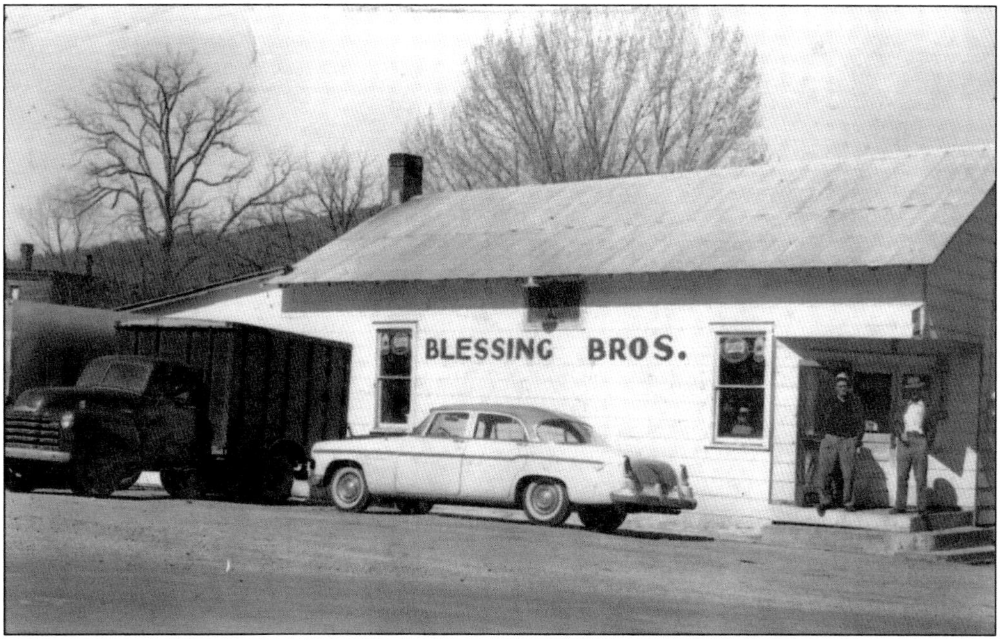

PRODUCE PRODUCTION. The Blessing Brothers store, located in Bastian, was a good source of produce and other staples for residents throughout the region. (Courtesy of Georgia Stacy Havens.)

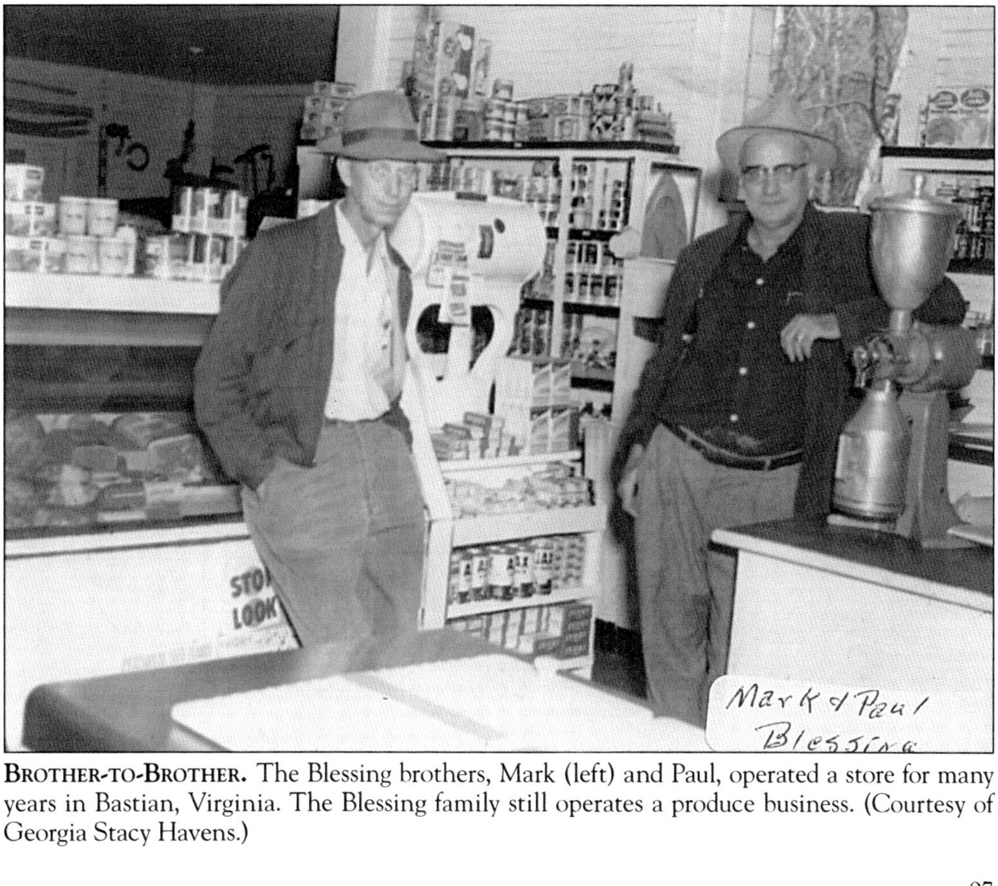

BROTHER-TO-BROTHER. The Blessing brothers, Mark (left) and Paul, operated a store for many years in Bastian, Virginia. The Blessing family still operates a produce business. (Courtesy of Georgia Stacy Havens.)

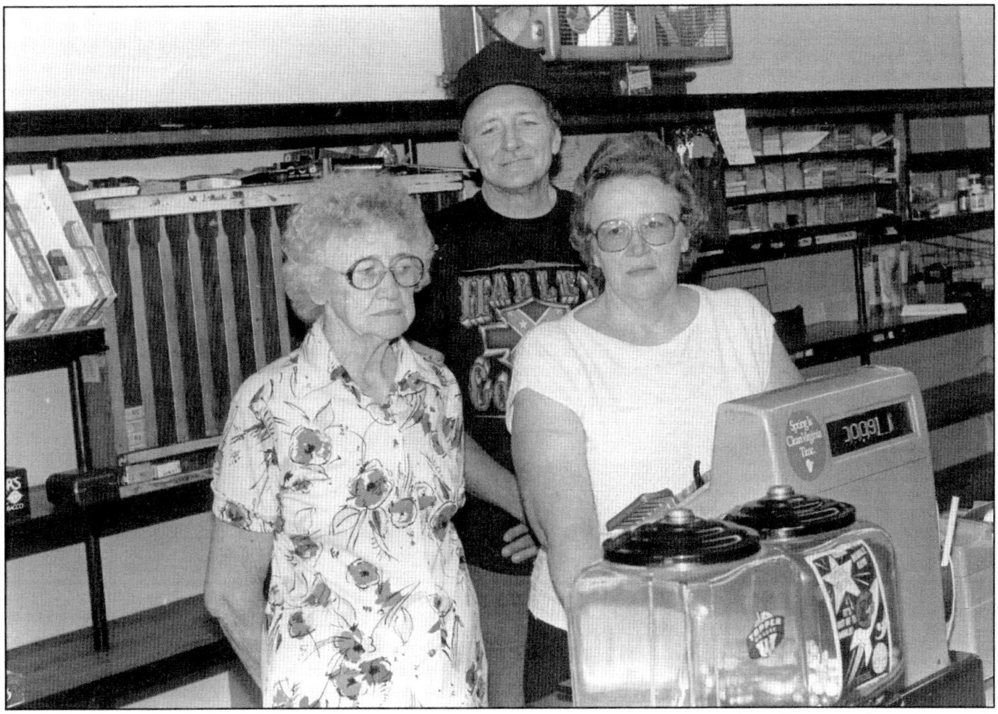

CARROLL BROTHERS' STORE. Marie Carroll (left of cash register), her daughter Pauline (at cash register), and her son Buddy Carroll are shown here in the Carroll Brothers' Grocery Store in Rocky Gap. (Courtesy of Buddy Carroll.)

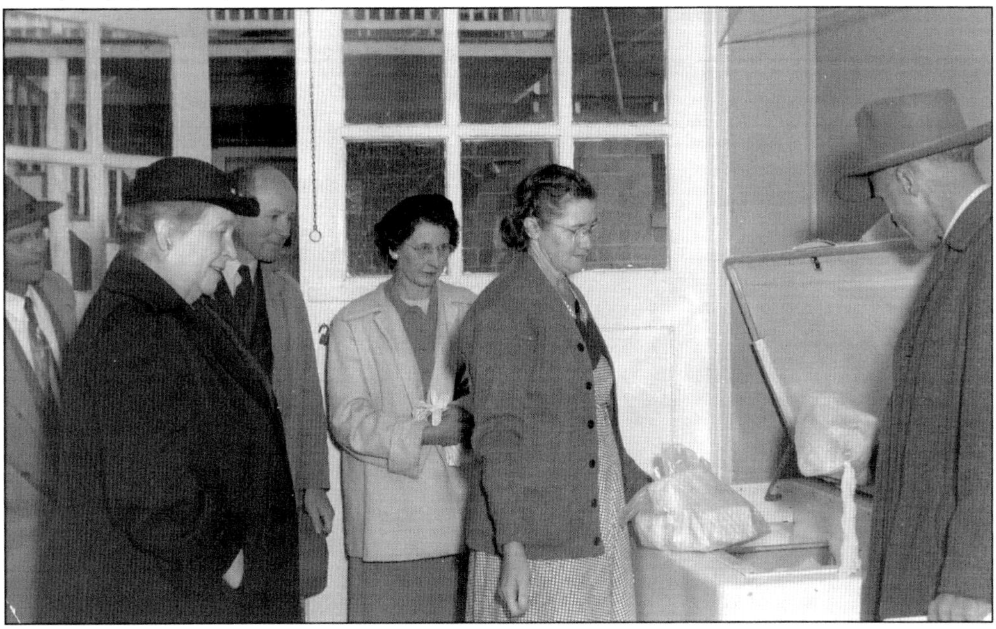

MODERN LIVING. A Bland County extension officer (right) is pictured above demonstrating the use of a food freezer to Marie Carroll (center) of Carroll Brothers' Grocery Store as several customers look on. Carroll Brothers' was the first grocery store in the county to have a food freezer. (Courtesy of Buddy Carroll.)

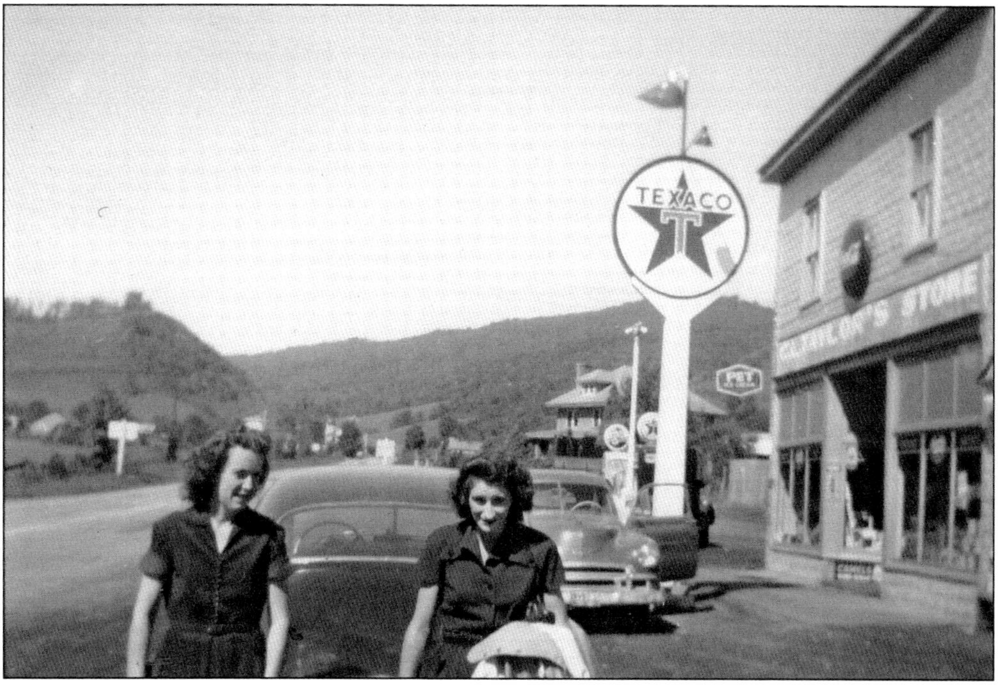

Good Day for a Stroll. Louise (left) and Gloria Tuggle are shown here taking a walk in front of Honaker's Store. Honaker's offered groceries and gasoline. (Courtesy of Nannie Rose Tiller.)

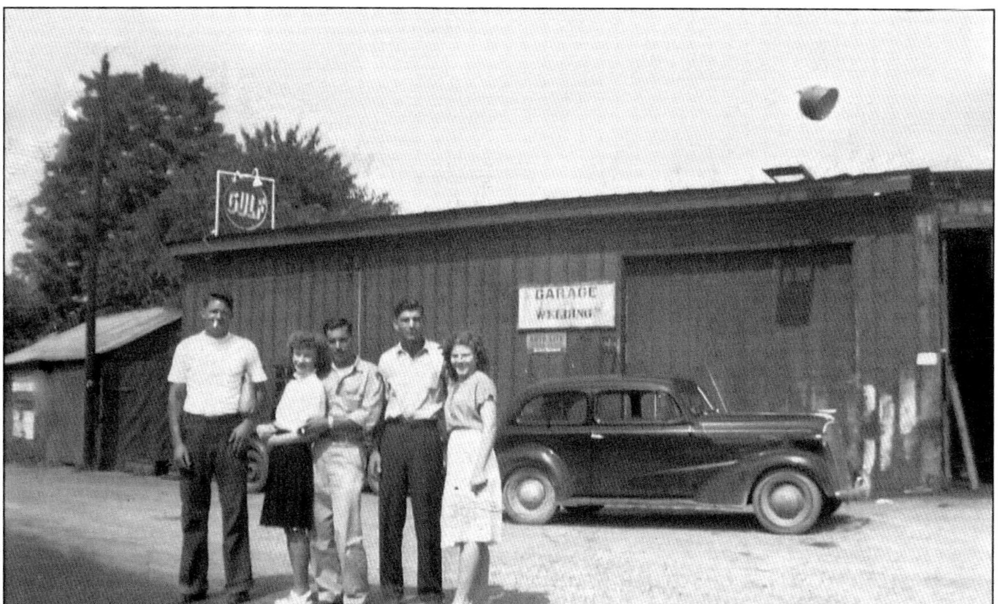

Ring Bell for Service. Five Bastian-area young people are shown here at the Gulf service station in Bastian. They are, from left to right, Byrd Kitts, Evona Pauley, Jewel Havens, Junior Stacy, and Georgia Stacy. (Courtesy of Georgia Stacy Havens.)

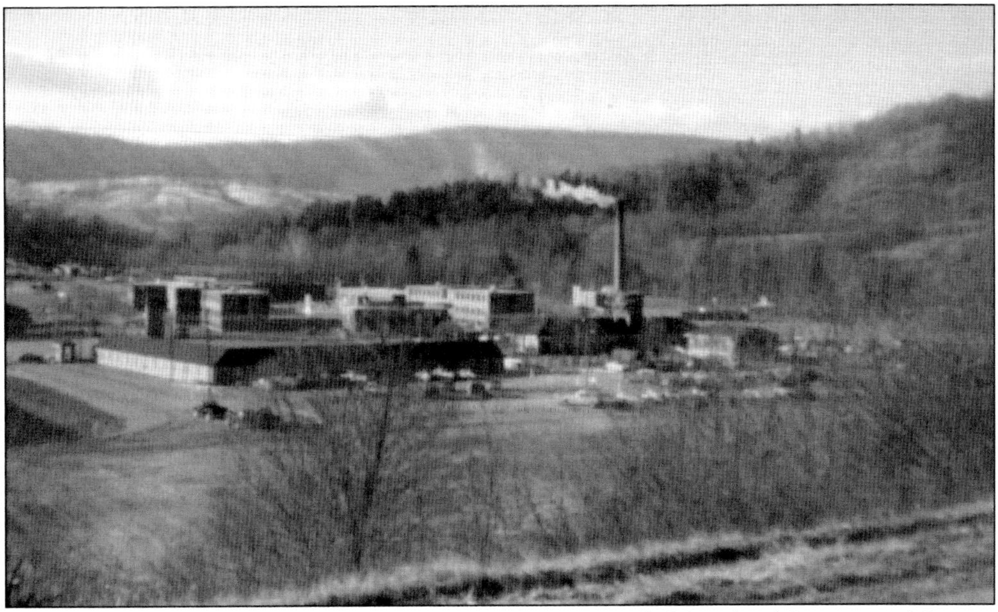

Correctional Center. The Bland Correctional Farm, now called the Bland Correctional Center, is located on State Route 42 in the extreme eastern end of the county. The center opened in October 1952. By the early 1960s, it had grown to more than 2,100 acres and housed 520 inmates. (Courtesy of Robert Waddle.)

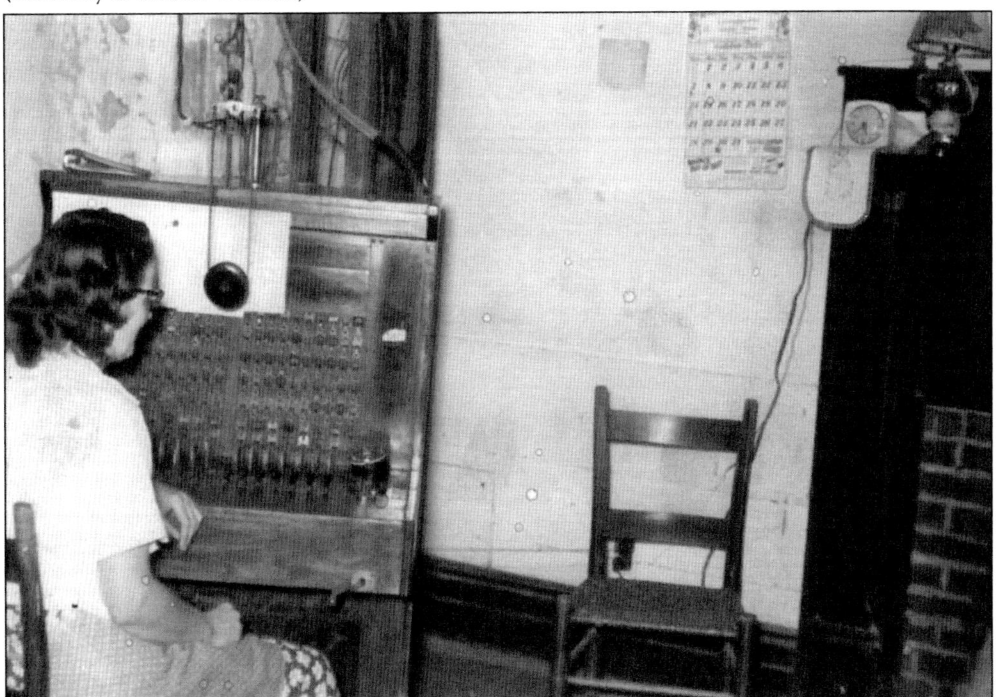

Hold the Phone. Betty Hubble is shown here operating the switchboard at the Ceres community telephone service. Ceres and Burke's Garden, Virginia, were connected via telephone service as early as 1895. (Courtesy of Betty Hubble.)

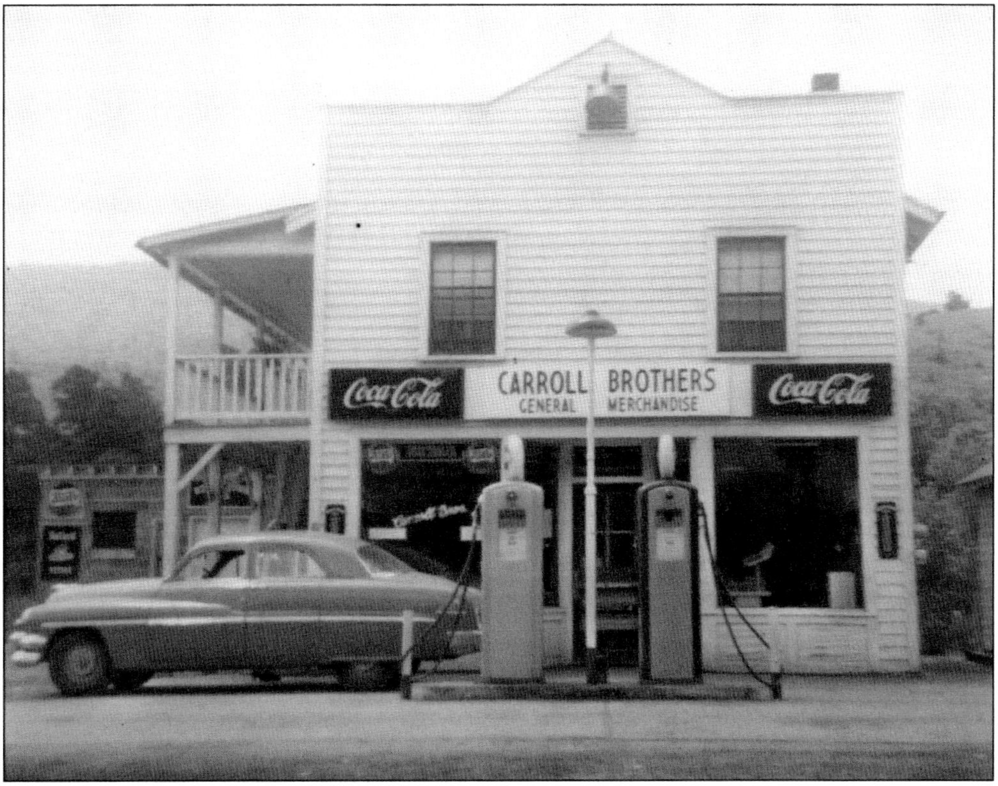

Gas And Grub. Carroll Brothers' Grocery in downtown Rocky Gap also sold gasoline to its customers. (Courtesy of Buddy Carroll.)

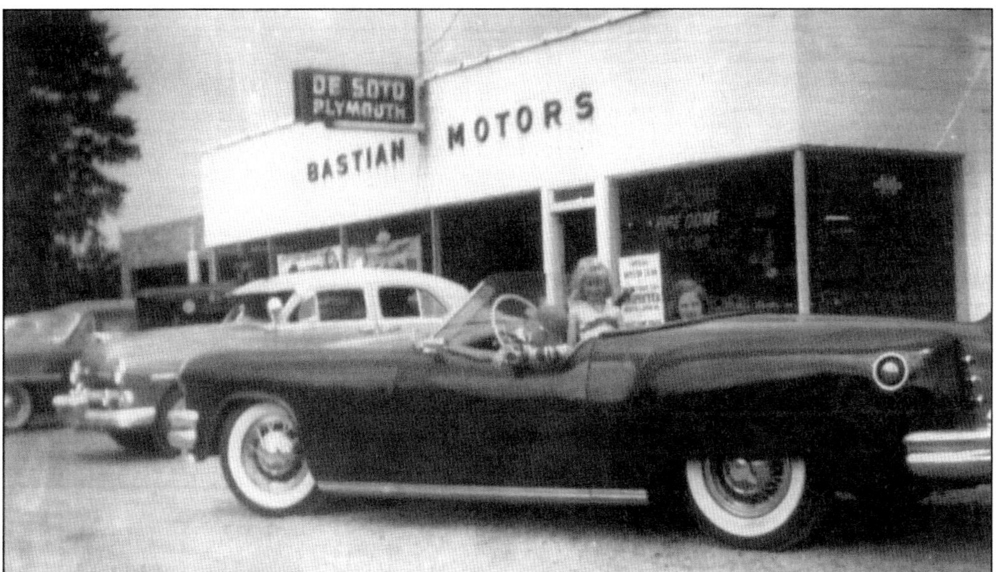

Happy Motoring. A Cadillac is pictured here in front of Bastian Motors in Bastian, Virginia. Bastian Motors was a De Soto and Plymouth dealership. (Courtesy of the Bland County Historical Society.)

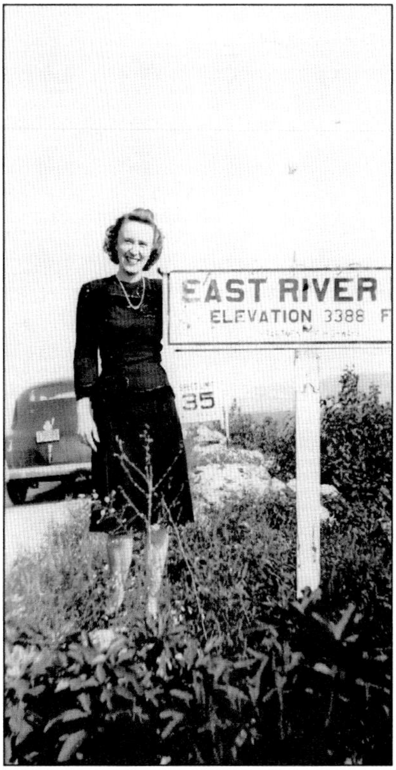

TOP OF THE MOUNTAIN. Margaret Imhoff Smith, the wife of Carl J. Smith, is shown atop East River Mountain in this 1940s vintage picture. (Courtesy of the Bland County Historical Society.)

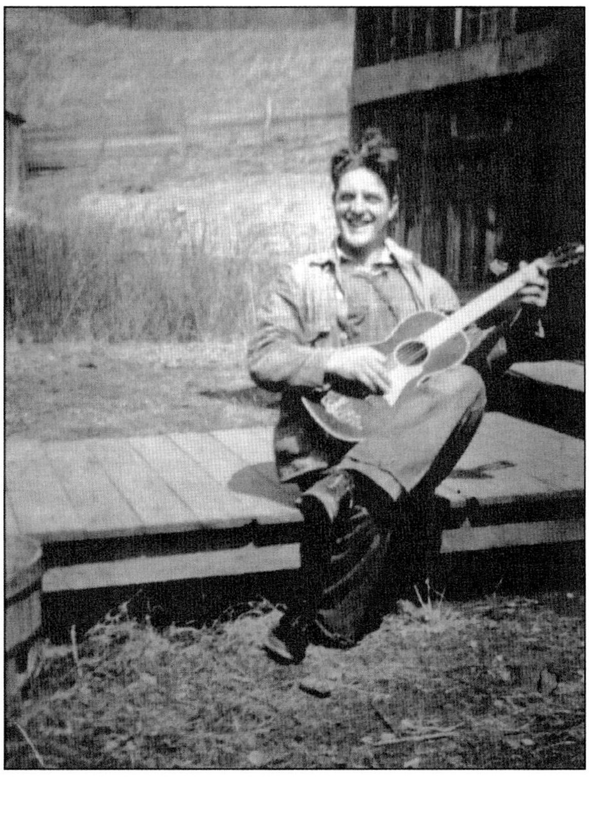

GOOD TIMES. Harry Frank Hall Jr. is shown here strumming on his guitar. (Courtesy of Georgia Stacy Havens.)

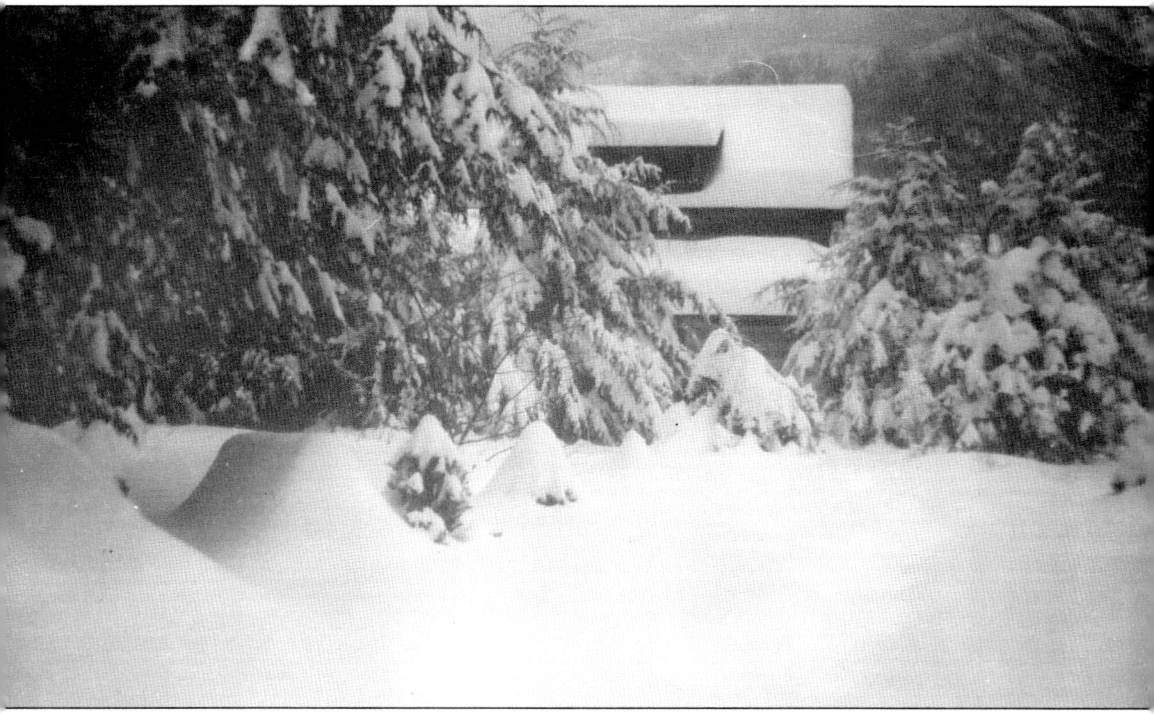

SNOW WHITE. The mountains of Southwestern Virginia can make for very picturesque scenes in all four seasons, as this winter scene photograph in 1948 of the home of Buford and Nannie Rose Tiller of Dry Fork demonstrates. (Courtesy of Nannie Rose Tiller.)

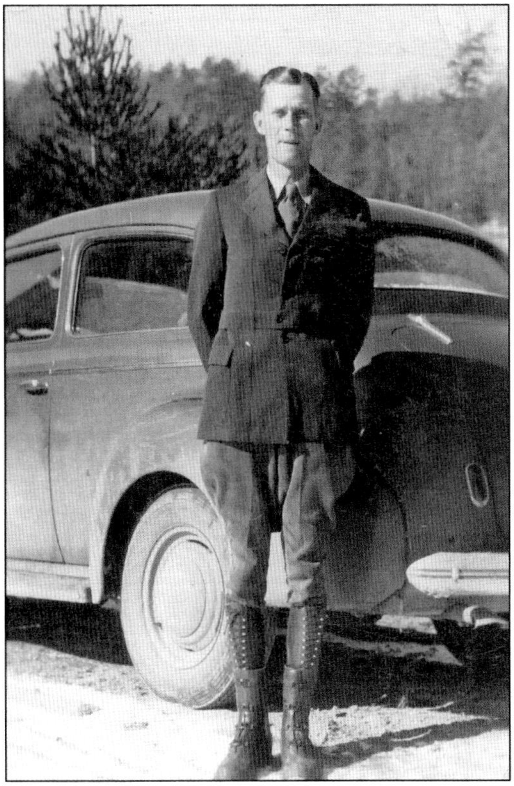

Ticket to Ride. Brown Johnston is shown here standing behind his automobile at his farm near Bastian, Virginia. Johnston was a foreman at the Bastian Civilian Conservation Corps camp. (Courtesy of Mary Jane [Johnston] Pennington.)

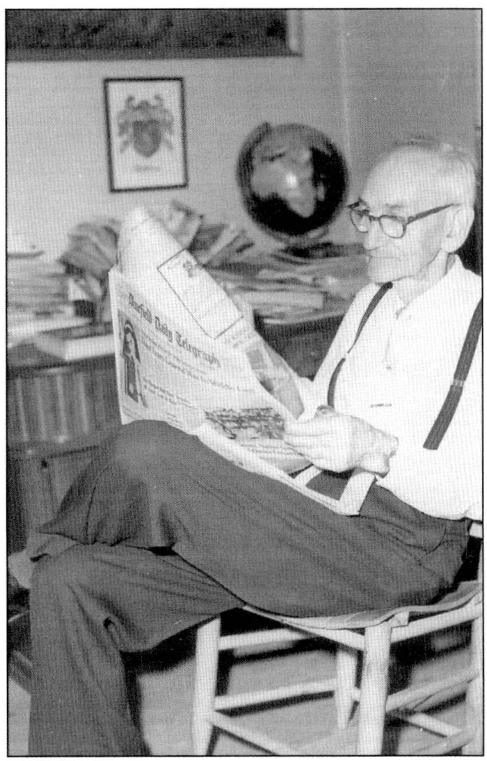

Easy Reader. William Arthur Guthrie is shown here reading his copy of the *Bluefield Daily Telegraph*. (Courtesy of Brenda King.)

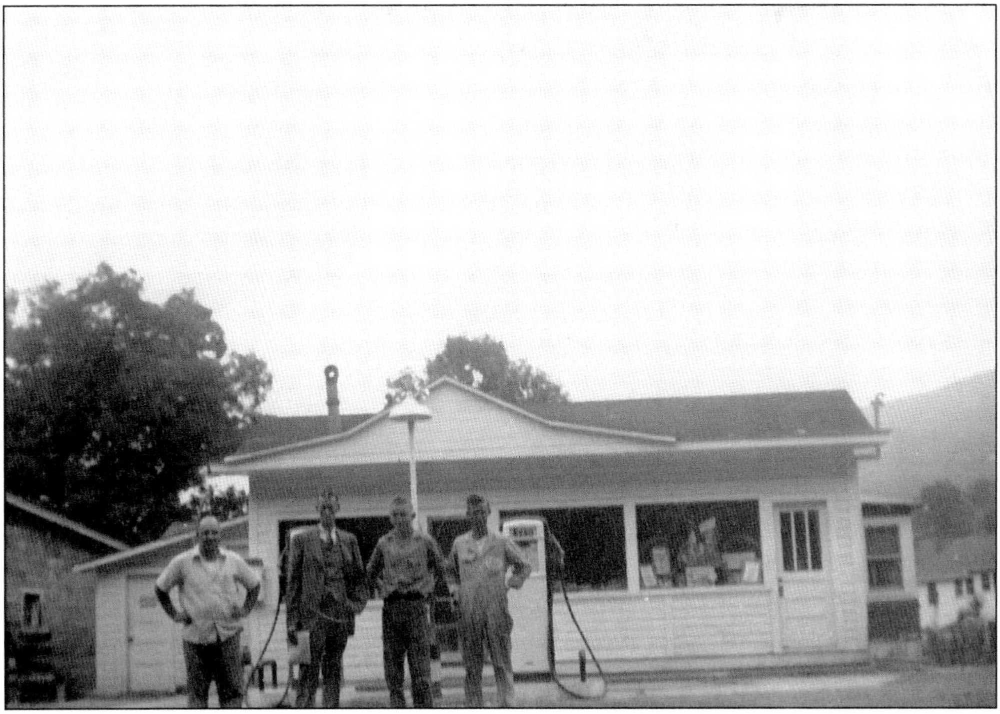

The Gap. Friends are shown here gathered at the North Gap service station that opened in 1946 and closed in 1958. Those pictured are, from left to right, Eugene Shufflebarger, station owner; Bill Walters; Corby Hounshell; and Arlie Sutphin. (Courtesy of Billy Jean [Walters] Carty.)

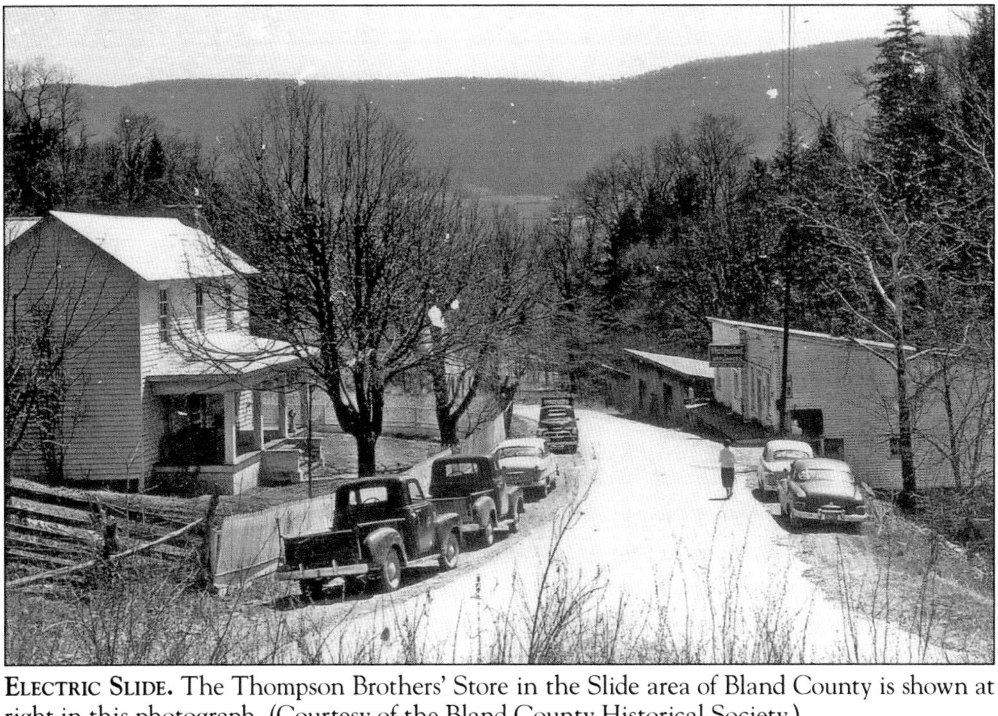

Electric Slide. The Thompson Brothers' Store in the Slide area of Bland County is shown at right in this photograph. (Courtesy of the Bland County Historical Society.)

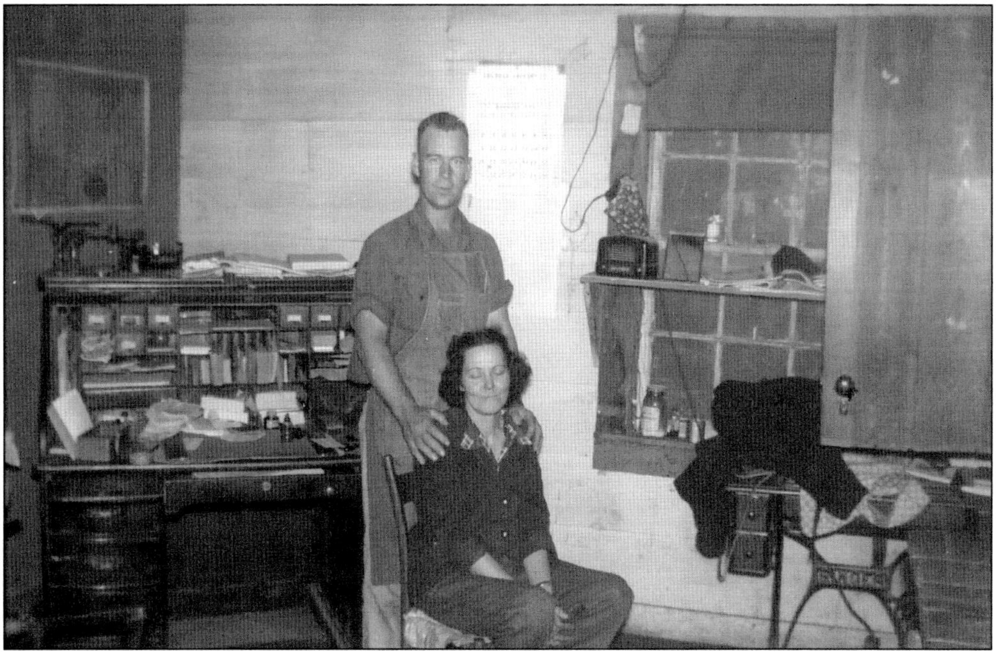

ONGOING MAIL. Buford Tiller (standing), the postmaster of the Rocky Gap Post Office, is shown here with mail carrier Bonnie French. (Courtesy of Nannie Rose Tiller.)

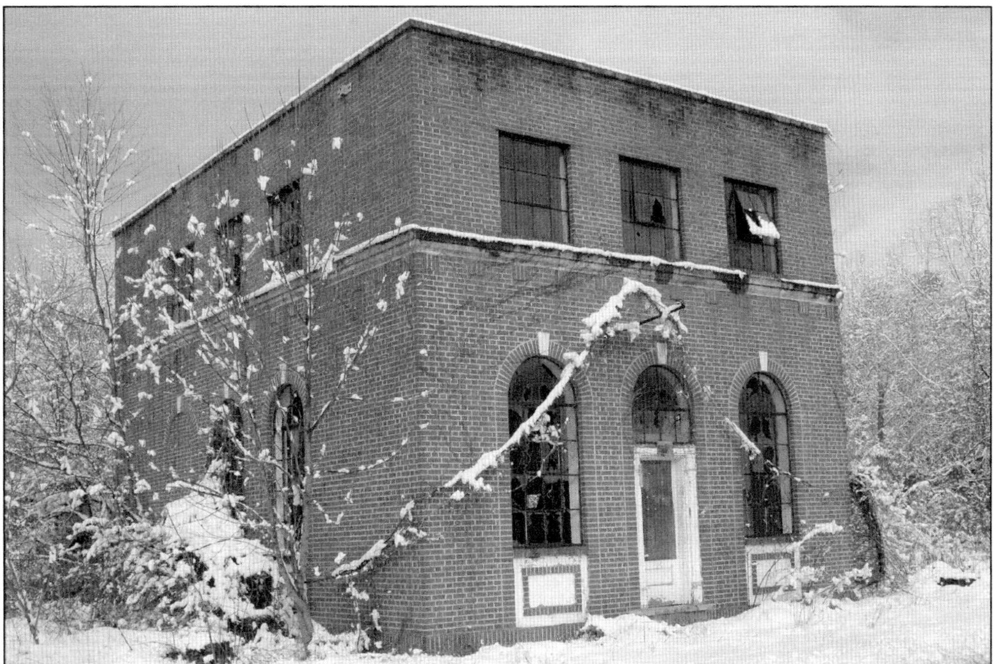

CHANGING TIMES. The Bank of Rocky Gap opened for business on January 8, 1923, and ended its decade-long run in 1933, when it merged with the Bank of Bland County. (Courtesy of Doris Sink.)

Seven

Opening Up New Opportunities

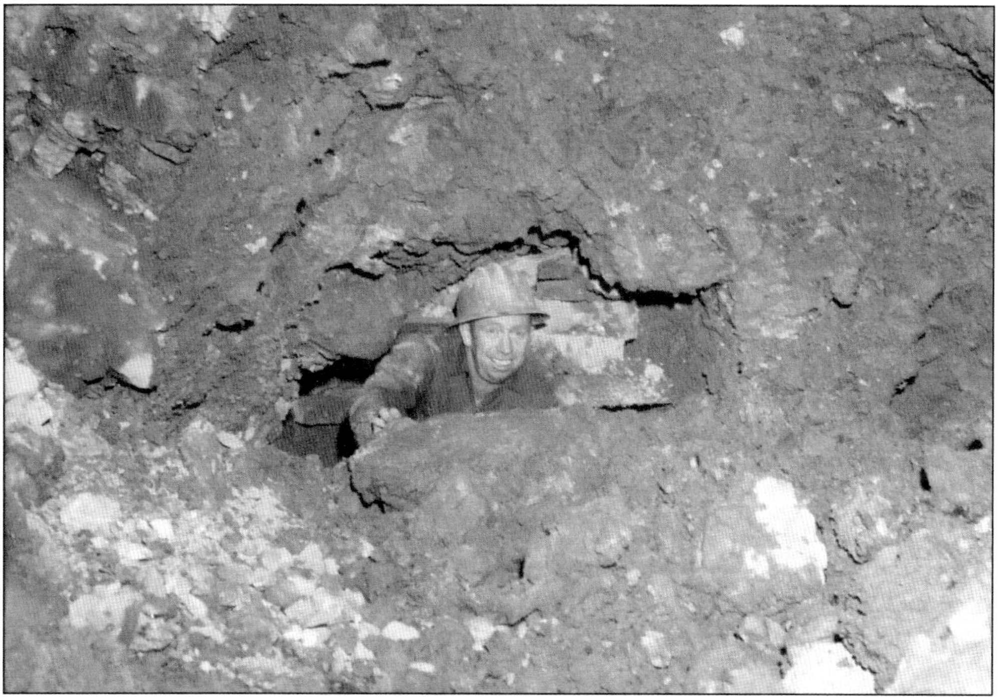

Peek-a-Boo. An unidentified worker for Gordon H. Ball, Inc., and the S.A. Healy Company, joint contractors on the East River Mountain Tunnel project, is shown here poking his head through the rubble. This photograph was taken shortly after the workers from the two crews met in the middle of the mountain at the state line dividing West Virginia and Virginia. This tunnel is located under hundreds of feet of mountain. Famed area photographer Melvin Grubb received a call early one morning during the early 1970s to immortalize this moment. (Photograph by Melvin Grubb.)

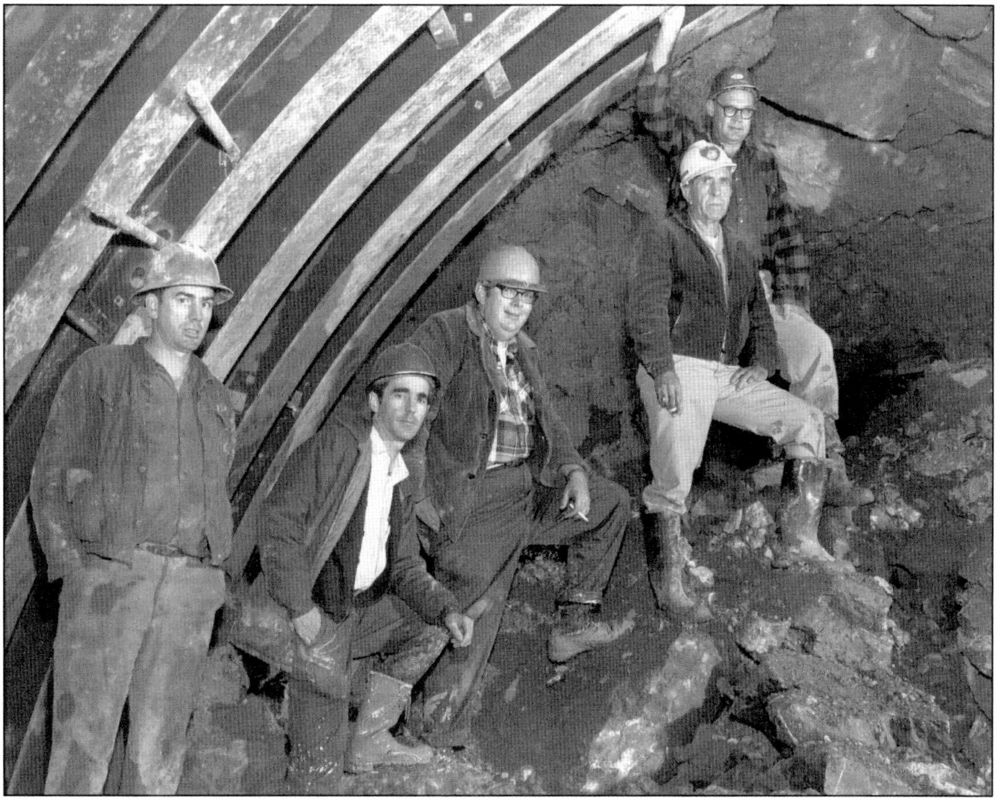

Rock on. Five unidentified employees of the joint contractor of California are shown here posing at the East River Mountain Tunnel project for a Melvin Grubb photograph. Grubb was an official photographer of the Lakes-to-Florida Highway Association. (Photograph by Melvin Grubb.)

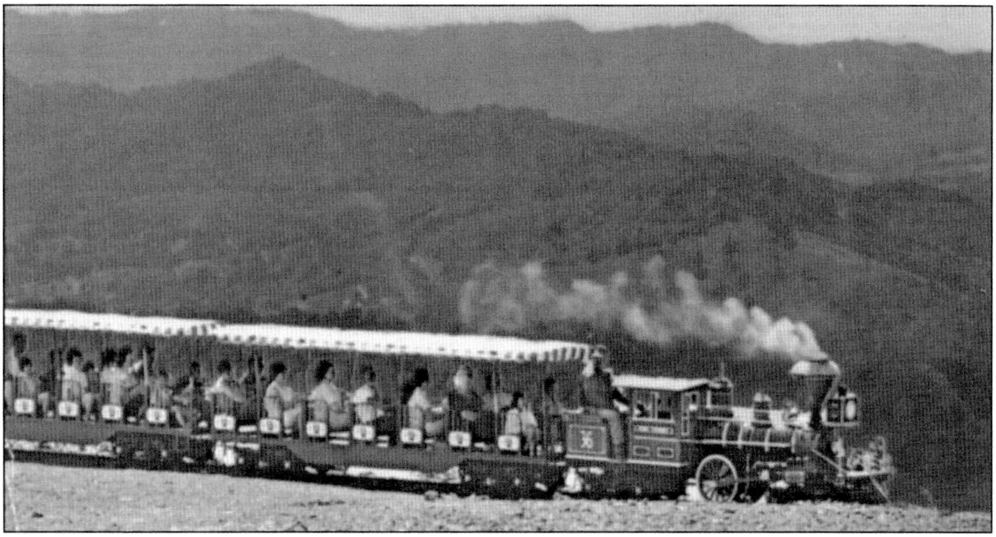

Ridge Runner Railroad. The Ridge Runner Railroad continued operating while the tunnel was under construction but closed a few years after traffic moved from old US Route 52 to Interstate 77. The Ridge Runner made a loop on top of East River Mountain, touching Bland County, Virginia, and Mercer County, West Virginia. (Courtesy of Jean Blevins.)

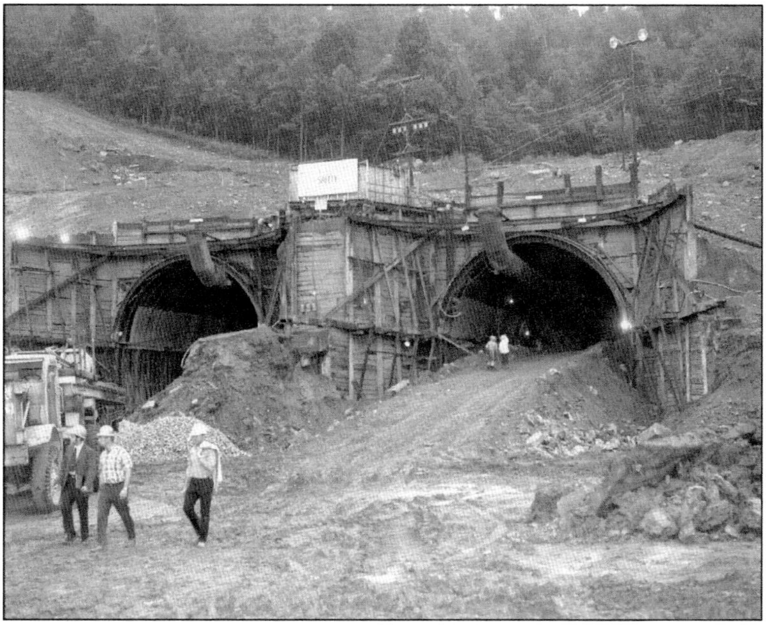

HOLE IN THE WALL. The south entrance to the East River Mountain Tunnel was one of the final pieces of the project that made Bland County "the light at the end of two tunnels," as former county administrator Gary Cutlip proclaimed. A companion tunnel, Big Walker Mountain Tunnel, was completed first. (Photograph by Melvin Grubb.)

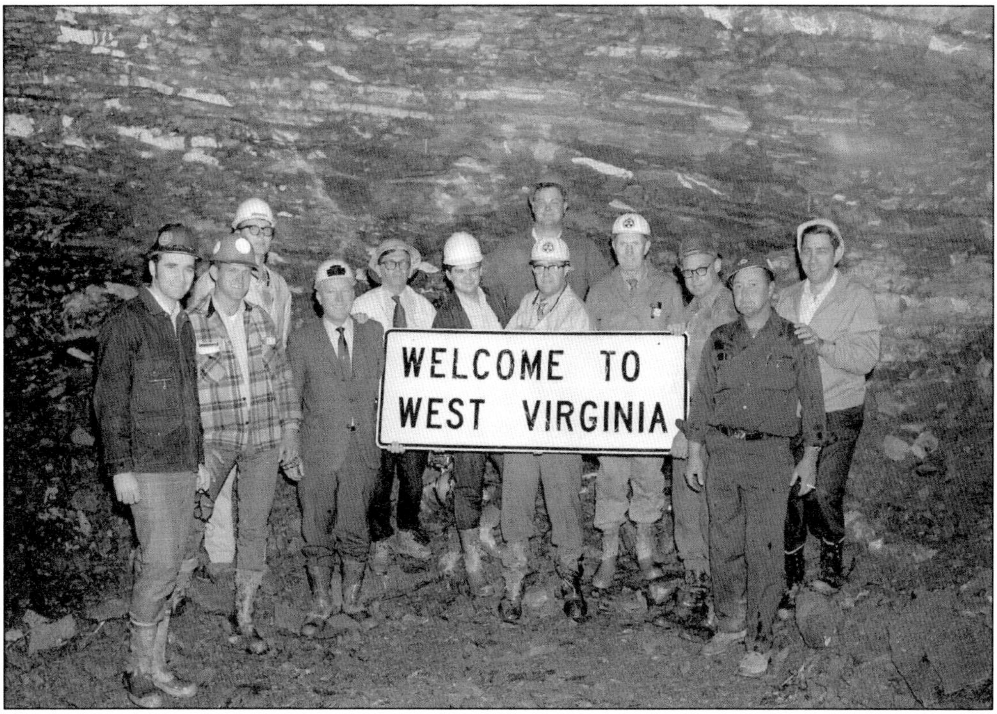

UNDERGROUND MOVEMENT. Tunnel officials and Lakes-to-Florida Highway Association members gathered underground to pose for a humorous photograph after workers from the south entrance reached the Virginia–West Virginia state line. *Bluefield Daily Telegraph* newsman H. Edward "Eddie" Steele, fifth from left, was honored in 2004, following his death the previous year, when the Bland Board of Supervisors voted to dedicate East River Mountain Tunnel to Steele's memory in recognition of his efforts to get the interstate routed through Bland County, Virginia. (Photograph by Melvin Grubb.)

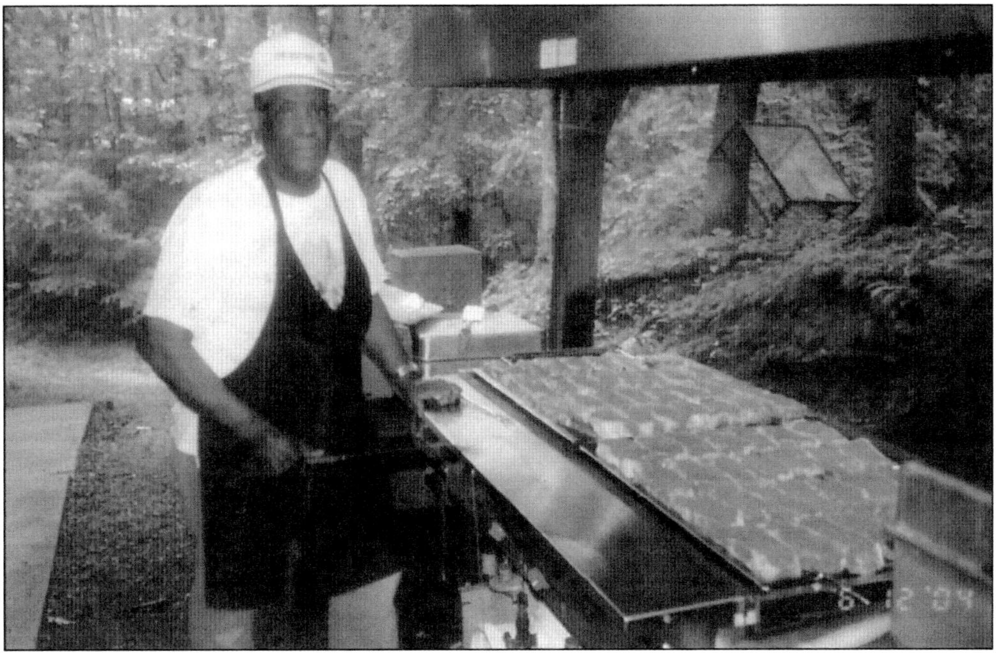

GREAT DEAL AT STEAK. Walter Lawson, a retired coal miner from Mercer County, West Virginia, has been cooking for many years for events hosted by Consol Energy at the Alexander Lodge, located west of Bastian and between Round Mountain to the south and Rich Mountain to the north. (Courtesy of Walter Lawson.)

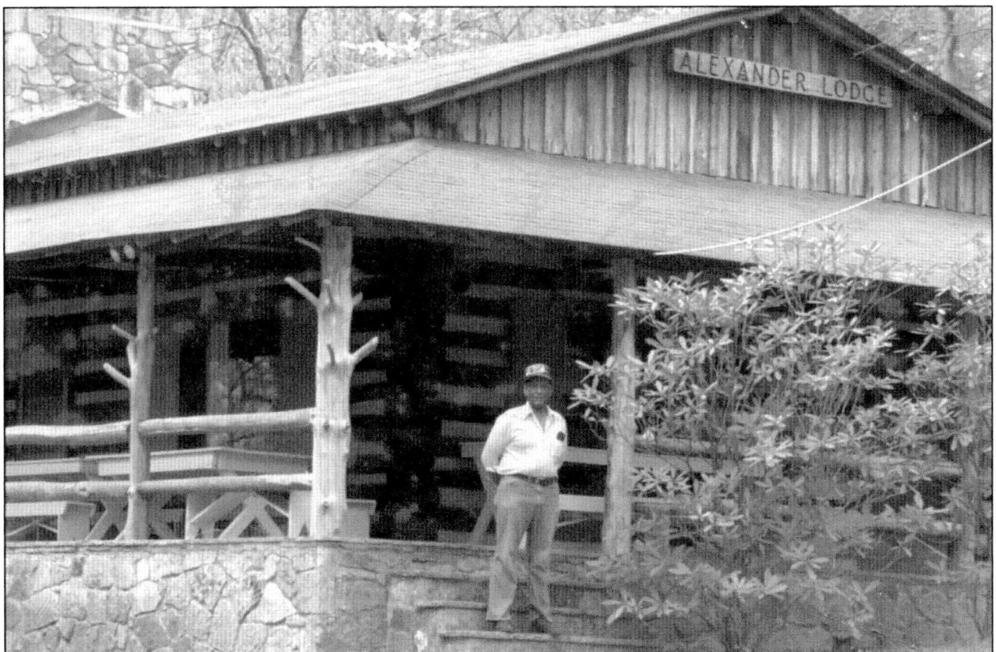

HUNTING CAMP. According to Walter Lawson, shown here, Consol Energy has retreats at Alexander Lodge for executives, customers, and associates through the spring, summer, and fall each year. (Courtesy of Walter Lawson.)

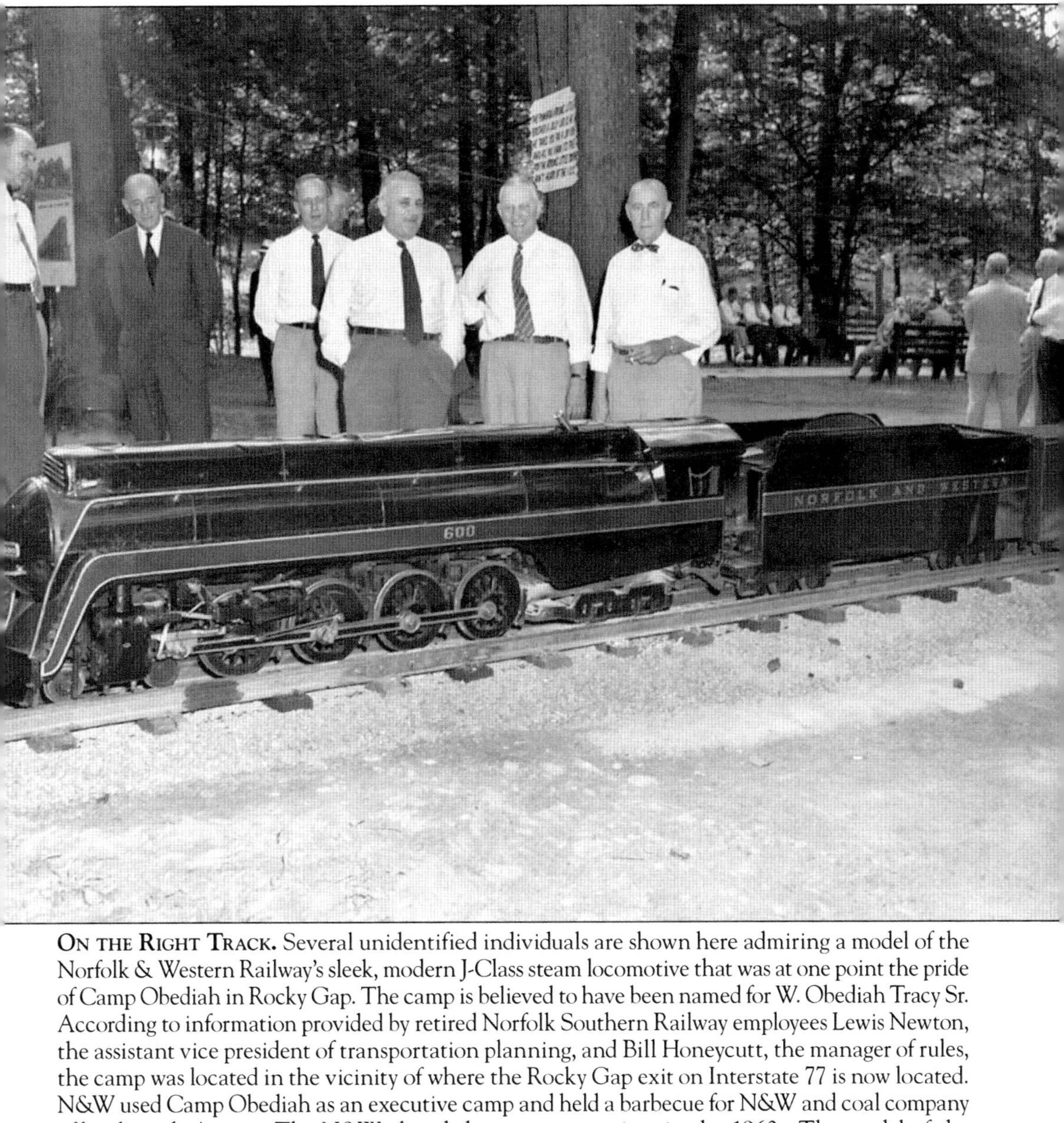

On the Right Track. Several unidentified individuals are shown here admiring a model of the Norfolk & Western Railway's sleek, modern J-Class steam locomotive that was at one point the pride of Camp Obediah in Rocky Gap. The camp is believed to have been named for W. Obediah Tracy Sr. According to information provided by retired Norfolk Southern Railway employees Lewis Newton, the assistant vice president of transportation planning, and Bill Honeycutt, the manager of rules, the camp was located in the vicinity of where the Rocky Gap exit on Interstate 77 is now located. N&W used Camp Obediah as an executive camp and held a barbecue for N&W and coal company officials each August. The N&W closed the camp some time in the 1960s. The model of the J-Class locomotive was built by Bluefield, West Virginia, machinist Willis Couling (or Cowling), who donated it to the City of Bluefield, West Virginia, upon his death with the stipulation that the city should display it for the pleasure of the public. When the city did not display the model, Couling's heirs sold it. Its last known owner was a man in Cincinnati, Ohio, who purchased it in the 1980s. (Courtesy of Gordon Hamilton.)

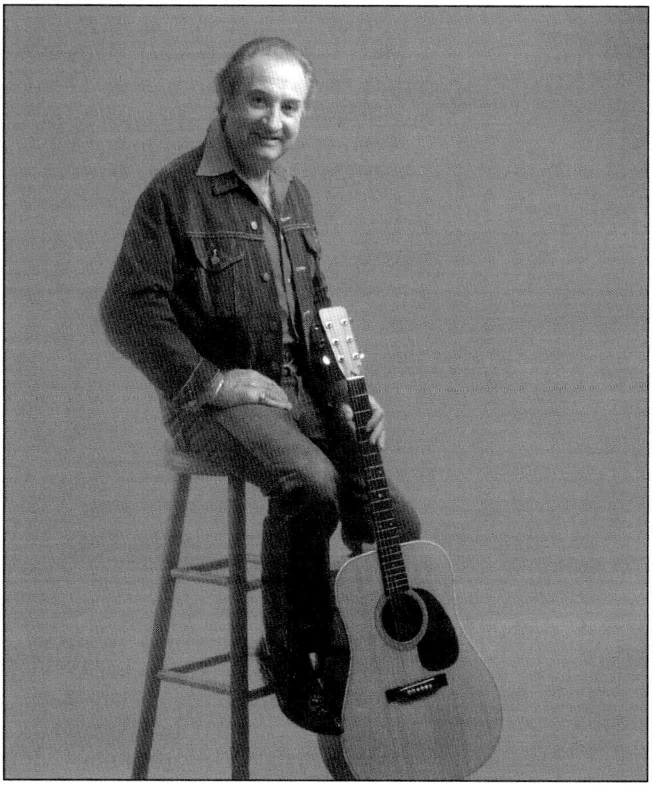

Hollybrook Harmonizer. Country music legend Darnell Miller was born, raised, and continues to live in the Hollybrook community of Bland County, Virginia. Miller started out performing live on Bluefield, West Virginia, radio in the mid-1950s. He was one of the regular artists on the WWVA Jamboree in Wheeling, West Virginia, and continues to perform and record. (Courtesy of Darnell Miller.)

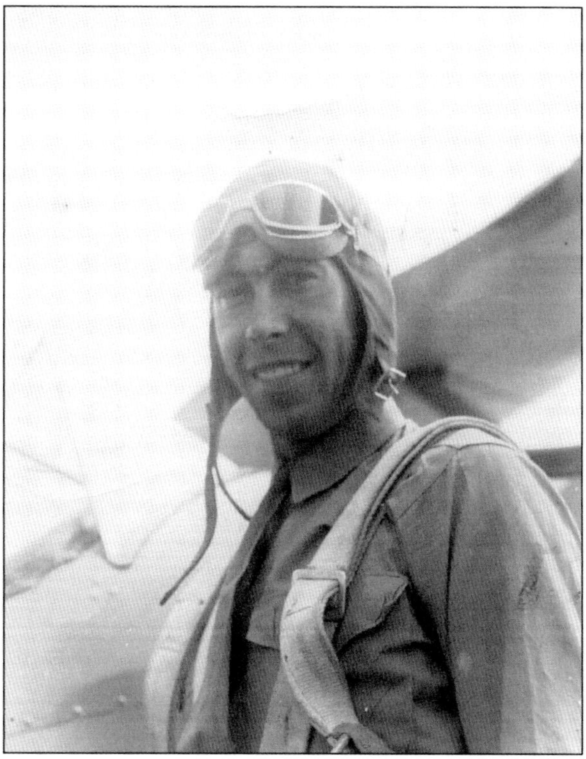

High Flier. James O. "Jim" Morehead is shown here in his pilot's gear. Morehead became superintendent of Bland County Schools in 1953 and was serving in that position during the centennial celebration. (Courtesy of the Bland County Historical Society.)

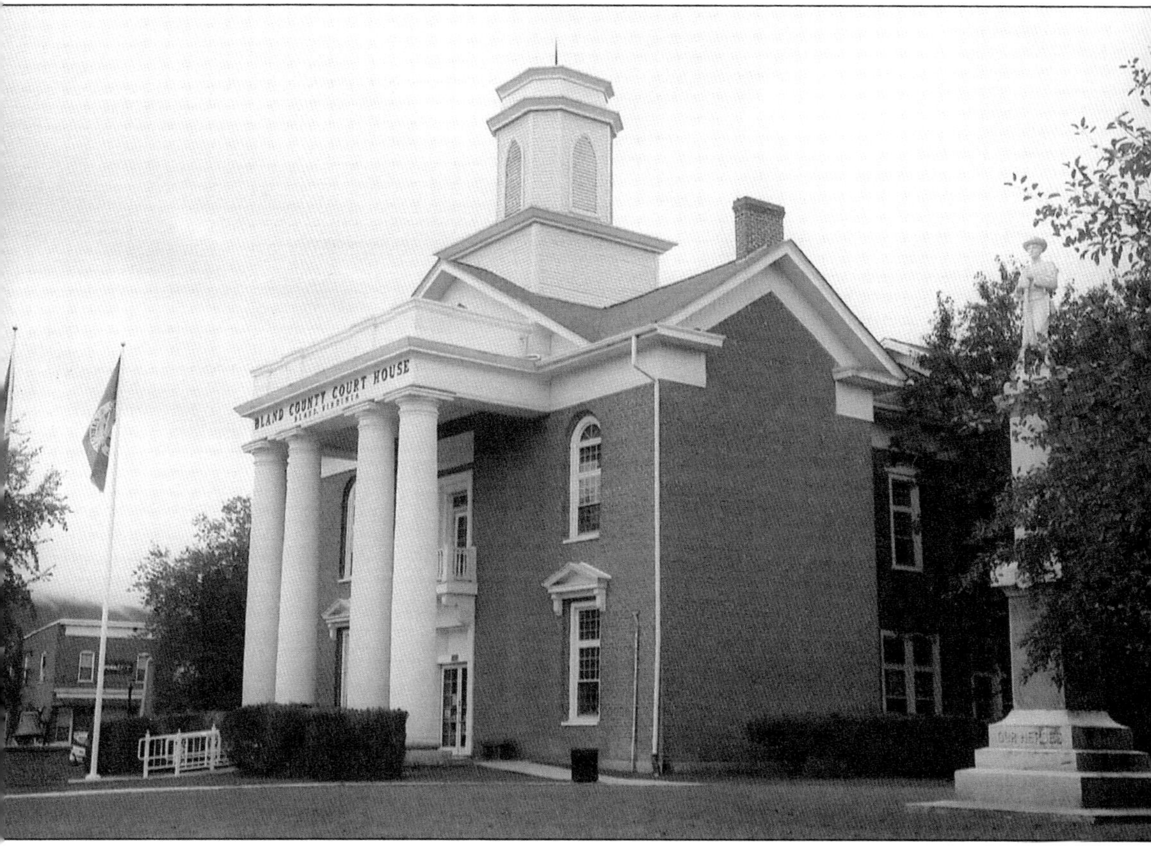

ORDER IN THE COURT. In 1862, James and Emily (Steel) Grayson donated the land where the Bland County Courthouse is located; however, plans to build the courthouse building did not start until about 1871, near the end of the post–Civil War Reconstruction period. Construction on the brick structure started on January 1, 1872, and was completed on October 22, 1874. The courthouse burned on December 5, 1888, but was rebuilt with new bricks laid on the old foundation. In addition to the Confederate monument erected by the United Daughters of the Confederacy, the complex includes a monument built to honor Thomas J. Muncy, who was serving as US attorney for the Western District of Virginia at the time of his death in 1922. Also, Muncy's French ancestors fought under Lafayette during the American Revolution. In 1949, builders put a new addition on the courthouse, and in the first decade of the 21st century, the Bland County Board of Supervisors undertook a major modernization and renovation project at the courthouse that was completed in 2007. (Author's.)

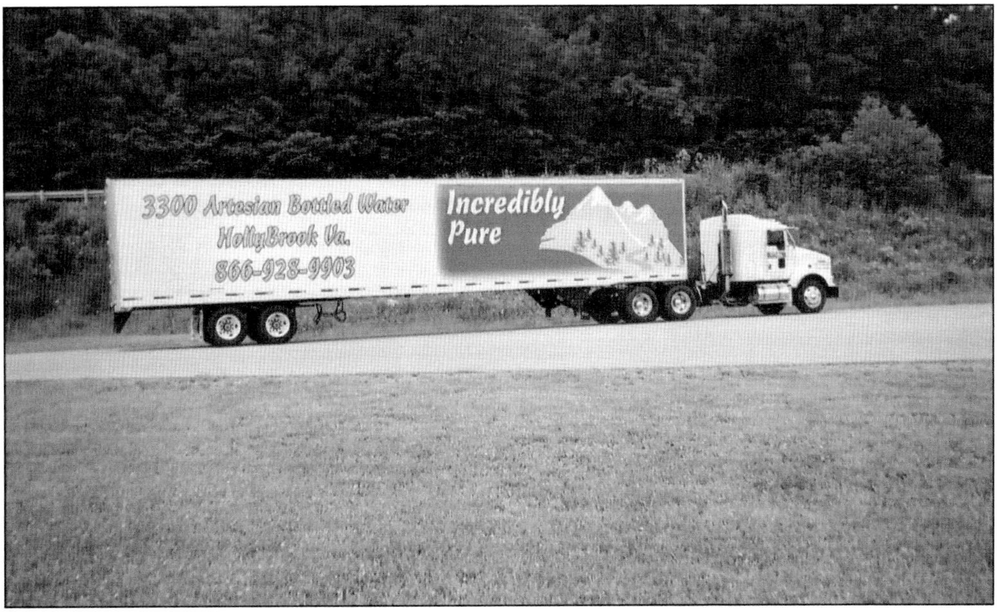

Wet Your Whistle. A tractor-trailer carrying 3300 Artesian water is shown here transporting bottled water from the plant near the well on Wilderness Road in the Hollybrook community. Hollybrook Oil & Gas attracted investors to the project, and a well was sunk 3,300 feet and hit the artesian well that has been pumping out pure water since 1921. (Courtesy of 3300 Artesian.)

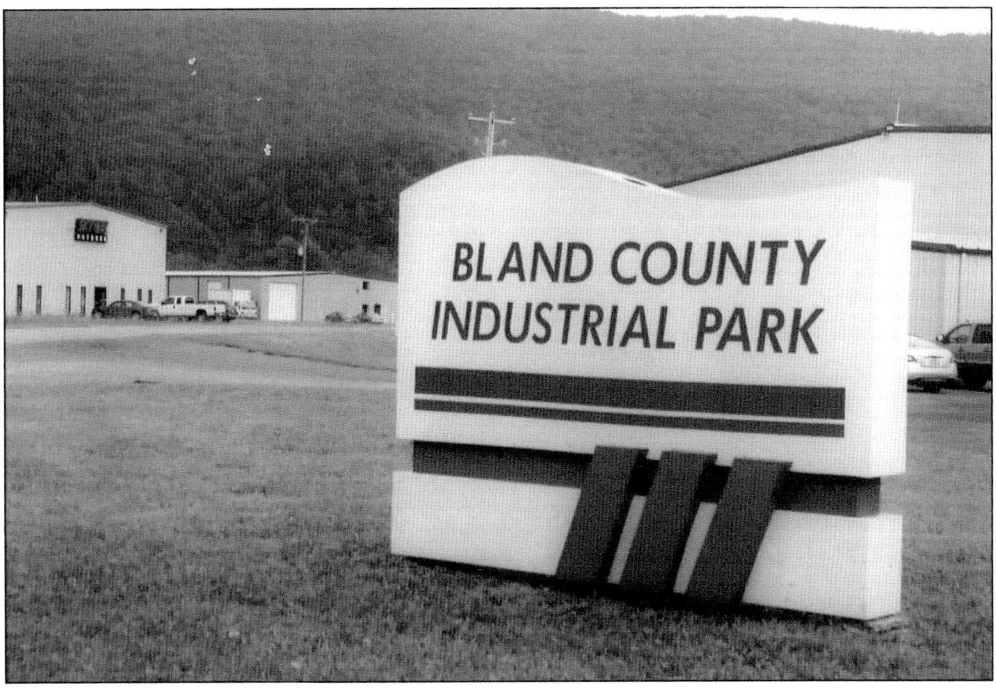

Industrious County. The entrance to Bland County's newest industrial park near Bastian is shown here. The county boasts of several manufacturing concerns that create a variety of products in an environmentally friendly manner and provide jobs for hundreds of county residents. (Author's.)

FARM LIVING. Rose Ferguson (left), Seewood Ferguson, and Reba Charlton are shown here on their Bland County farm. Many African American farming families continue to till the county's fertile soil. (Courtesy of Mary Little.)

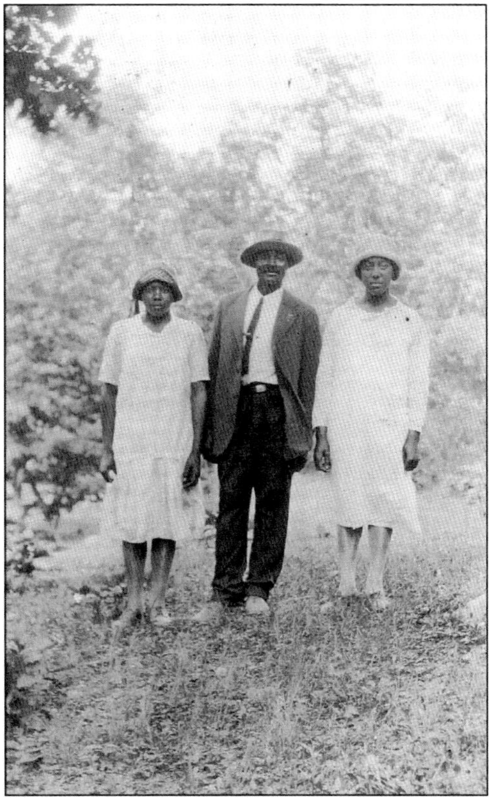

FRIENDS. Charles Morehead (left) and John Lambert are shown in this 1961 photograph enjoying a little visit. Bland County residents enjoy keeping up on the latest events in the community. (Courtesy of Nannie Rose Tiller.)

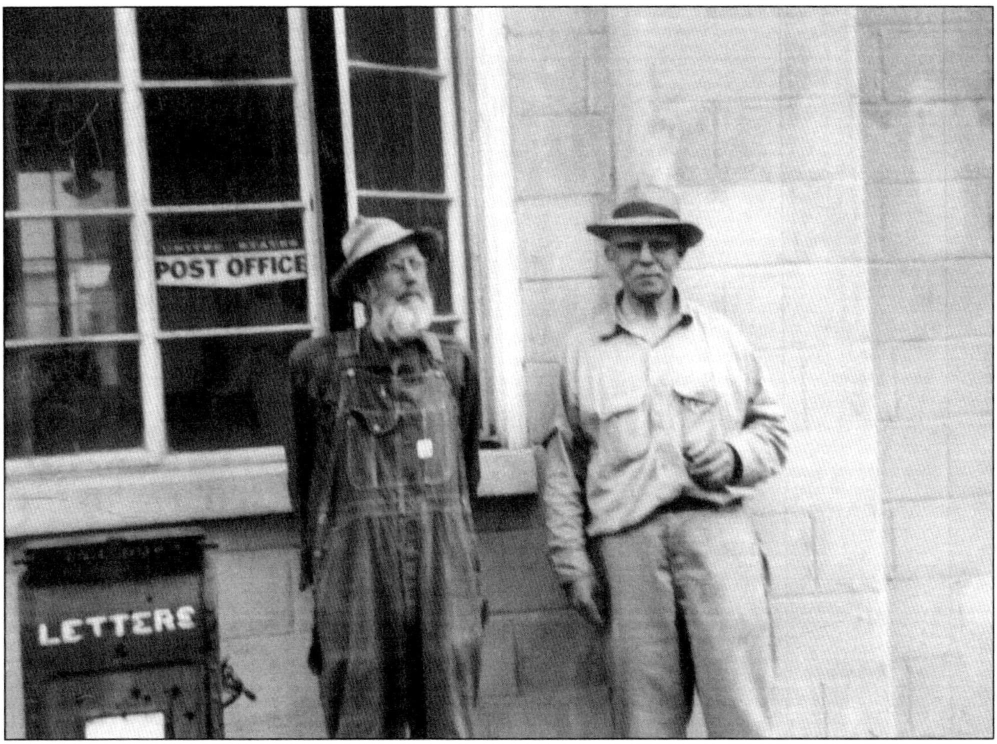

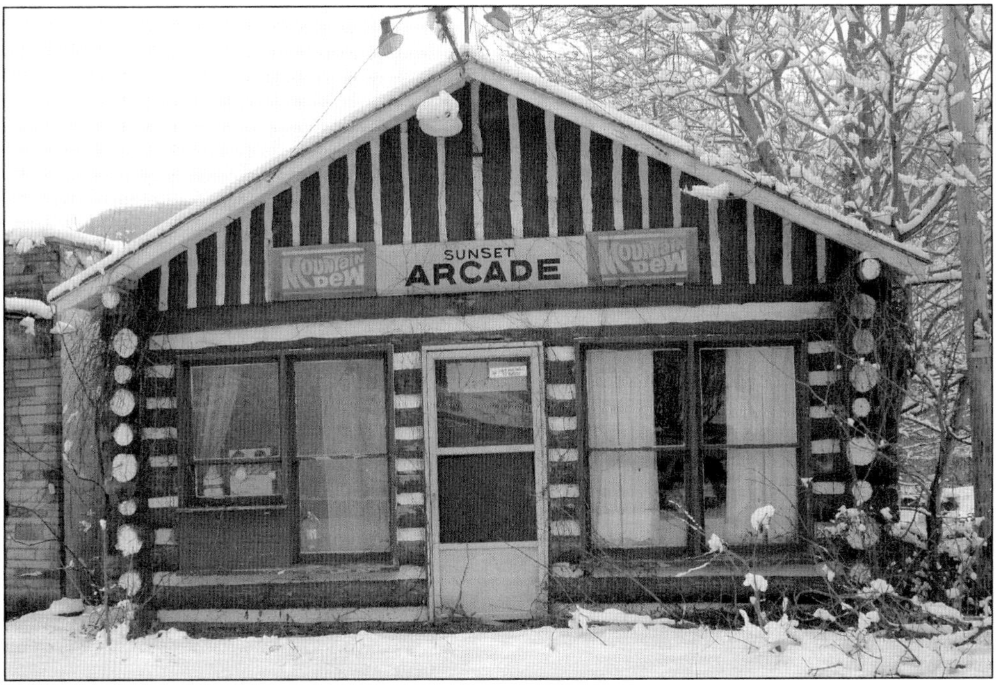

New Again. The old Sunset Arcade, located in downtown Bland, mixed old and new with a modern arcade in a log structure. (Courtesy of the Bland County Historical Society.)

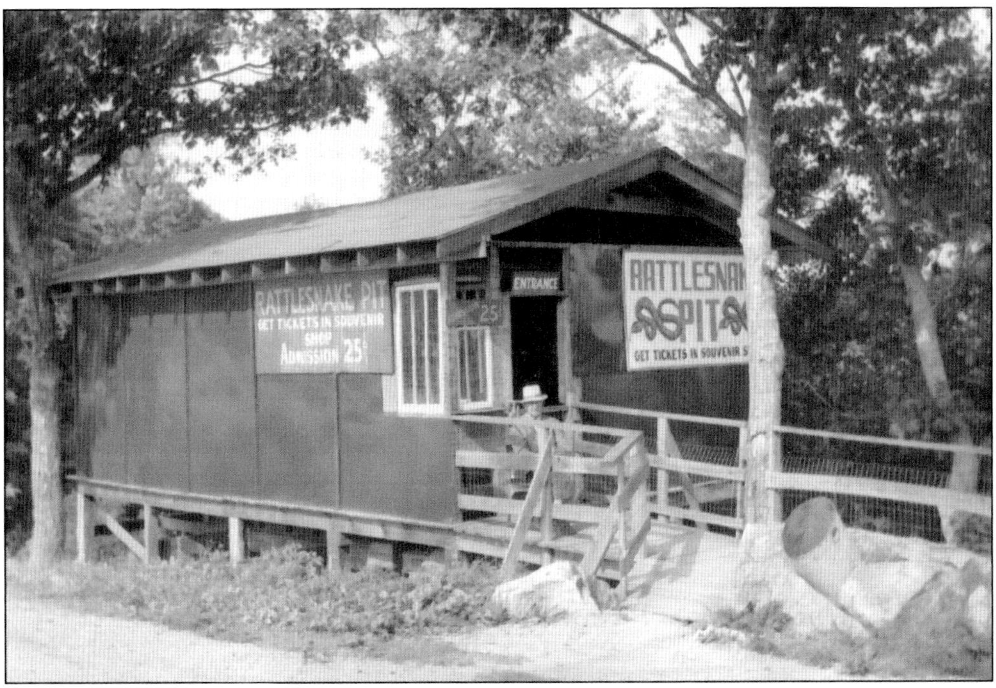

Attractions. Stuart and Abbie Kime developed many attractions at Big Walker Lookout, including a reptile pit. The pit is gone, but Monster Rock Trail, which was part of the original Appalachian Trail System, remains as one of the location's attractions. (Courtesy of Ron Kime.)

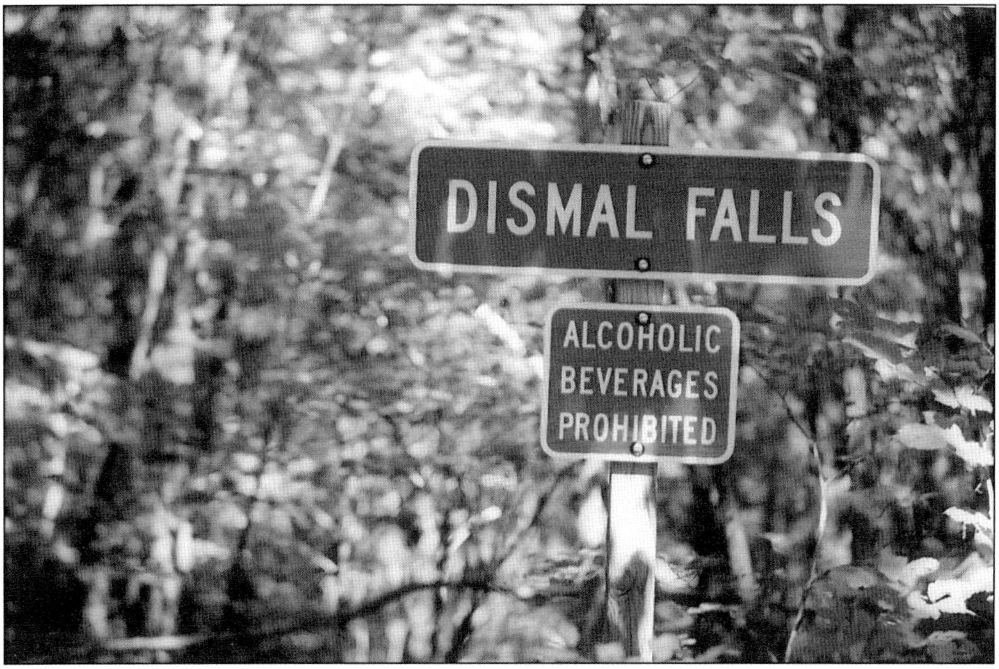

WORLD-CLASS HIKING TRAILS. There are many entries into the famous Appalachian Trail System in Bland County. The Dismal Falls area provides access to the trail and other activities in a rustic setting. (Author's.)

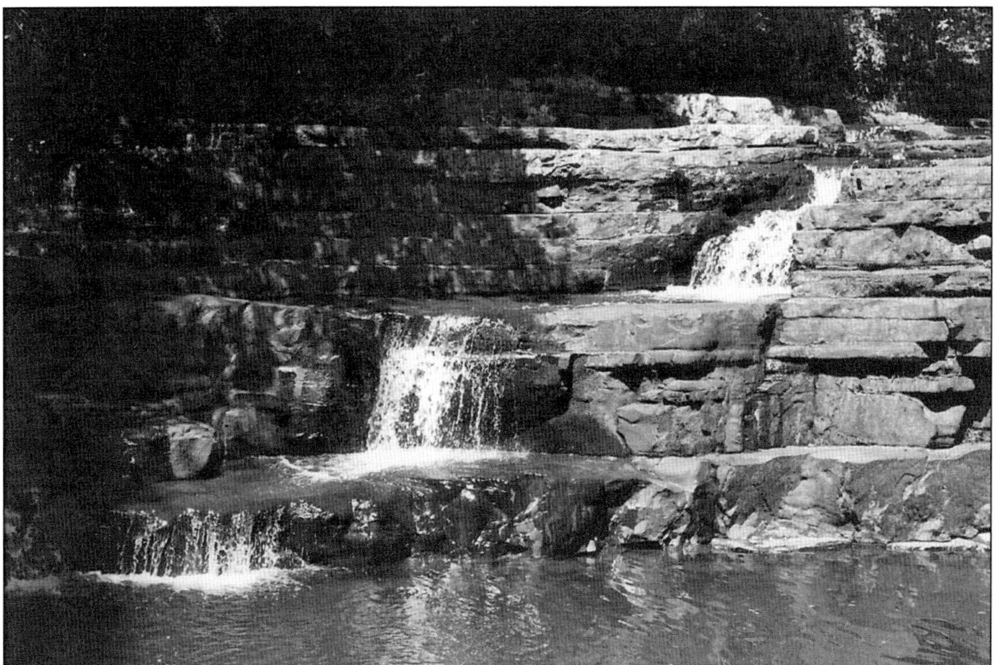

LEGENDS OF THE FALLS. Dismal Falls, located a short distance from State Route 42 and part of the Blue Grass Trail in eastern Bland County, is one of the region's most remote and beautiful waterfalls. (Author's.)

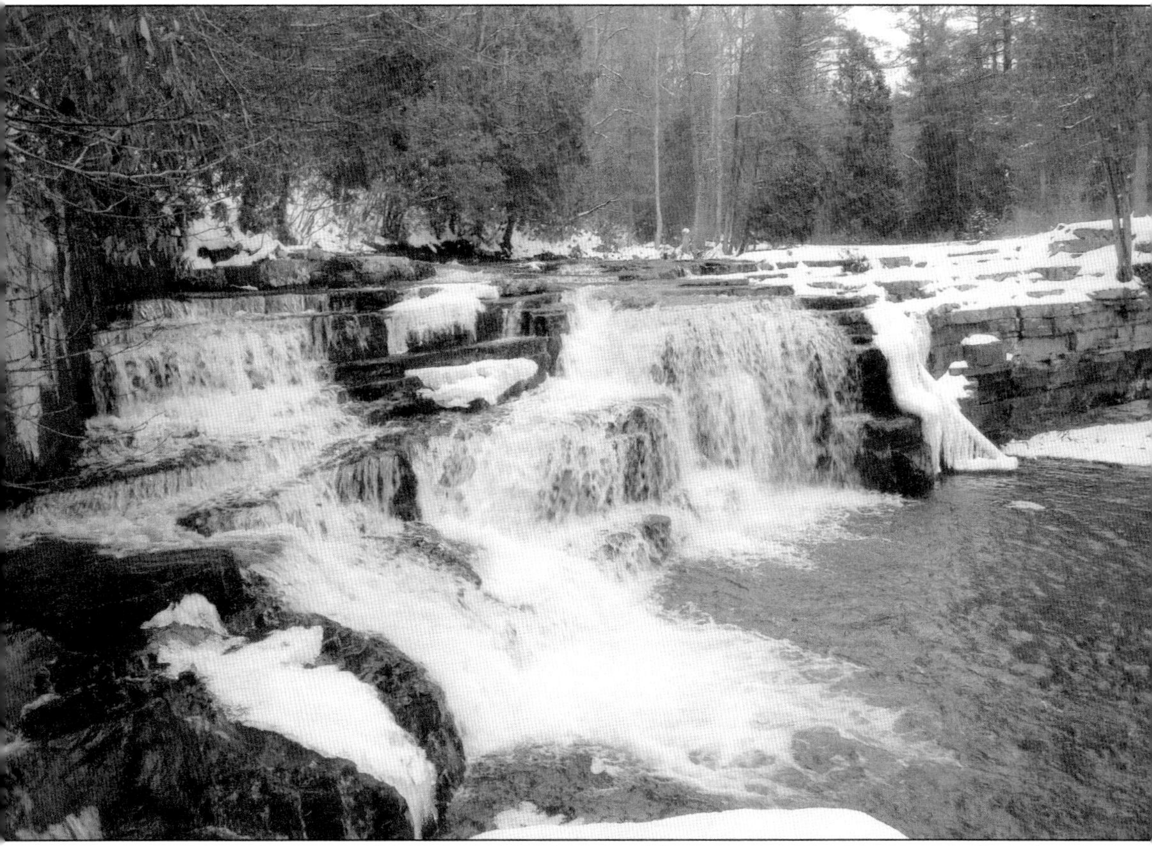

A Natural. The winter of 2009–2010 brought several feet of snow to the mountains of Southwest Virginia, and the melt-off provided a steady flow to streams like Dismal Creek in the Jefferson National Forest. Dismal Falls, shown here, is located in an isolated, secluded area where the creek is 40 feet wide, and the falls have created a natural swimming pool that is popular with hikers on the Appalachian Trail as well as with students from Virginia Tech in Blacksburg, not far from the location. The waters of Dismal Creek drain into Kimberling Creek before heading into the New River. (Photograph by James Pruett.)

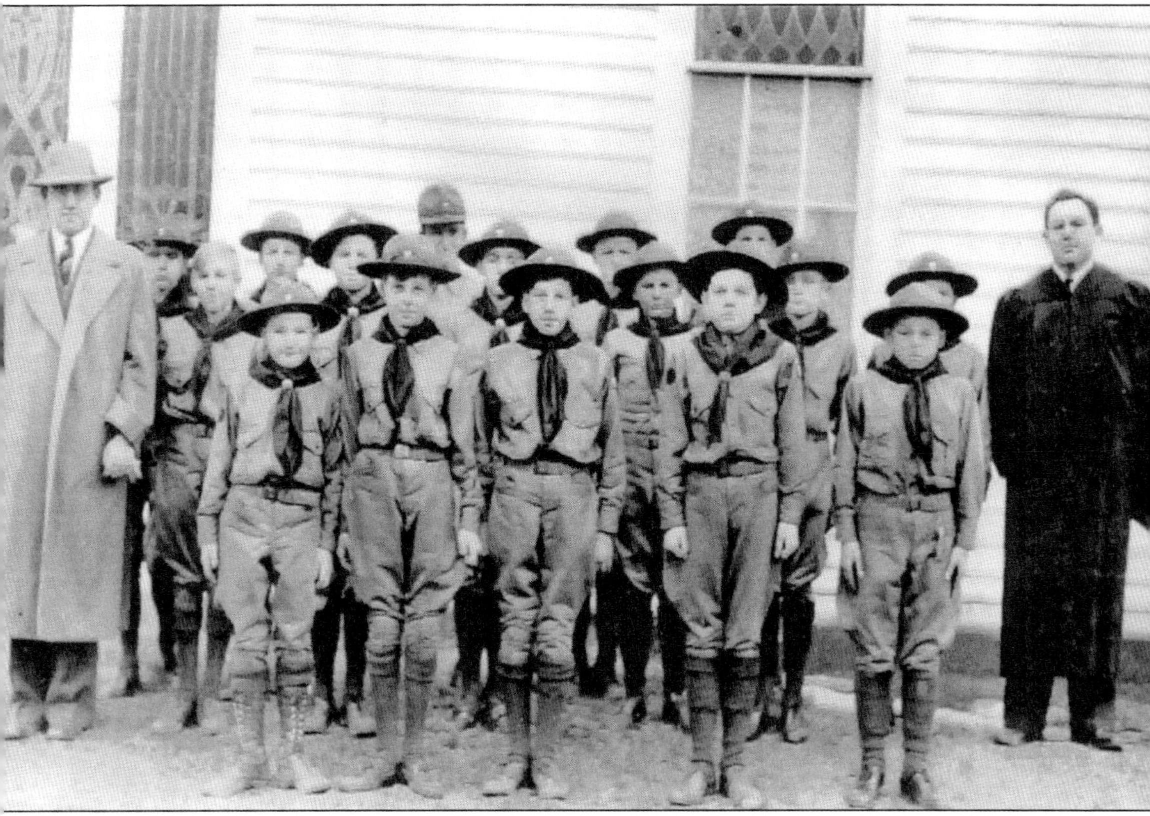

Good Scouts. The Bland County Boy Scouts of America troop, shown here, is just one of scores of regional Boy Scout troops that have enjoyed a camping and outdoor experience in Bland County. Boy Scout Camp Roland on Wolf Creek, near Bastian, remains a popular camping area for Boy Scouts year-round. (Courtesy of the Bland County Historical Society.)

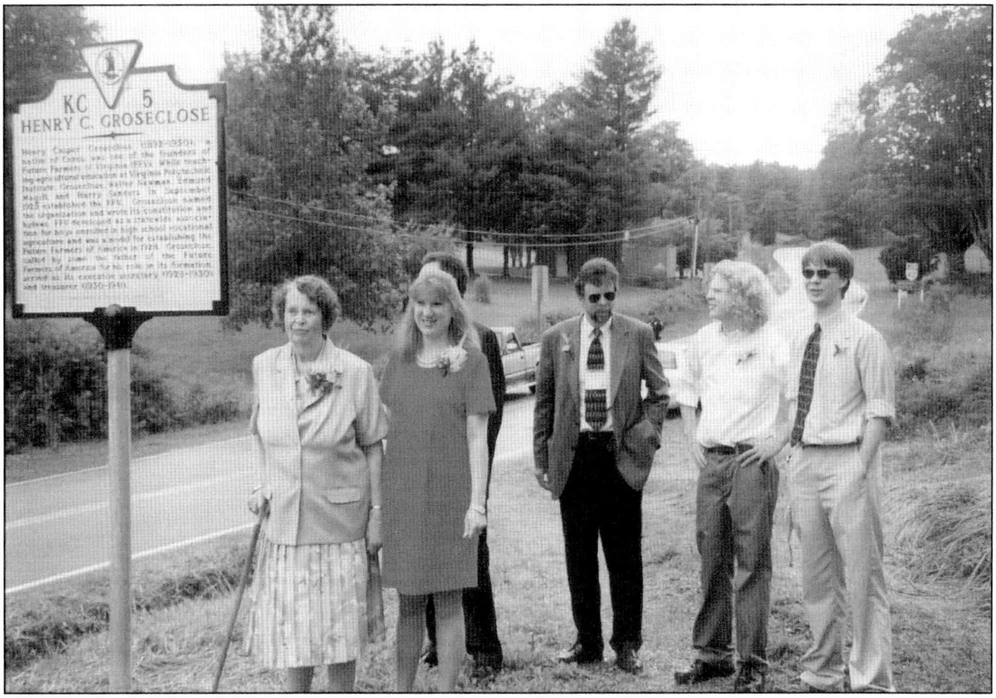

HISTORY REMEMBERED. In July 2003, family members of Henry C. Groseclose gathered at Ceres for the dedication of the highway marker recognizing Groseclose as the father of the Future Farmers of America. Those pictured are, from left to right, Henry's widow, Marie Groseclose; grandchildren George P. Groseclose (face obscured) and Virginia Groseclose Atkinson; great-grandsons Stuart and Nicholas Groseclose; and grandson Tom Saxton Groseclose Jr. (Courtesy of Marie Groseclose.)

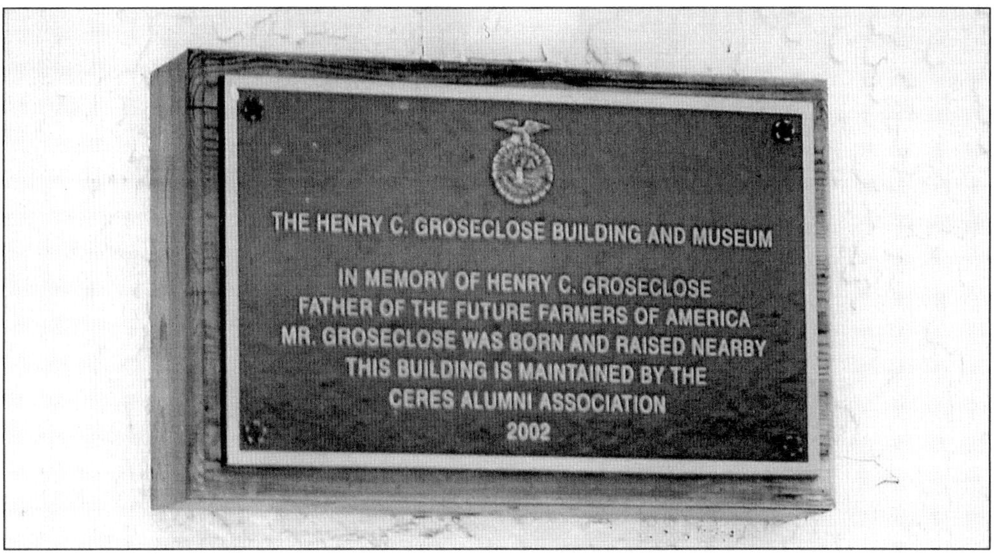

CONTINUING EDUCATION. The Ceres Alumni Association continues its work to tell the story of the importance of Ceres High School to the community, to Bland County, and to the world by preserving artifacts and images of the school as well as telling the story of Henry C. Groseclose. (Author's.)

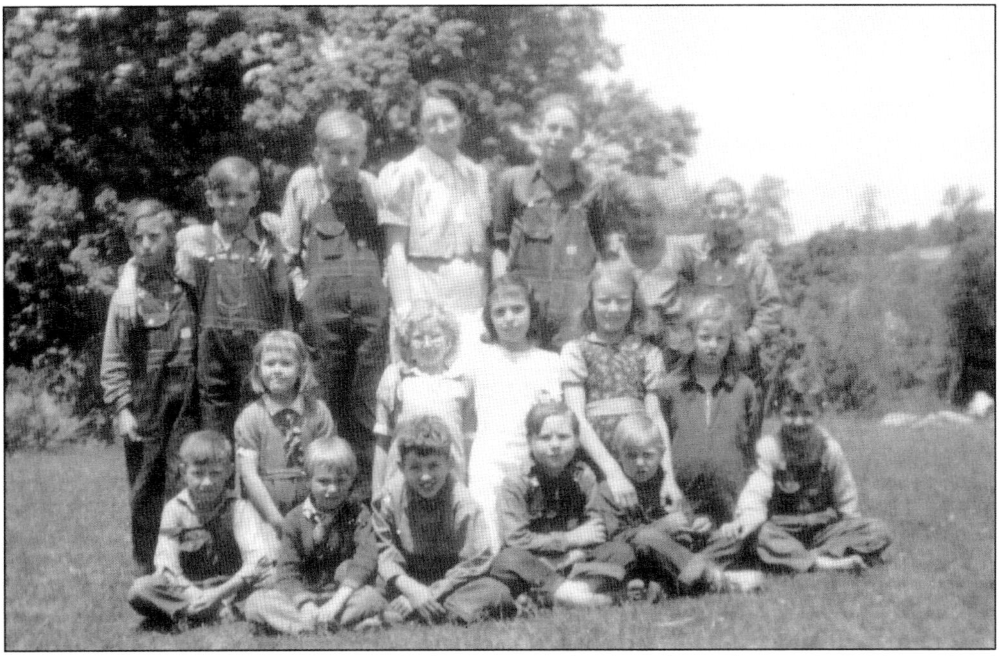

School Days. Students of Silver Creek Elementary School are shown here gathered for a school photograph. Bland County educators have a long history of providing an excellent education to students in the county. (Photograph from the Bogle Library Collection; courtesy of the Bland County Historical Society.)

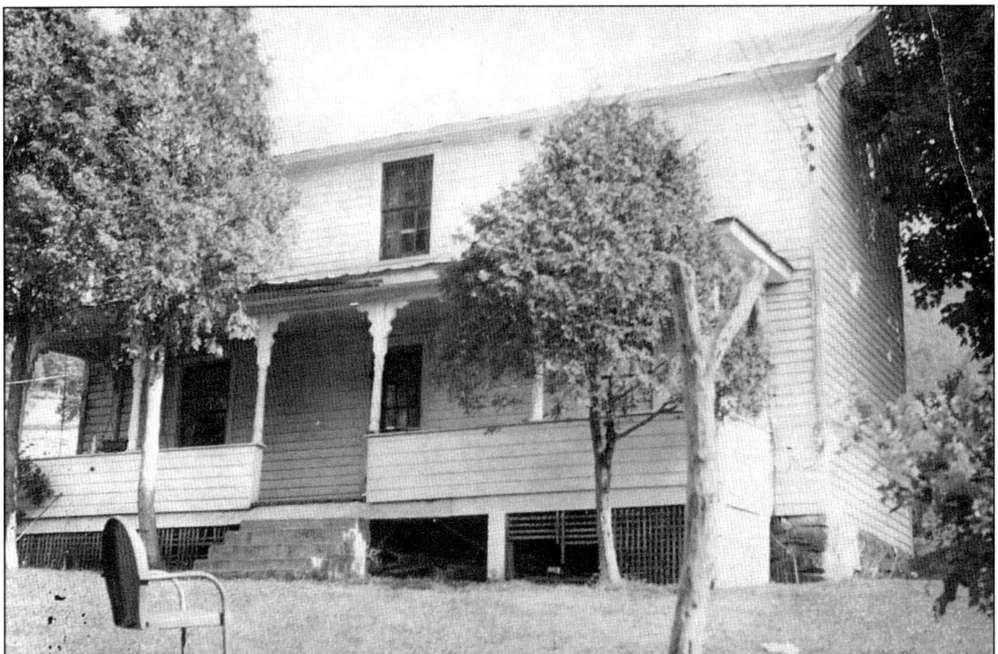

Old Home Place. As part of its efforts to tell the story of the community, the Ceres Alumni Association would like to restore the historic Groseclose home in Ceres. (Courtesy of the Ceres Alumni Association.)

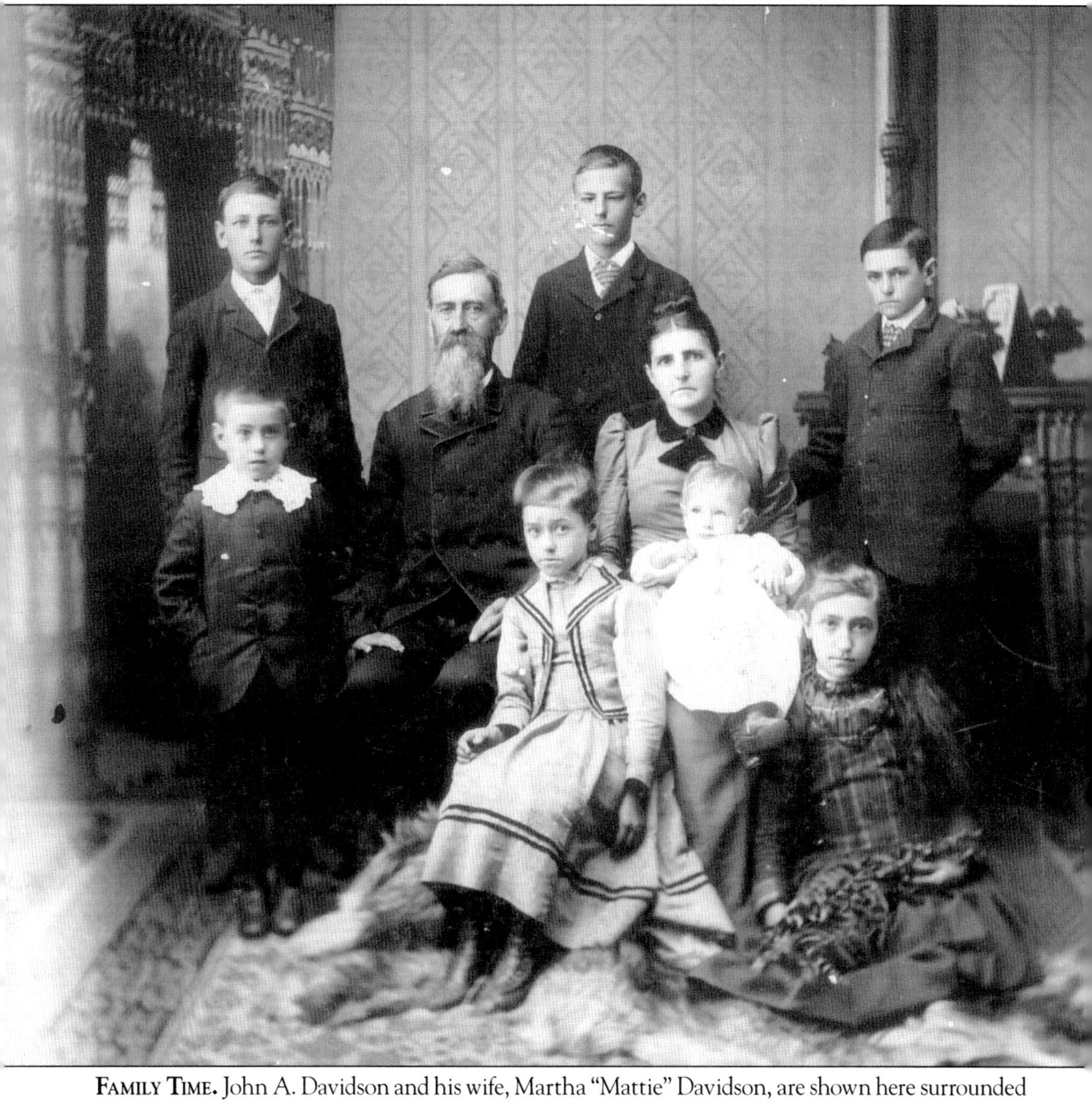

FAMILY TIME. John A. Davidson and his wife, Martha "Mattie" Davidson, are shown here surrounded by their family. John A. Davidson was a grandson of John Goolman Davidson, who was killed by Indians in 1793. The Davidsons shown above were married on December 24, 1872, and had seven children: John Henry, James Joseph, Julia Ann, Eugene, William Alexander, Bessie Rose, and Grady Doak. (Courtesy of Harry Thompson.)

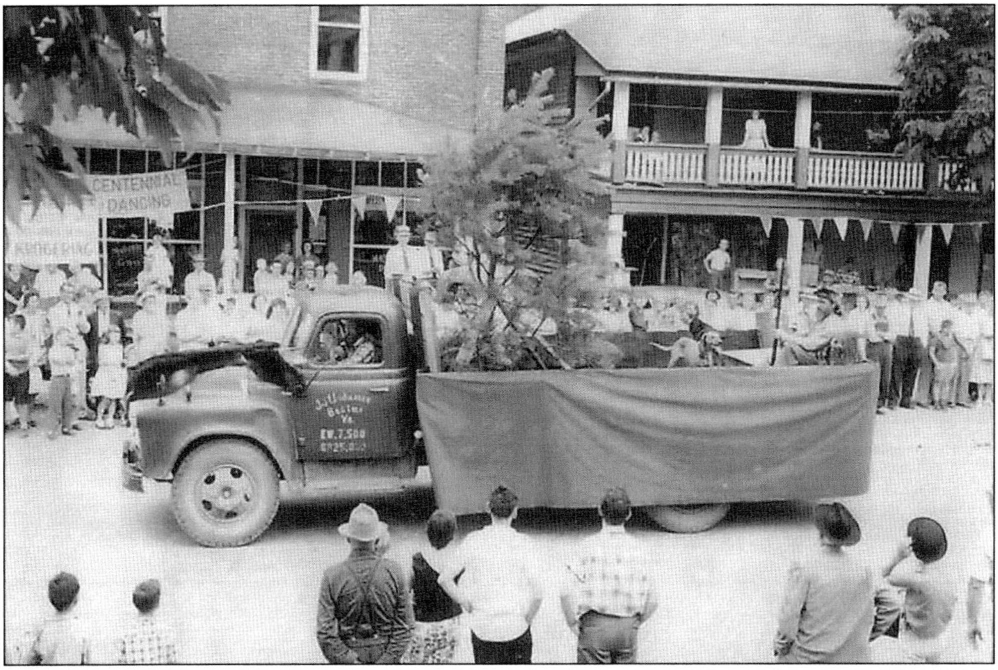

Truck Show. Bland County residents turned out for the centennial parade in 1961. The Bland County Board of Supervisors and other groups have many surprises ready for the sesquicentennial celebration in 2011. (Photograph from the Bogle Library Collection; courtesy of the Bland County Historical Society.)

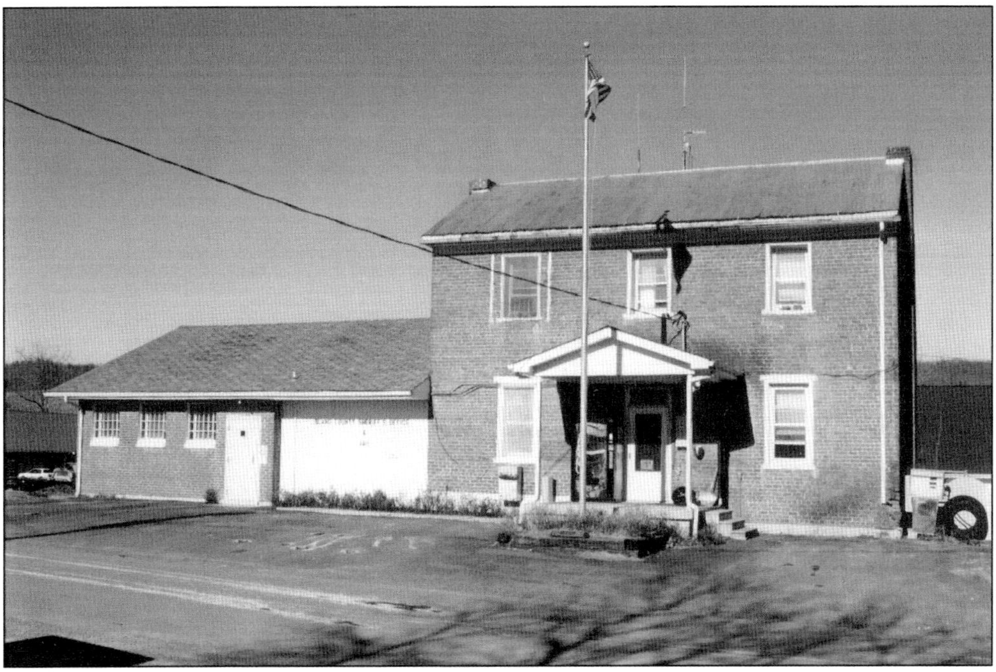

Jail No More. Volunteers of the Bland County Historical Society have been working to transform the old Bland County Jail, shown here, into a resource center for historical research in Bland County. (Courtesy of the Bland County Historical Society.)

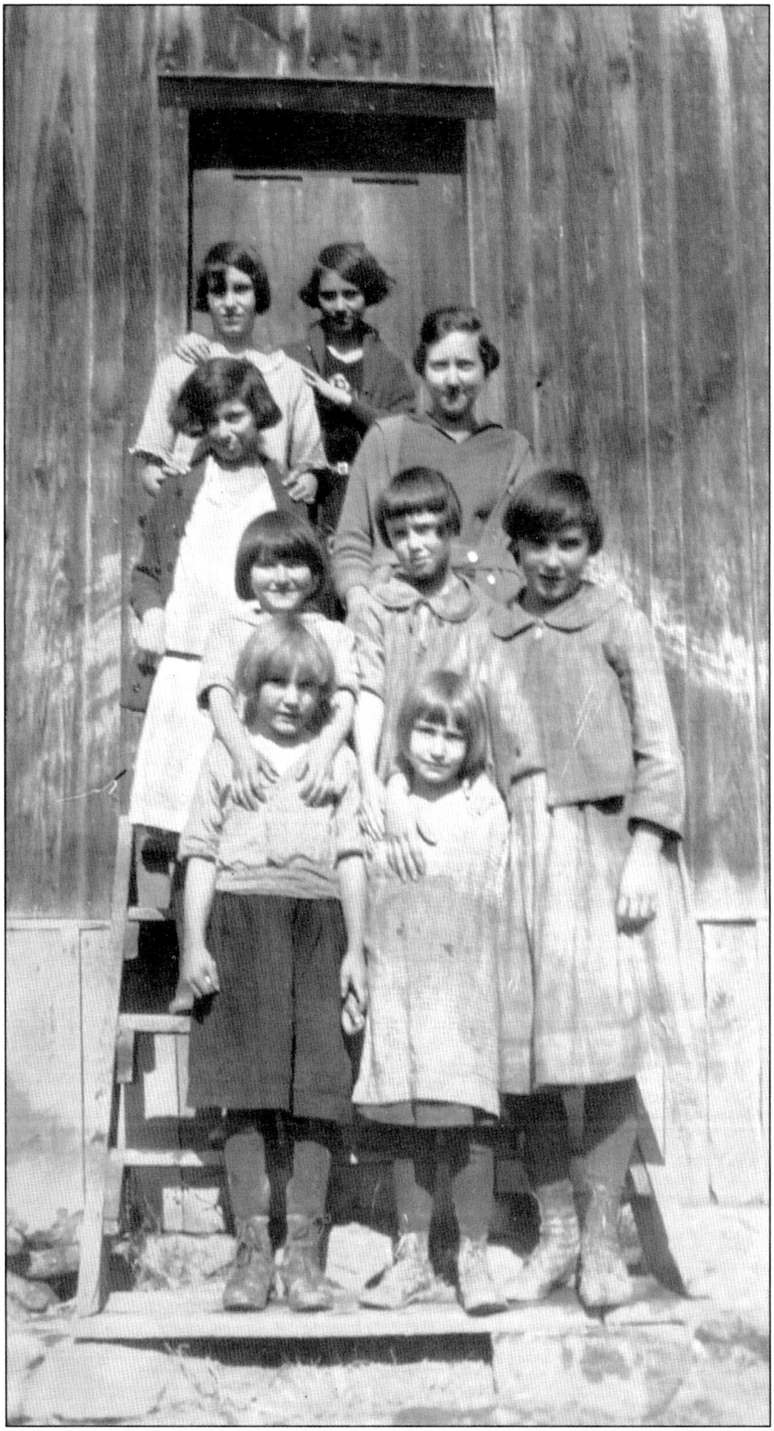

Children Are the Future. Students of the old Bogle School are shown here posing for a class photograph. The Bogle School was erected in 1858—three years before Bland County came into existence. The Bland County School Board erected this frame building in 1887, and the school provided an education to children and adults alike. (Courtesy of Billy Jean [Walters] Carty.)

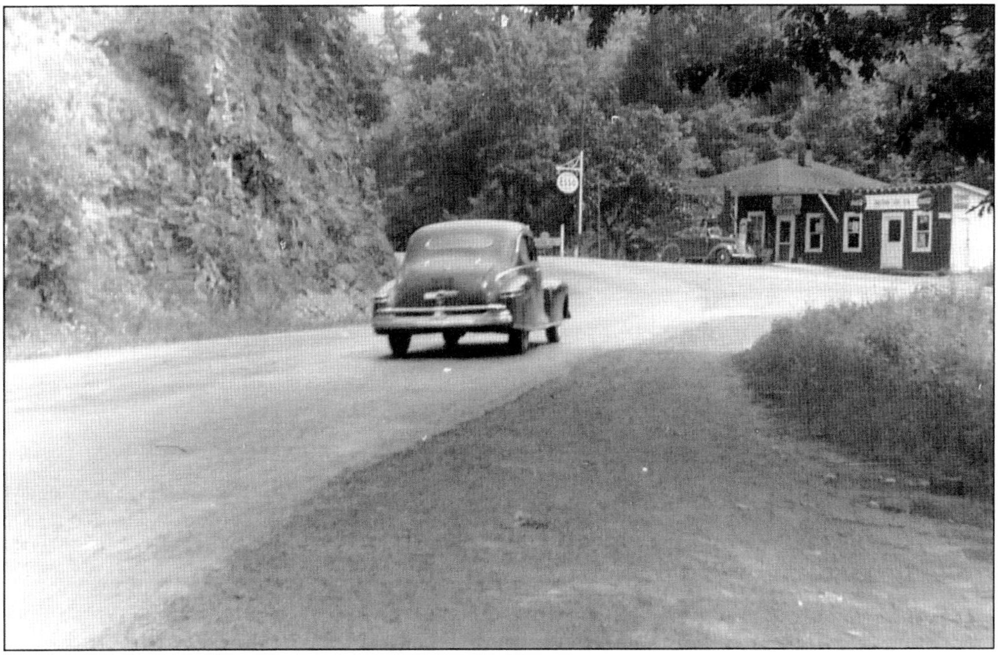

A Long and Winding Road. Don Bruce's filling station is shown here on old US Route 52 between Bastian and Bland, Virginia, on Brushy Mountain. Times have changed, but Bland County still has a great deal of mountain charm. (Courtesy of the Bland County Historical Society.)

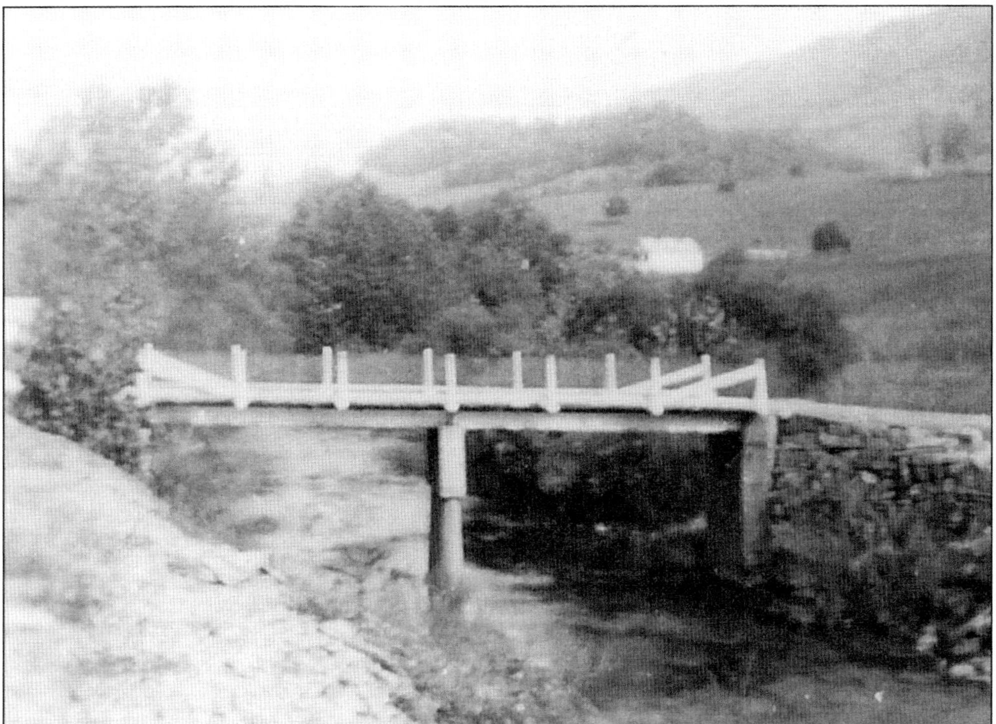

Clearfork. The old US Route 52 Bridge over Clearfork, shown here, was replaced in about 1951. New highways have changed the Bland County profile. (Courtesy of Doris Sink.)

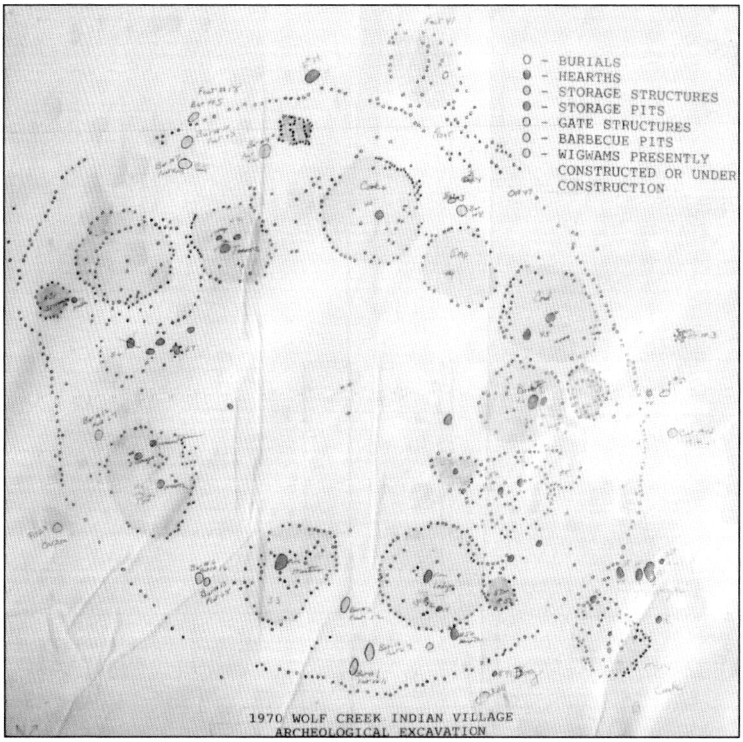

MAKING HISTORY. History is made each day at the Wolf Creek Indian Village in Bastian. Local volunteers and staff members are working from the actual Indian village map (shown at left) to set posts and fire pits to recreate the Woodland Period village. (Photograph by Eric DiNovo.)

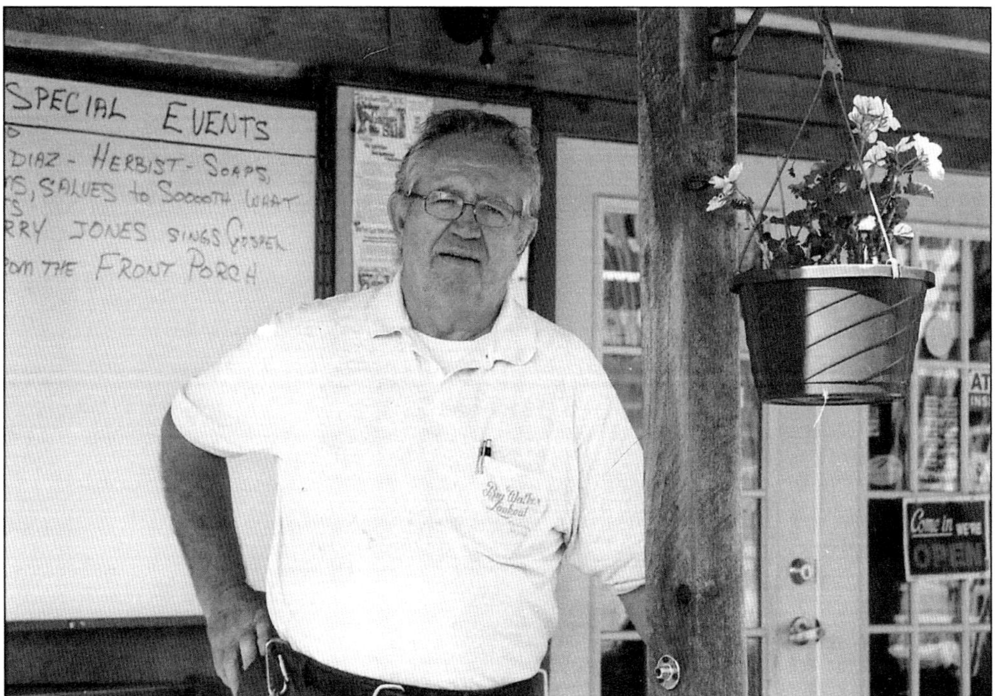

FAITH OF THE FATHERS. Ron Kime, shown here standing on the front porch of the Big Walker Lookout store, has carried on the dream that his parents built on top of Walker Mountain. Ron and his wife, Dee Kime, make the old attraction an exciting stop year-round. (Author's.)

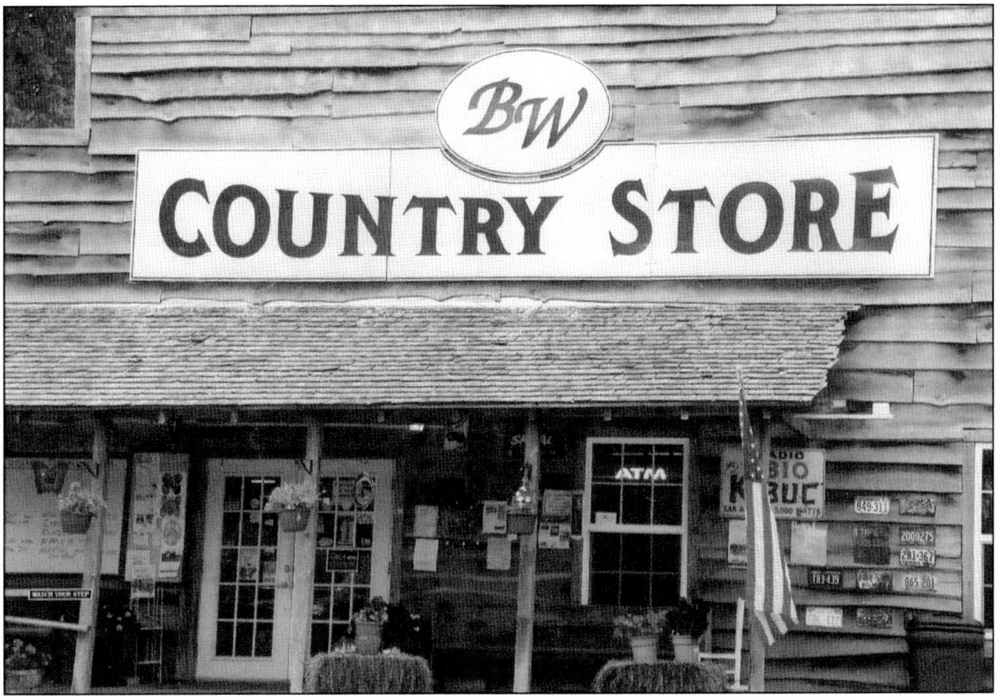

A Wide Assortment. The Big Walker Country Store prides itself on its selection of merchandise available that is produced by artists, artisans, and crafters from Bland County and the surrounding area. (Author's.)

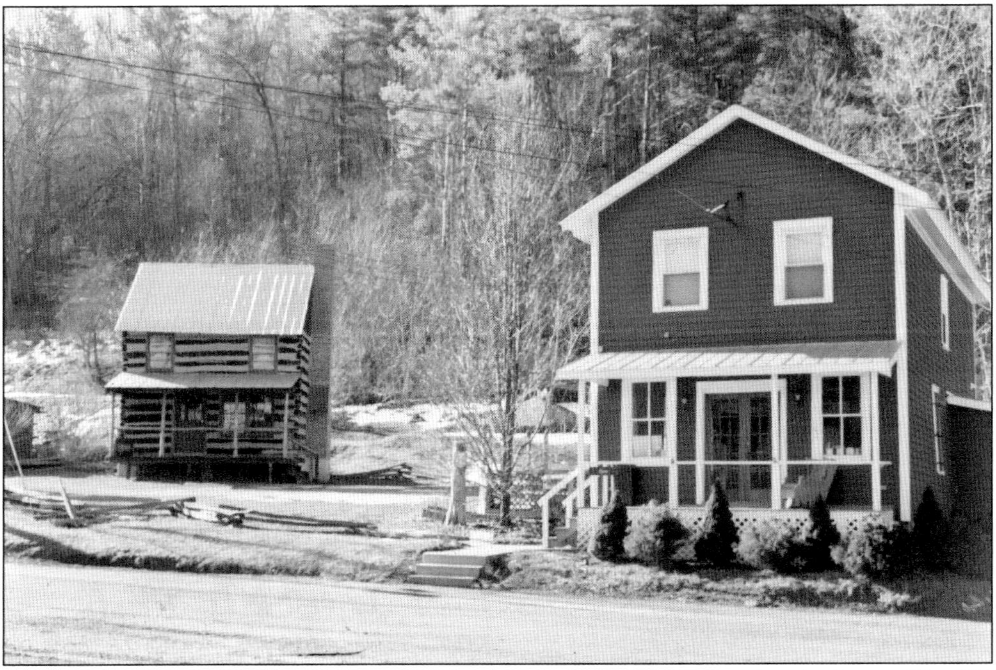

Shopping Center. Bland, Virginia, celebrates its past while looking ahead to the future. The Old Post Mercantile (above right) and restored log cabin coexist with the newly renovated courthouse just across the street. (Courtesy of the Bland County Historical Society.)